PRIEST AND LEVITE
IN MALACHI

SOCIETY
OF BIBLICAL
LITERATURE

DISSERTATION SERIES
David L. Petersen, Old Testament Editor
Pheme Perkins, New Testament Editor

Number 121

PRIEST AND LEVITE
IN MALACHI

by
Julia O'Brien

Julia M. O'Brien

PRIEST AND LEVITE
IN MALACHI

Scholars Press
Atlanta, Georgia

PRIEST AND LEVITE
IN MALACHI

Julia M. O'Brien

Ph.D., 1988
Duke University

Advisor:
Eric Meyers

Library of Congress Cataloging in Publication Data

O'Brien, Julia M.
    Priest and Levite in Malachi / Julia M. O'Brien.
    p. cm. — (Dissertation series / Society of Biblical
    Literature ; no. 121)
    Thesis (Ph. D.)—Duke University, 1988.
    Includes bibliographical references.
    ISBN 1-55540-438-3 (alk. paper). — ISBN 1-55540-439-1 (pbk.)
    1. Bible. O.T. Malachi—Criticism, interpretation, etc.
2. Priests, Jewish. 3. Levites. I. Title. II. Series:
Dissertation series (Society of Biblical Literature) ; no. 121.
BS1675.6.P7035 1990
224'.99067—dc20   90-47687
                                          CIP

Printed in the United States of America
on acid-free paper

CONTENTS

LIST OF TABLES vii

LIST OF ABBREVIATIONS viii

ACKNOWLEDGEMENTS ix

PREFACE... xi

INTRODUCTION.. xiii

I. MALACHI AND THE PRIESTHOOD... 1

    Overviews of the History of the Priesthood
       Traditionalist View
       Wellhausen and the Developmental Model
       After Wellhausen
       Synthesis of Histories of the Priesthood
    Understandings of Malachi's View of the Priesthood

II. *LĒWÎ* AND *KŌHĒN*: A SYNTACTICAL STUDY........................ 27

    Problem
    Methodology
    Occurrences
    Comparison of the Descriptions

III. THE FORM OF THE BOOK OF MALACHI 49

    Form Criticism and the Prophets
    The Unity & Integrity of the Book
    Suggestions of Form
    The *Rîb* Form
    Malachi as *Rîb*
    The Significance of this Thesis
    Implications for the Book's Unity

The *Sitz im Leben* of the *Rîb*
Significance of Form for Priest and Levite in Malachi
Conclusion

IV. THE SOURCES USED BY THE BOOK OF MALACHI 85
Introduction to the Problem
Deuteronomy and the Priestly Code
    General Language
    Technical Cultic Language
    Cultic Institutions
    Language for Describing Priests
    Conclusions Regarding D and P
Other Biblical Traditions
The Canon Known to Malachi
Conclusions

V. MALACHI AND THE PRIESTHOOD IN CONTEXT 113
Date of the Book
    Historical References
    Similarities to the Historical Situation of Ezra/Nehemiah
    Linguistic Analysis
    Quotes from Other Literature
    Genre and Style
    Conclusions Regarding Date
Malachi's Description of the Priesthood Compared with
    other Literature
    Deuteronomistic History
    Jeremiah and Ezekiel
    Miscellaneous Prophetic Writings
    Haggai and Zechariah 1-8; Zech. 9-14
    Ezra and Nehemiah
    Chronicles
    Old Testament Pseudepigrapha
    Qumran
    Conclusions Regarding Context

VI. CONCLUSIONS AND IMPLICATIONS 143

BIBLIOGRAPHY 149

LIST OF TABLES

1. Terms in Mal. 3:5 Compared with Other Sources 92-93
2. Chronological Order of Works as Constructed by Hill 128
3. Chronological Order of Works Based on Hill's Statistics 129

LIST OF ABBREVIATIONS

ASOR	American Schools of Oriental Research
BA	*Biblical Archaeologist*
BASOR	*Bulletin of the American Schools of Oriental Research*
BDB	Brown-Driver-Briggs lexicon (see bibliography under Brown)
BZAW	*Beihefte zur Zeitschrift für die alttestamentliche Wissenschaft*
CBQ	*Catholic Biblical Quarterly*
GKC	Gesenius-Kautzsch-Cowley grammar (see bibliography under Gesenius)
HUCA	*Hebrew Union College Annual*
JBL	*Journal of Biblical Literature*
JPS	Jewish Publication Society translation of <u>Tanak</u>
JSOT	*Journal for the Study of the Old Testament*
JSOTS	*Journal for the Study of the Old Testament, Supplement Series*
JTS	*Journal of Theological Studies*
KAI	*Kanaanäische und aramäische Inschriften* (see bibliography under Donner and Röllig)
KAT	*Kommentar zum Alten Testament*
PEQ	*Palestine Exploration Quarterly*
VT	*Vetus Testamentum*
VTS	*Vetus Testamentum, Supplements*
ZAW	*Zeitschrift für die alttestamentliche Wissenschaft*

ACKNOWLEDGEMENTS

I am grateful to all those persons whose encouragement and support have made this dissertation possible. My discussion and collaboration with Dr. Eric Meyers has proven most fruitful, and I look forward to the publication of his forthcoming work on Malachi. Dr. Jack Sasson has provided much support and many helpful comments.

I also thank my fellow students in the Department of Religion at Duke University, and particularly Kenneth Hoglund; these friends have exemplified the meaning of the term "colleague."

Finally, I thank my husband William for his enduring faith in me and—above all—for helping me to keep my sense of humor.

PREFACE

Biblical studies is, in essence, the art of asking heuristic questions. The array of methodologies and approaches currently being employed in our field (and others) underscores that we share no consensus that "correct" answers and "accurate" history can be unearthed from biblical texts.

This dissertation, completed in 1988, explores one avenue of reasoning—that of traditional source criticism. It asks a relatively simple question: If one accepts the Documentary Hypothesis, what does this assumption entail for reading the Book of Malachi?

I hope to have demonstrated that source-critical questions, while valuable in suggesting the interplay between various biblical texts, have often been posed in ways that ignore—and often obscure—much of what reading the Book of Malachi can offer. My subsequent exploration of other methodologies and other questions has corroborated these findings, as well as my belief that by exploring the implications of our approaches and assumptions we learn not only about the texts we read but also about ourselves as readers.

Julia M. O'Brien
July 1990

INTRODUCTION

Since the work of source critics in the eighteenth and nineteenth centuries, most biblical scholars have maintained that Israel's priesthood, far from receiving its eternal form at Sinai, experienced change over time. According to Julius Wellhausen's *Prolegomena to the History of Israel*,[1] which undergirded earlier source criticism with an argument based upon Israel's institutions, this development can be traced within the individual sources that comprise the Pentateuch. Each source, written by a different author at a different time, reflects a unique stage in the development of the priesthood.

According to Wellhausen's source–critical scheme, while the J source reveals that Israel had no established priesthood in its earliest history, the Book of Deuteronomy (D) and the Blessing of Moses (Deut. 33) indicate that by the time of Josiah's reign priesthood belonged to the tribe of Levi, such that the term "Levite" served as a clan title for the priest. The Priestly source (P) demonstrates that by the post-exilic period priests were known as the "sons of Aaron," while the term "Levite" denoted an inferior cultic servant. Subsequent scholars have heatedly debated the manner in which these changes occurred, and yet even many traditional biblical critics agree with Wellhausen that priesthood underwent development during Israel's history.

This developmental scheme, as well as most studies of the priesthood, are formulated on the basis of Pentateuchal texts and major works such as Ezekiel. Other biblical texts are then analyzed to discern their place within the scheme: does a biblical book, for example, grant the privilege of priesthood to all Levites or to the sons of Aaron?

Problematic in this regard is the Book of Malachi. Usually dated to ca. 450 B.C.E. on the basis of linguistic analysis and situational affinities with the Books of Ezra and Nehemiah, Malachi stands firmly within the

---

[1] Julius Wellhausen, *Prolegomena to the History of Israel*, preface by W. Robertson Smith (Gloucester, MA: Peter Smith, 1973 [reprint of 1878 ed.]).

time frame of the Aaronide assertion of priestly power proposed by Wellhausen. Ultimately concerned with the priesthood, its failings and its ideal, the book should offer prime information for evaluating theories of the status of priesthood in the post-exilic period. Its language should indicate which priestly group wields power and, if Wellhausen is correct, then too the sources upon which the prophetic book is based. And yet, a clear depiction of the nature of the priesthood in Malachi is obscured by the fact that the terms used do not fit clearly into either a Deuteronomic or Priestly scheme.

In describing the priesthood, Malachi uses several terms: it refers to the "priests" (*hakkōhănîm*), "the sons of Levi" (*bĕnê-lēwî*), and to a "covenant with Levi" (*bĕrît-ʾet-lēwî*) without relating these terms syntactically. It does not use the term "sons of Aaron" (*bĕnê-ʾahărōn*), which is distinctive to the Priestly Code, nor Ezekiel's designation "sons of Zadok" (*bĕnê ṣadôk*), yet neither does Malachi use the common Deuteronomic compound designation "the Levitical priests" (*hakkōhănîm hallĕwiyyîm*).

Malachi's terminology for the priesthood, for this reason, has been interpreted in contradictory ways. On the one hand, most scholars have argued that in Malachi "priests" and "sons of Levi" are synonymous and that Malachi therefore predates P. A second position maintains that since Malachi may share several isolated cultic regulations with P the book may be seen as transitional in the move from D to P. According to a third position, Malachi reflects the unique language of the post-exilic period. A fourth view sees within the Book of Malachi a bitter struggle between the Aaronide priest and the Levite.

This dissertation attempts to evaluate these differing explanations of the Book of Malachi and to ascertain what information it may provide for understanding the priestly groups and the priestly terminology of the post-exilic period. In so doing, it will offer an overview of scholarly study of the priesthood and of Malachi's treatment of the priesthood; it will study the language and form of the book; it will attempt to determine the sources which underlie it; and it will attempt to suggest the context for the book's treatment of the priesthood.

CHAPTER I

MALACHI AND THE PRIESTHOOD

OVERVIEWS OF THE HISTORY OF THE PRIESTHOOD

Traditionalist View

According to a traditionalist view, the present shape of the biblical canon provides a faithful description of Israel's priesthood throughout its history. As recorded in the Book of Exodus, although the patriarchs performed sacrifice out of personal piety, true priesthood did not begin until Moses, himself from the tribe of Levi, set apart his brother Aaron as priest. After ordaining Aaron and his sons, Moses then consecrated the remainder of the tribe of Levi to be cultic servants, subject to the sons of Aaron. From the very founding of the cult at Sinai, then, the service of the LORD was entrusted to the Levitical tribe which was subdivided into the Aaronide priests and the remaining Levites, who acted as cultic servants.

The traditional position moreover assumes that the nature of these two ranks of priesthood did not vary in substance from the time of their Mosaic origin until the fall of the Israelite state in 70 C. E . The entire Pentateuch, as well as all other biblical writings, understand the term "priest" as synonymous with "the descendent of Aaron." The term "Levite" usually refers to the non-Aaronide cultic servant but also may be used in a general sense to refer any member of the tribe. Accordingly, in the books of the Former Prophets, "priests" are understood to be Aaronide priests . By the phrase "the Levitical priests," Deuteronomy intends the sons of Aaron, and when Deuteronomy mentions "Levites" it may refer either to the lower clergy or the whole tribe. Ezekiel's description of the priests as the "sons of Zadok" and its apparent attempt to limit the priesthood to this subset within the sons of Aaron marks no change in the priesthood but rather arises from the prophet's idiosyncratic conviction that due to their sinfulness all non-Zadokite Aaronides have abrogated their right to the priesthood.[1]

Wellhausen and the Developmental Model

The work of biblical scholars in the eighteenth and nineteenth centuries revolutionized the study of the Hebrew Bible and ancient Israelite institutions. Ignoring the canonical presentation of biblical material, these scholars instead isolated disparate sources within it, each source composed by a different author and each reflecting a different period in Israelite history.

Julius Wellhausen's *Prolegomena to the History of Israel,* first published in 1878, represents the full flowering, though not the origin, of the source–critical enterprise. While, indeed, others before him had isolated discrete sources within the Pentateuch,[2] Wellhausen's accomplishment was to place these sources in order and to buttress the ensuing developmental scheme with an argument based on an analysis of Israel's institutions. According to Wellhausen's reconstruction, rather than representing the origin of Israel's cultic life, the Pentateuch instead stands as the final product of a long process of development. Underlying its narrative are three different documents—the Jehovist (J), the Deuteronomist (D) and the Priestly Code (P)—penned at different times over a period spanning from the monarchy to the post-exilic era. Regulations governing the cult and the priesthood derive only from the latest document: their origins are neither Mosaic nor Israelite, but—in Wellhausen's estimation—"Jewish" and post-exilic.

Wellhausen's separation and chronological ordering of these sources led him to postulate a history of Israel's priesthood far different than that portrayed by the biblical text. Within this scheme, the priesthood developed from a simple to an increasingly-complex institution.

EARLY PERIOD

According to Wellhausen's scheme, the nature of the priesthood in the early period of Israel's history is outlined by the oldest literary stratum, J. This source reveals that at the time of its composition Israel knew

---

[1] Among those who support such a traditional position are Samuel I . Curtiss, *The Levitical Priests: A Contribution to the Criticism of the Pentateuch,* preface by F. Delitzsch (Edinburgh: T & T Clark, 1877).

[2] For the contributions of those such as Witter and Astruc, see Otto Eissfeldt, *The Old Testament: An Introduction,* trans. P. R. Ackroyd (New York: Harper & Row, 1965), 160-166.

no elaborate priesthood responsible for proper sacrifice, as is described in the later sources.

Priesthood only arose with the development of public worship centers within Israel. The early priests who officiated at these centers were not responsible for proper sacrifice, but only for the consultation of oracular devices. All persons, not only prominent figures such as Elijah and Samuel, sacrificed for themselves. Entrusted with consulting the oracle were members of a priestly guild associated with the name of Levi. These "Levites" bore no genealogical connection with the tribe of that name since the secular tribe of Levi died out during the period of the judges, leaving only a few isolated survivors. The guild formed independently, deriving its name from the lineage of Moses.[3]

MONARCHY

With the founding of the monarchy and the establishment of royal chapels arose the need for an organized priesthood. While members of the Levitical guild usually were preferred as priests, priesthood in the early period of the monarchy was not limited to any one group. King David himself acted as priest and appointed non-Levitical priests for his clergy, including his own sons and Ira the Jairite.

David's most important priestly appointment was that of Zadok, who was not only non-Levitical but also, in Wellhausen's estimation, non-Israelite. Early in David's reign Zadok shared the priestly office with the Levite Abiathar, but in the course of events following David's death, Abiathar was ousted, leaving the control of the Jerusalemite clergy to Zadok and his descendents. During the reign of Solomon, the Zadokites exercised control over the Jerusalemite priesthood, although members of the Levitical guild continued to serve local sanctuaries in the countryside.

According to Wellhausen's reconstruction, the reign of Josiah marked a watershed in the development of the priesthood. Josiah's reform of the cult mandated the centralization of worship in Jerusalem and the abolition of all local sanctuaries at which members of the Levitical guild served. The Book of Deuteronomy, which is identified by Wellhausen as the basic document of this reform, champions the cause of the Levites so affected, requiring that they be granted the right of equal service in the Jerusalem Temple alongside the sons of Zadok.

---

3 Wellhausen, *Prolegomena*, 143-144. According to Welhausen, the Blessing of Moses in Deuteronomy 33 indicates that at the time of its composition the guild was sufficiently cohesive to be considered a tribe on par with other tribes (*Prolegomena*, 143).

The theoretical equality of Zadokite and Levite championed by the Book of Deuteronomy did not materialize. The Zadokite clergy refused to forgo their hegemony in the Temple, and hence the Levites, deprived of work by centralization and barred from Jerusalem, became equal to the widow, orphan and sojourner.[4] Hence, while law declared illegal any distinction in rank between the Zadokite and the Levite, such a distinction *de facto* arose at the close of the pre-exilic history.

EZEKIEL

This consequence of Deuteronomic reform—that is, the improper distinction between ranks of the clergy—is given prophetic legitimation in the Book of Ezekiel. Ezekiel lambasts the members of the Levitical guild who had served sanctuaries outside Jerusalem and punishes them for their sin by demoting them to temple servants. In contrast, the sons of Zadok, who had since appropriated the Levitical genealogy, are praised by Ezekiel as the true and faithful priests.

POST-EXILIC ERA

Within the developmental scheme of Wellhausen, the post-exilic era witnessed a further entrenchment of the Zadokite priesthood and a further distancing of the cult from the everyday lives of individual Israelites. During this period the final document of the Pentateuch, the Priestly source (P), was added to J and D, imposing upon the earlier material detailed ritual and legalistic requirements. P also granted to the Zadokite priesthood a new designation—"the sons of Aaron"—to provide a more ancient legitimization for their exclusive claims to the priesthood. The Book of Chronicles rewrites Israel's history from the perspective of the P source, attempting to demonstrate the antiquity of cultic regulations; according to Wellhausen, it is of no value for the reconstruction of the true events of Israel's history.[5]

After Wellhausen

The influence of Wellhausen's reconstruction of the history of Israel's cult upon the field of biblical studies scarcely can be overstated. His work defined the parameters of discussion by identifying the major issues bearing upon the priesthood—issues which subsequent scholars must address. Both those who would attempt a defense of the traditional

---

4 Denying the historical validity of the Levitical cities, Wellhausen views the Levites as relying solely on charity for their support (*Prolegomena*, 159f.).

5 Wellhausen, *Prolegomena*, 171-227.

viewpoint and those who would offer an even more radical reconstruction can do so only by debating the tenets set forth by Wellhausen in his developmental scheme.[6]

The scholarly debate bearing upon an understanding of the Israelite priesthood during the more than one hundred years since the publication of Wellhausen's *Prolegomena* is not easily synthesized. The issues that Wellhausen addressed encompassed source identification, source dating, sociological analysis, as well as evaluation of the historical accuracy of the Former Prophets and of later literature and tracing the history of Israelite institutions. Few scholars today attempt such broad syntheses and instead focus on component parts of the larger discussion. The following is an attempt to summarize post-Wellhausian scholarship that bears upon each stage of the developmental scheme that he proposed. Study concerning the priesthood in the Early Period, the Monarchy, Ezekiel and the Post-Exilic Era will be considered in turn.

EARLY PERIOD
THE PRESENT STATUS OF SOURCE CRITICISM ON J AND E.

While Wellhausen dated J ca. 800 B.C.E., subsequent scholars have contested this date. Gerhard von Rad, in the course of his study of the theological message of the Yahwist, argued that the source hails from the reign of Solomon, when "enlightenment" ideals held sway.[7] Many scholars since von Rad have adopted his earlier dating of J to the period ca. 1000 B.C.E.

J has been placed, conversely, much later than Wellhausen's 800 B.C.E. date by both Kennett and John van Seters. Kennett is alone in maintaining that J, not Deuteronomy, was the book found in the Temple during Josiah's reign.[8] According to van Seters, J does not accurately reflect the earliest period of Israel's history but rather betrays its origin in the exilic period.[9] While van Seters' thesis has been accepted by various

---

6 This assessment of Wellhausen's work is shared by Menahem Haran, *Temples and Temple Service in Ancient Israel: An Inquiry into the Character of Cult Phenomena and the Historical Setting of the Priestly School* (Oxford: Clarendon Press, 1978), vi-vii (hereafter Haran, *Temples*).

7 Gerhard von Rad, *Old Testament Theology*, trans. D. M. G. Stalker (New York: Harper & Row, 1962), I: 3-102.

8 R. H. Kennett, "The Origin of the Aaronite Priesthood," *Journal of Theological Studies* 6 (1905): 184.

9 John van Seters, *Abraham in History and Tradition* (New Haven: Yale University Press, 1975).

German scholars, the majority of source critics continues to deal with J based on the assumption of its monarchical origins.

Wellhausen acknowledged the presence of a fourth source, the Elohist (E), which is "...in his manner and in his manner of looking at things most closely akin to the Jehovist."[10] As in Wellhausen, however, the E source receives little attention in modern scholarly circles. Martin Noth has attempted to account for the similarities between J and E by postulating a common source which he calls G, and Frank Cross considers J and E to be variants of a larger Epic tradition.[11] Indeed, many doubt the existence of E: Mowinckel considers E as a collection of supplements to J,[12] and the computer analysis of Radday and others suggest no statistically-significant difference between J and E.[13]

PATRIARCHAL PERIOD.

The majority of scholars supports the position of the biblical text and of Wellhausen that Israel had no priesthood in the patriarchal era. According to M. Haran, who argues that throughout Israelite history priests officiated only at temples, the absence of Yahwistic temples in the period of the patriarchs accounts for the absence of priests.[14] The accuracy with which the early narratives of J and E describe the patriarchal period also has been questioned; while the American school of archaeology has attempted to verify the plausibility of the patriarchal narratives,[15] many such as Gottwald and van Seters have despaired of using biblical data to reconstruct the period of the patriarchs.[16]

---

10 Wellhausen, *Prolegomena*, 7.

11 Martin Noth, *A History of Pentateuchal Traditions*, trans. Bernhard W. Anderson (Englewood Cliffs, NJ: Prentice-Hall, Inc., 1972), 38-41; F. M. Cross, *Canaanite Myth and Hebrew Epic: Essays in the History of the Religion of Israel* (Cambridge, MA: Harvard University Press, 1973), 6 (hereafter Cross, *Myth*).

12 S. Mowinckel, *The Two Sources of the Predeuteronomic Primeval History (JE) in Gen 1-11* (Oslo: J. Dybwad, 1937); quoted in Ernst Sellin and George Fohrer, *Introduction to the Old Testament*, trans. David E. Green (Nashville: Abingdon, 1965), 146; 154.

13 Yehuda Radday and others, "Genesis, Wellhausen and the Computer," *ZAW* 94 (1982): 467-481.

14 Menahem Haran, "Priests and Priesthood," in *Encyclopaedia Judaica* (Jerusalem: Keter Publishing House, 1971), 13: 1071-1072.

15 For example, John Bright, *A History of Israel*, 3rd ed. (Philadelphia: Westminster Press, 1981).

16 N. K. Gottwald, *The Hebrew Bible: A Socio-Literary Introduction* (Philadelphia: Fortress Press, 1985), 146-147; van Seters, *Abraham*, conclusions on 309-312.

MOSAIC PERIOD.

While scholars largely agree that the origins of priesthood are not to be found in the patriarchal period, no such consensus characterizes discussions regarding the Mosaic era. According to Wellhausen's reconstruction, Israel's priesthood was not regulated in the wilderness; the accounts of the cult's origins at Sinai appear only in the P source, and hence are late and untrustworthy.

In a move away from Wellhausen's position, a significant minority of scholars is now willing to suggest that priesthood had elementary beginnings in the wilderness. They do so in at least two ways: first, many are willing to acknowledge that the P source preserves much ancient material and may be utilized in a study of the early period.[17] Secondly, many argue that JE presumes a priesthood in Israel's early history. R. Abba, as well as W. R. Smith, for example, maintain that JE presumes the existence of a priesthood while it yet acknowledges that non-priests also offer sacrifice.[18] Similarly, Haran explains that JE knows the priesthood of Aaron and considers ark-bearing a priestly activity, although it recognizes that non-Aaronides offered sacrifice.[19] According to Lattey, the presence of priests in Exodus 19:22—assigned by him to these early sources—suggests that JE presumes the existence of Israelite priests.[20]

Wellhausen's assertion that the tribe of Levi bears no genealogical connection with the priestly guild likewise has been a focus of debate. Accepting Wellhausen's position, Smith and Bertholet consider Levi an eponymous ideal, devoid of any historical moorings;[21] Gunneweg traces the origins of Levitism to the amphictyony;[22] and, according to L. Waterman, the Levites were never in Egypt and Moses was never a Levite.[23]

Within recent years more scholars have suggested an historical connection between the Levitical tribe and the priestly guild. Haran has

---

17 To be discussed below, 19, 20; 109.
18 R. Abba, "Priests and Levites," in *Interpreter's Dictionary of the Bible*, ed. George Buttrick and others (Nashville: Abingdon, 1962), vol. K-Q, 881; W. R. Smith, *The Old Testament in the Jewish Church* (New York: D. Appleton and Company, 1881), 358.
19 Haran, *Temples*, 66-76.
20 Cuthbert Lattey, "The Tribe of Levi," *CBQ* 12 (1950): 279.
21 W. R. Smith and A. Bertholet, "Levites," in *Encyclopaedia Biblica*, ed. T. K. Cheyne and J. Black (New York: MacMillan and Co, 1902), III: 2775.
22 A. H. J. Gunneweg, *Leviten und Priester* (Göttingen: Vandenhoeck and Ruprecht, 1965), 81.
23 Leroy Waterman, "Moses the Pseudo Levite," *JBL* 59 (1940): 397.

taken this position,[24] as has Cody, who contends that the name Levite originally referred to a member of the tribe and later came to describe the member of the priestly profession.[25] In the same vein, Kaufmann considers the Levites to be a tribe dedicated to guarding the *tôrâ* during the wilderness experience,[26] and Sklba stresses the Levitical link with Qadesh.[27] Both Baudissin and Polk maintain that one was included into the Levitical professional caste by virtue of either genealogy or choice.[28]

According to Wellhausen, while Israel in the pre-monarchic period did not maintain an elaborate priesthood as described by P, individual priests did serve local sanctuaries. These priests were not primarily responsible for sacrifice (as P suggests) but rather were known for the manipulation of oracular devices. Most scholars have agreed with Wellhausen that the role of the Israelite priest was not to sacrifice but to give instruction. Cody, Baudissin, Kelly, and Gray take this position;[29] similarly, Weaver contends that the original responsibility of the priest was *tôrâ* and oracles, although over time the duties of the priesthood changed.[30]

---

[24] Haran, *Temples*, 81-82. In an earlier period, Curtiss also took this position (*Levitical Priests*, ch.2).

[25] Aelred Cody, "An Excursus on Priesthood in Israel," in *Ezekiel*, The Old Testament Message: A Biblical-Theological Commentary (Wilmington, DE: Michael Glazier, 1984), 260-261.

[26] Ezekiel Kaufmann, *A History of Israelite Religion: From Antiquity to the End of the Second Temple* (Tel Aviv: Dvir, 1937-1948); quoted in Moshe Greenberg, "A New Approach to the History of the Israelite Priesthood," *JAOS* 70 (1950): 45 (hereafter Greenberg, "New Approach") .

[27] R. J. Sklba, "The Teaching Function of the Pre-Exilic Israelite Priesthood" (Ph.D. diss., Rome: Pontifica Studiorum Universitas A. S. Thomas Aq. in Urbe, 1965), 32.

[28] W. Baudissin, "Priests and Levites," in *Hastings Dictionary of the Bible*, ed . James Hastings (New York: Charles Scribners' Sons, 1902), IV: 70; Timothy Polk, "The Levites in the Davidic-Solomonic Empire," *Studia Biblica et Theologica* 9:1 (April, 1979): 4.

[29] A. Cody, *A History of Old Testament Priesthood* (Rome: Pontifical Biblical Institute, 1969), 11-14 (hereafter Cody, *History*); Baudissin, 73; James C. Kelly, "The Function of the Priest in the Old Testament," Pontificium Athenaeum Antoninianum, Facultas Theologicae, dissertation no. 242 (Rome: Pontificium Athenaeum Antoninianum. Sectio Biblica Hierosolymitana, 1973), 20, 22; George B. Gray, *Sacrifice in the Old Testament: Its Theory and Practice* (Oxford: Clarendon Press, 1925), 200.

[30] Horace Robert Weaver, "The Priesthood of Judaism in the Persian Period" (Ph. D. diss., Boston University Graduate School, 1949), 66.

PERIOD OF THE JUDGES AND EARLY MONARCHY.

Except for a few adherents to the traditional position, scholars largely agree with Wellhausen's assessment that non-Aaronides functioned as priests in the period of the judges. Pointing to priestly figures in the narratives of the Book of Judges, they support the contention that the priestly hegemony of Aaronide priests was unknown in the early period.

The non-Levitical character of these priests is contested, however. In light of the priestly activities of David, his sons and Ira the Jairite, Gray, Baudissin, Weaver, and Rowley contend that non-Levites were accepted into priestly roles.[31] De Vaux and Sklba concur with this thesis, although they utilize Judges 17-18 to suggest that while others served, Levites were preferred as priests.[32] Another point of view is presented by McConville, who argues that there is little evidence of non-Levitical priestly *families* in the early period, although non-Levitical individuals occasionally functioned as priests.[33] Abba concurs, attributing the priesthood of David to his royal privilege and describing the priesthood of his appointees as constituting royal rather than cultic service.[34]

MONARCHY

ZADOK.

All but a few dissenters such as Bartlett continue to view David's appointment of Zadok and Solomon's ousting of Abiathar as crucial events in the development of the priesthood. Bartlett argues that Zadok's priestly position never became the exclusive right of his descendants.[35] Most other scholars, however, have concurred with Wellhausen that after Abiathar's banishment, priesthood in Jerusalem belonged solely to the sons of Zadok for at least several centuries.

Wellhausen's description of Zadok as non-Levitical has been supported by Baudissin, North, and suggested by Cody;[36] Weaver, following Arnold, suggests that Zadok was Gibeonite.[37] A large number of scholars

---

[31] Gray, 240-241; Baudissin, 70; Weaver, 78; H. H. Rowley, *Worship in Ancient Israel: Its Forms and Meaning* (London: SPCK, 1967), 95-96.

[32] Roland de Vaux, *Ancient Israel: Its Life and Institutions* (New York: McGraw-Hill Book Co., 1961), 362; Sklba, 44.

[33] J. G. McConville, *Law and Theology in Deuteronomy*, JSOTS 33 (Sheffield: Department of Biblical Studies, University of Sheffield, 1984), 131.

[34] Abba, 882.

[35] J. R. Bartlett, "Zadok and his Successors at Jerusalem," *JTS* n.s. 19 (1968): 8-9.

[36] Baudissin, 72; Francis S. North, "Aaron's Rise in Prestige," *ZAW* 66 (1954): 194; Cody, *History*, 91-93.

[37] Weaver, 85.

has gone further to suggest that Zadok was not only not a Levite but also not an Israelite: Aberbach and Hauer have maintained that Zadok served as a Jebusite priest prior to his inclusion by David into the Israelite priesthood.[38]

The ascription to Zadok of a non-Levitical origin has not escaped challenge, however. Abba and Haran argue that Zadok was from the Levitical line.[39] Cross, using P and Chronicles in his historical reconstruction, posits that Zadok may indeed be an Aaronide;[40] many such as Polk have considered Cross' suggestion a sufficient basis to assert Zadok's Aaronide lineage.[41]

LEVITICAL CITIES.

While Wellhausen discounted the reality of the Levitical cities, numerous scholars have challenged this assessment. Baudissin explains these locations as ancient worship centers,[42] while McConville understands them to be residential centers for the unlanded Levites.[43] B. Mazar, who has focused much attention on these cities, argues that they were provincial administrative centers developed by Solomon.[44] Polk builds upon Mazar's thesis and suggests that the centers were staffed by Levites.[45] Haran, who agrees with Wellhausen that the description of the cities contains various utopian elements, nonetheless claims that the accounts also preserve historical components.[46]

THE BLESSING OF LEVI (DEUTERONOMY 33:8-11).

The Blessing of Levi in Deuteronomy 33 serves as an important document for the history of the Israelite priesthood. It defines the role of the priest as that of guarding *tôrâ* and of offering sacrifice, and it appears to grant priesthood to the entire tribe of Levi, recognizing no distinctions within it. According to Wellhausen, this passage—an independent document of the the northern kingdom—indicates that at the time of its composition the priesthood had become

---

[38] Moses Aberbach and Leivy Smolar, "Aaron, Jeroboam, and the Golden Calves," *JBL* 86 (1967): 136; Christian E. Hauer, Jr., "Who was Zadok?" *JBL* 82 (1963): 90.

[39] Abba, 882; Haran, *Temples*, 77-78.

[40] Cross, *Myth*, 207-15.

[41] Polk, 10.

[42] Baudissin, 71.

[43] McConville, 134.

[44] B. Mazar, "The Cities of the Priests and Levites," *VTS* 7 (1959 Congress Volume, 1960): 202.

[45] Polk, 17-19.

[46] Haran, *Temples*, 122-131.

...so fixed and influential, so independent and exclusive...that it takes a place of its own alongside the tribes of the nation [and] is itself a tribe, constituted, however, not by blood, but by community of spiritual interests.[47]

Scholars such as Kelly, Gray, and Smith and Bertholet have supported Wellhausen's dating of Deut. 33:8-11 and his separation of the passage from the rest of the Book of Deuteronomy. Along with Abba, they place the passage earlier than the rest of the book, in a period between the tenth and eighth centuries B.C.E.[48] Haran accepts a similar date and considers the entire Blessing of Moses to be a J document.[49] Cross and Freedman consider verses 8-11, which describe the role of the priest, to be later additions to the Blessing and therefore of no value in describing the priesthood during the monarchy.[50]

Most who consider the Blessing as a independent document inserted into Deuteronomy accept the conclusion that the passage grants priesthood to the whole tribe of Levi. Kelly and Gray take this position,[51] and even Hoppe, who denies that the Book of Deuteronomy itself demands equality of priest and Levite, yet contends that the Blessing of Levi does support Levitical claims to the priesthood.[52] Following Wellhausen, Smith and Bertholet argue that the passage refers only to the Northern priesthood and hence does not describe the status of priesthood in Judah.[53]

Those who consider the Blessing of Moses in Deuteronomy 33 to be an integral part of the book rather than a distinct document maintain that this passage treats the priesthood in the same manner as does the book as a whole. The various positions taken on Deuteronomy's priestly program will be discussed below.

DEUTERONOMY.

According to Wellhausen, by advocating that all members of the Levitical tribe may serve at the central sanctuary Deuteronomy seeks to to insure that the centralization of worship does not impoverish the Levites scattered throughout the land. Hence, while Deuteronomy dis-

---

47 Wellhausen, *Prolegomena*, 136.

48 Kelly, 9; Gray, 213; Smith and Bertholet, "Levites," 2771; Abba, 881.

49 Haran, *Temples*, 67.

50 Frank M. Cross and David Noel Freedman, "The Blessing of Moses," *JBL* 67 (1948): 204.

51 Kelly, 9-10; Gray, 213.

52 Leslie Hoppe, "The Origins of Deuteronomy" (Ph. D. diss., Northwestern University, 1978), 196-198.

53 Smith and Bertholet, "Levites," 2771.

tinguishes between the "Levitical priests" (*hakkōhănîm hallĕwiyyîm*—the Jerusalemite clergy) and the "Levites" (*hallĕwiyyîm*—the country priests), it insists that any Levite may serve as priest if he comes to Jerusalem.

That Deuteronomy champions—at least theoretically—the ability of all Levites to be priests has become almost axiomatic in biblical studies, as frequently assumed as it is argued. This position is supported by scholars of such diverse theological and methodological backgrounds as Haran, Greenberg, and Polk.[54] Even Milgrom, who argues for the temporal priority of P over D, understands Deuteronomy as a northern, pro-Levitical document.[55] Baudissin, while contending that Deuteronomy reveals that foreign slaves served as Temple servants, yet maintains that Deuteronomy does not recognize distinctions of rank within the tribe of Levi itself.[56] Cody, Gottwald, Kennett and Weaver agree that the equality of all Levites—although a major platform of Deuteronomy—was never actualized.[57]

While Wellhausen did acknowledge the terminological distinction between the "Levitical priests" and the "Levites," many subsequent scholars have proposed that these terms are synonymous. Buber and Rowley have asserted the equality of these terms, but the case has been set forth most strongly by J. A. Emerton in his response to G. E. Wright.[58]

Despite the popular consensus that Deuteronomy grants priesthood to the entire tribe of Levi, a persistent minority has continued to argue otherwise. From his syntactical study of the terms in the book, Wright maintains that Deuteronomy understands the phrase "the Levitical priests" to refer to altar clergy and the term "Levites" to refer to lay teachers of *tôrâ* scattered throughout the countryside. He therefore concludes that Deuteronomy's use of terms varies little from that of P.[59] Curtiss and Lattey interpret Deuteronomy's language in a more general way: in Deuteronomy's imprecise terminology, "Levite" describes both

---

54   Haran, *Temples*, 61; M. Greenberg, "New Approach," 45; Polk, 16.

55   Jacob Milgrom, "Profane Slaughter and a Formulaic Key to the Composition of Deuteronomy," *HUCA* 47 (1976): 16.

56   Baudissin, 75.

57   Cody, *History*, 134; Gottwald, 388; Kennett, 172; Weaver, 113.

58   Martin Buber, "Priest," in *The Jewish Encyclopedia*, ed. Isidore Singer and others (New York: Funk and Wagnalls, 1905), X: 193-194; Rowley, *Worship*, 96; J. A. Emerton, "Priests and Levites in Deuteronomy," *VT* 12:2 (April 1962): 129-138.

59   G. E. Wright, "The Levites in Deuteronomy," *VT* 4 (1954): 325-330. This view is shared by E. M. Meyers in his article "Priestly Language in the Book of Malachi," *Hebrew Annual Review* (1987): 225-237 (hereafter Meyers, "Priestly Language").

ranks of the clergy.[60] Similarly, Hoppe considers Deuteronomy as a "diplomatically-worded compromise" that permits non-Aaronides to perform limited priestly functions.[61] According to McConville, the theological agenda of the book accounts for its imprecise terminology; seeking to stress the unity of all Israel, Deuteronomy consciously blurs— although it is aware of—distinctions between groups.[62]

Wellhausen's assessment of Deuteronomy's agenda is based upon his conviction that the "Levites" of the book are the priests of the country *bāmôt*, denied their rightful place in Jerusalem by the sons of Zadok. Abba supports this view that the Levite is the *bāmâ* priest,[63] but Baudissin, Haran and Kaufmann disagree. According to Baudissin, the Levite in the country did not function as a priest but was an unemployed recipient of charity.[64] Similarly, Haran contends that Deuteronomy expresses no concern for those serving the very *bāmôt* which it prohibits, and that the priests of the *bāmôt* were non-Levitical; true Levites outside of Jerusalem differed little from the laity.[65] Kaufmann, although agreeing that Josiah banished only defiled priests, differs from Haran and Baudissin in suggesting that the Levites during the period of Josiah were a new class. Deuteronomy rehabilitates a long-dead Levitical class in order to fulfill newly-found Scripture.[66]

EZEKIEL

According to Wellhausen, the distinction in rank between Jerusalemite priest and country Levite, although prohibited by the Deuteronomic reform, became a reality by the close of the pre-exilic history. Chapters 40-48 of Ezekiel, in this scheme, provide prophetic sanction to this distinction, demoting the Levites because of their sin—a demotion assumed by P.

Scholarly attention to the importance of Ezekiel in the study of the priesthood has centered on three major issues: the respective dates of Ezekiel and P; the identification of the parties involved; and the outcome of Ezekiel's program.

---

60 Curtiss, 9-21; Lattey, 288-291.
61 Hoppe, 186.
62 McConville, 151-152 (summary).
63 Abba, 883.
64 Baudissin, 76.
65 Haran, *Temples*, 100.
66 Kaufmann, in Greenberg, "New Approach," 46.

DATES.

Although Welch places Ezekiel 40-48 in the years after the Return,[67] most scholars continue to date Ezekiel sometime during the exilic period. Wellhausen's post-exilic dating of P, however, integral in his understanding of Ezekiel, has engendered lively debate. The arguments for the date of P will be discussed in greater detail below, yet it is important to note here that a growing number of scholars—especially those from Israel—advocate a pre-exilic date for the major portions, if not the entirety, of the Priestly source. Hence, while Hanson concurs with Wellhausen's position and places Ezekiel before P, Haran and Milgrom—as well as Baudissin, Curtiss and Lattey—maintain that Ezekiel builds upon P.[68]

PARTIES.

A large majority of scholars, especially those who accept the chronological priority of Ezekiel over P, follow Wellhausen in describing Ezekiel's program as providing prophetic legitimation for the *de facto* subordinate status of the Levite. Emerton, Gray, de Vaux, Weaver and Smith and Bertholet adopt this position and interpret Ezekiel as banishing from the Temple all non-Zadokite Levites.[69]

While Abba concurs on this dating of Ezekiel, he however understands the book's goal differently: rather than demoting the entire Levitical class, Ezekiel downgrades only those who have practiced idolatry.[70] Lattey argues this same case from an alternate position on dating, for he asserts that by chastising idolatrous Levites Ezekiel upholds P's earlier insistence on the sole worship of Yahweh.[71]

OUTCOME.

But while Lattey attempts to support both the priority of P *and* Ezekiel's continuity with it, Curtiss, Haran, and Kaufmann—who also place P prior to Ezekiel—do not. They acknowledge that Ezekiel's exclu-

---

67 Adam Welch, *Post-Exilic Judaism* (London: William Blackwood and Sons, Ltd., 1935), 237.

68 Paul Hanson, *The People Called: The Growth of Community in the Bible* (San Francisco: Harper & Row, 1986), 224 (hereafter Hanson, *People Called*); Haran, *Temples*, 102; Jacob Milgrom, *Studies in Levitical Terminology, I: The Encroacher and the Levite. The Term ʿAbodah* (London: University of California Press, 1970), 83f.; Baudissin, 90; Curtiss, 68ff.; Lattey, 291.

69 Emerton, 136; Gray, 227; de Vaux, 365; Weaver, 114; Smith and Bertholet, "Priest," *Encyclopaedia Biblica* (New York: MacMillan and Co., 1902), III: 3845.

70 Abba, 883.

71 Lattey, 291.

sion of all non-Zadokite priests conflicts with P's inclusion of all descendents of Aaron. Consequently, these scholars contend that Ezekiel's vision of restoration in chapters 40-48 was never accomplished.[72] Haran deems the plan an "imaginary" attempt to turn those true priests outside of Jerusalem into temple servants.[73] Kaufmann labels the prophet/priest "idiosyncratic"—a lone voice calling for the limitation of the priesthood to one branch of the Aaronide clan.[74]

Hanson, a bit differently, distinguishes between the original Book of Ezekiel and what he believes to be a Zadokite revision. Despite its chastisement of the country priests, he believes that the original book was conciliatory, still regarding all priests as Levites. On the contrary, a Zadokite revision of the book introduced a sharp anti-Levitical polemic. The presence of various strata within Ezekiel, therefore, accounts for its often inconsistent use of the term "Levite."[75]

POST-EXILIC PERIOD

GENERAL DESCRIPTION.

The post-exilic period, as described by Wellhausen, marked the final entrenchment of the ruling priestly party. Claiming for itself Mosaic legitimacy, this group both squelched all rivals and exerted its hegemony over the community. Although Wellhausen bases his presentation of the development of the Pentateuch upon this understanding of priestly control during the post-exilic era, he offers no detailed discussion of the struggles preceding that control.

This task has been undertaken by Paul Hanson, who endeavors to clarify the post-exilic segment within Wellhausen's larger scheme. Hanson explains that the pre-exilic tension between a Mushite group (represented in Abiathar) and a Zadokite group grew bitter in the early years after the Return as competing plans for the restoration of Israel clashed. The Levites, most of whom had remained in the land, envisioned a new theocratic Israel, in which all persons would be equal; the Zadokites, however, advocated their own hierocratic government as formulated in Babylon and as negotiated with the Persian government.[76]

---

[72] Curtiss, 77-78.
[73] Haran, *Temples*, 107.
[74] Kaufmann, in Greenberg, "New Approach," 44.
[75] Paul Hanson, *The Dawn of Apocalyptic: The Historical and Sociological Roots of Jewish Apocalyptic Eschatology*, revised ed. (Philadelphia: Fortress Press, 1979), 263-269.
[76] Hanson, *People Called*, 253-290.

These two competing plans of restoration precipitated acrimonious struggle in the years after the Return. The Zadokites co-opted earlier literature in defense of their position. For example, while the Priestly Code had been written in the exile as a sensitive response to crisis, the Zadokites appropriated P's separation of an upper clergy ("the sons of Aaron") and a lower clergy ("the Levites") in their battle against the Levitical theocratic party. Hanson maintains that echoes of this battle still resound in Third Isaiah, and, as will be discussed later, Malachi.

In this struggle, the Zadokites were victorious. The canon preserves the record of their accomplishments not only in the Books of Haggai and Zechariah, but also in their pro-Zadokite revisions of the originally conciliatory Book of Ezekiel and of such portions of the Priestly Code as the account of the sons of Korah.[77]

According to Hanson, in the decades after the Zadokite victory, this bitter polemic between the Zadokites and Levites weakened, disappearing by the time of the Chronicler. With all rivals effectively squelched and with most of the "deplorable" conditions of the restoration community improved by Ezra, the hierocratic party could, ca. 400 B.C.E. adopt a more conciliatory position toward its rivals.

One component of this tolerance is found in Chronicles' development of a new genealogy in which both Zadokites and Levites share an Aaronide ancestry and through which all priests are the sons of Aaron. Hence, Hanson maintains, while in Chronicles the Zadokites retain superiority over all others and continue to control the high priesthood, the "...Ithamarides and the Levites have been restored to the hierocratic cult in good favor." [78]

SONS OF AARON.

As seen in Hanson's discussion, the designation "sons of Aaron" served an important legitimizing function both in the Priestly Code and in Chronicles. Hanson's view that the term was created by P and then utilized by the Chronicler is not unilaterally accepted by scholars, and, thus, differing explanations of the origin and significance of the term "sons of Aaron" are here offered.

According to Wellhausen, the term is the creation of the Priestly Code, intended to grant to the Zadokite group a more venerable legitimacy. It is but a new name for an old group.[79] Hanson takes this same

---

[77] Hanson, *Dawn*, 268-269.
[78] Ibid., 273.
[79] Wellhausen, *Prolegomena*, 126.

position, maintaining that P's "sons of Aaron" are the same group that Ezekiel and Chronicles call the "sons of Zadok."[80]

Curtiss and Kaufmann agree that during the post-exilic period the existing priesthood was renamed the "sons of Aaron," and yet they, unlike Wellhausen and Hanson, see no real change in the character of the Israelite priesthood from the time of its inception. Curtiss places the division between priest and Levite in the wilderness;[81] similarly, Kaufmann suggests that the tension between Aaronides and Levites surfaced—and was resolved—in the wilderness period.[82]

More usually, however, the term "sons of Aaron" is viewed as a designation first developed during the post-exilic (or exilic) era as a compromise between at least two groups. Smith and Bertholet, for example, argue that the expanded genealogies of Chronicles indicate that the "sons of Aaron" included a larger group than the previous "sons of Zadok."[83]

While Hanson posits that P penned the term "sons of Aaron" in the exilic period and that Chronicles extended the designation in the post-exilic period to include non-Zadokites, many consider the term to have actually originated in a compromise achieved in the restoration community. Accordingly, Judge understands this term as a compromise label developed to include both the Zadokites who had returned from Exile and the Levitical circles who had remained in the land.[84] This position is shared by Welch, who explains that this compromise allowed all descendents of Aaron to serve as priests; and, while it did not give the Levites full priestly privileges, it yet refused to degrade them as had Ezekiel.[85]

But while Judge and Welch view this compact as binding large factions within the community, other scholars view the conflict as one solely between priestly families—in Gottwald's words, "a battle of priestly pedigrees."[86] Bartlett, for example, understands the "sons of Aaron" compromise as ending the bitter post-exilic rivalry between the Ithamarides and the Eleazarides.[87] Abba and de Vaux, positing tension

---

80 Hanson, *People Called*, 231-232.
81 Curtiss, in preface by Delitzsch, viii.
82 Kaufmann, in Greenberg, "New Approach," 45.
83 Smith and Bertholet, "Priest," 3844.
84 H. G. Judge, "Aaron, Zadok and Abiathar," *JTS* n. s. 7 (1956): 70-74.
85 Welch, *Post-Exilic Judaism*, 239.
86 Gottwald, 461.
87 Bartlett, "Zadok," 16.

between these same groups, maintain that the compromise was reached in Babylon and brought by Ezra to Yehud upon his return.[88]

A yet different third position holds that the term "sons of Aaron," rather than a genealogical legitimization or a compromise title, was indeed the name for an actual group of priests.[89] Most vocal in maintaining that the sons of Aaron were a separate group of priests to which others later attached themselves are Cody, Haran, Kennett and North.

Noting in Joshua's descriptions of the Levitical cities that the Aaronides are given only southern locations, Cody and Haran conclude that the sons of Aaron originally were a subgroup of Levites who resided in proximity to Jerusalem. When the Deuteronomic reforms established the Temple as the sole legitimate sanctuary, only these sons of Aaron among the non-Zadokites were sufficiently close to Jerusalem to be affected. The reigning Zadokites did not welcome the Aaronides during the time of Josiah, say Cody and Haran, but sometime during or after the exile they found it necessary to merge genealogically with the sons of Aaron.[90]

Kennett and North, quite differently, argue that the sons of Aaron were originally the priests of the shrine at Bethel that had been founded during the divided monarchy and to which various biblical texts such as Exodus 32 link the figure of Aaron. According to Kennett, the sanctuary at Bethel continued to operate after the fall of the Northern kingdom and, when the destruction of Judah destroyed the Temple cultus, those Judaeans remaining in the land turned to the sanctuary at Bethel for religious leadership.[91] North extends this thesis even further, asserting that during the exile Bethel supplanted Jerusalem as the country's sole worship center. According to North and Kennett, upon their return from the exile the Zadokites were forced to join themselves to the established Aaronide priesthood.[92]

THE PRIESTLY CODE (P).

Because the Priestly Code consistently uses the term "sons of Aaron" for Israel's priests and because it draws clear distinctions between priests and Levites, scholars have perceived this legislation as central in under-

---

88   Abba, 885; de Vaux, 395-396.

89   Baudissin (89) stands practically alone in insisting that even before the exile some Zadokite priests traced their lineage back to Aaron.

90   Cody, *History*, 156-166; Haran, *Temples*, 84-92.

91   Kennett, 161-186.

92   F. S. North, 194.

standing Aaronide priestly claims. As with other issues, Wellhausen's thesis regarding P has served as the basis for most subsequent debate. According to Wellhausen, P was written by Israel's priests in the post-exilic period (ca. 400 B.C.E.) as an attempt to establish the restoration community as a religious body—as opposed to a nation—and to fortify their own control over it. P both grants Mosiac legitimacy to the subordination of the Levite and, asserted Wellhausen, estranged Israel's faith from its natural connection with human life through its minute regulation of everyday practices such as sacrifice.[93]

Scholarly discussion bearing upon the Priestly Code has concentrated on two areas of Wellhausen's presentation. It evaluates both his dating of P and his assessment of P's theological and political goals.

Wellhausen's post-exilic dating of P has long enjoyed consensus within the field of biblical studies, often tacitly accepted where not overtly defended. Weaver, Rivkin, and Eissfeldt—as well as a vast multitude of thinkers—treat the Priestly Code as a product of the post-exilic community.[94]

Within recent years, however, this consensus has been shaken by those who vigorously defend a much earlier date. Baudissin and Kennett shift P's date to the period of the exile, but both traditionalists and a circle of Israeli scholars have gone further to maintain that P is pre-exilic, and perhaps even pre-Deuteronomic. Curtiss—though writing several years prior to the publication of the *Prolegomena*—responds to Wellhausen's arguments. He defends the priority of P over D and attempts to demonstrate that the Book of Hosea reflects a completed Pentateuch.[95]

Kaufmann and Haran, as well as Milgrom, offer at least three grounds for their pre-exilic dating of P. First, they maintain that the Priestly Code, especially in its original form, does not reflect knowledge of the Temple in Jerusalem. According to Haran, this legislation pertains primarily to the cult at Shiloh and was only later reworked to refer to the Jerusalem Temple.[96] Kaufmann contends that P does not presume the centralization of the cultus but rather reflects the period of the *bāmôt*.[97]

[93] Wellhausen, *Prolegomena*, e.g., 102.

[94] Weaver, 48; Ellis Rivkin, "Aaron, Aaronides," in *Interpreter's Dictionary of the Bible*, Supplementary Volume, ed. Keith Crimm and others (Nashville: Abindgon, 1976), 1-3; Eissfeldt, 207-208.

[95] Curtiss, 175-181.

[96] M. Haran, "Shiloh and Jerusalem: The Origin of the Priestly Tradition in the Pentateuch," *JBL* 81 (1962): 21-23.

[97] Kaufmann, in Greenberg, "New Approach," 45.

Second, they argue that P does not fit the post-exilic period. Presenting a terminological argument, Milgrom maintains that the priestly terminology found in P appears elsewhere in the Hebrew Bible only in pre-exilic texts.[98] Kaufmann, who like Wellhausen traces the development of Israel's institutions, posits that P's regulations such as the tithe antedate the legislation of Deuteronomy.[99] Haran, a bit differently, acknowledges that although P should be dated early many of its regulations were not observed until the post-exilic period. In an ingenious attempt to preserve an early date for P and to account for its early lack of influence, Haran theorizes that while P was written during the reign of Hezekiah, it remained the exclusive property of the priests until it was promulgated by Ezra as part of the Pentateuch.[100]

Third, these scholars maintain that literature written before the post-exilic period quotes directly from the Priestly Code. Not only do all of these scholars attempt to demonstrate Ezekiel's knowledge of P,[101] but also Milgrom, having analyzed D's formula for quoting sources on which it relies, concludes that Deuteronomy quotes not only from E but also from P.[102]

Vink, venturing in quite a different direction than most of current scholarship, has attempted to defend a date for P that is even later than that proposed by Wellhausen. He maintains that P was written in the late post-exilic period, not in the restoration community of Yehud but rather in the Dispersion.[103]

The goal of the Priestly Code, theorized Wellhausen, was to seal the Aaronide control of the priesthood and the inferior status of the Levite that was introduced in Ezekiel. Wellhausen, because he dates P early in the post-exilic period and Chronicles later, therefore views P as the first major authoritative writing to provide justification for the priestly program instigated by the prophet Ezekiel.[104]

---

98 Jacob Milgrom, *Studies in Cultic Theology and Terminology*, Studies in Judaism in Late Antiquity, ed. Jacob Neusner (Leiden: E. J. Brill, 1983), summary, ix (hereafter, Milgrom, *Cultic Theology*).

99 Kaufmann, in Greenberg, "New Approach," 45.

100 M. Haran, "Behind the Scenes of History: Determining the Date of the Priestly Source," *JBL* 100 (1981): 326-327.

101 Milgrom, *Levitical Terminology*, 8, n. 25; Haran, *Temples*, 94

102 Milgrom, "Profane Slaughter," 1-17.

103 J. G. Vink, "The Date and Origin of the Priestly Code," in *The Priestly Code and Seven Other Studies*, Oudtestamentische Studiën, no. 15 (Leiden: E. J. Brill, 1969), 80-144.

104 Wellhausen, *Prolegomena*, 124-125.

The theories concerning the program of P vary greatly according to the date assigned to the document. As noted above, those who date P in the pre-exilic years believe that it attempts to regulate first the Shiloh sanctuary and then the First Temple[105] or the individual *bāmôt*.[106] As also noted, Hanson—who dates the finalization of P to the exile—distinguishes between the program of the original document and its later utilization by the Zadokite hierocratic group. While Hanson concedes that P did distinguish between upper and lower clergy, he attributes to it none of the vehemence which characterized those who utilized it in the post-exilic community. Hanson moreover defends the vitality of P's theology and its utter necessity in the years after the destruction of the Temple.[107]

Even those who agree with Wellhausen in dating P in the post-exilic period differ in their evaluations of its goals. Weaver characterizes P's treatment of the Levites as less demeaning than does Wellhausen. He argues that although in P the Levitical status is lower than that of the priests, such status is not treated as a punishment as it is in Ezekiel.[108]

CHRONICLES.

Wellhausen regarded Chronicles as a totally untrustworthy attempt to rewrite Israel's history according to the post-exilic notions of P. Around the same time period, Curtiss argued that Chronicles used reputable documents,[109] and, within recent years, more scholars have shown themselves willing to accept the possibility that Chronicles, although a late document, preserves some ancient traditions. While a great number of scholars such as de Vaux consider the Chronicler's genealogies to be artificial, Cross has defended its description of Zadok as a descendant of Aaron.[110]

Chronicles' high estimation of the Levites is perhaps its outstanding characteristic. According to Hanson, this attention to the Levite is evidence of the conciliatory character of the book.[111] Milgrom believes that by granting the Levites such a prominent role and by designating them as *kādôš* Chronicles in fact defies the Priestly Code.[112]

---

105 E.g., M. Haran, "Shiloh and Jerusalem," 21.
106 E.g., Kaufmann, in Greenberg, "New Approach," 45.
107 Hanson, *People Called*, 224-233.
108 Weaver, 288 .
109 Curtiss, 100-120.
110 de Vaux, 373-374; Cross, *Myth*, 208-209.
111 Hanson, *People Called*, 302-303.
112 Milgrom, *Levitical Terminology*, 13, n. 46.

Synthesis of Histories of the Priesthood

The length of the preceding section and the number of its subsections demonstrate the degree to which scholars vary in their understanding of the priesthood. Their ideas are not easily categorized or traced developmentally. Since all interpret each of the many components of the study differently, they have produced a bewildering array of theories and permutations of theories that may—or may not—relate to other priestly scholarship. The following, however, attempts to identify several matters of consensus among most scholars, in order to determine major areas of significant controversy and to ascertain which of those factors in the study of the priesthood are integral to the study of Malachi.

MATTERS OF GENERAL CONSENSUS

Despite their disagreements, most scholars acknowledge several key points:

1. *Priesthood changed over time.* While biblical scholars assess differently the manner and the time frame of significant changes, the majority accept Wellhausen's thesis that the priesthood did not remain static throughout Israel's history.

2. *JE does not reflect the same detailed priesthood described by P.* Although they disagree over whether JE acknowledges the existence of priesthood at all and over the date of J, scholars agree that P's priesthood is more ordered than that presented in JE.

3. *At some time in Israel's history, priesthood was understood to belong to the entire Levitical tribe.* Even those such as McConville, who argue that Deuteronomy does not allow all Levites to be priests, concur that in an earlier period Levites were priests.

4. *Power was consolidated in Jerusalem during the monarchy.* Both those who deem David's appointment of Zadok as significant and those who contend that Josiah's program of centralization put the Levites in the countryside out of work agree that Jerusalem became a major center of priestly power.

5. *The Priestly Code advocates the priesthood of a smaller and/or different group than the entire Levitical tribe.* Although the identification of the "sons of Aaron" varies greatly, few are willing to suggest that this group includes the entire tribe of Levi.

While all these tenets do not receive unanimous approval, they are accepted by most scholars, at least in general terms. The majority of those studying the priesthood suggests that, at some point in Israel's history, priesthood became no longer the right of all members of the tribe of Levi and instead became the prerogative of a smaller group.

KEY ISSUES

Because this shift in priestly privilege is seen as a crucial stage in the history of the priesthood, the date and manner of this occurrence remains a vital issue of study. Since the Priestly Code is usually viewed as the first authoritative document to effectively prescribe this change, the date and the program of P likewise are central issues.

Due to the scholarship of the past few decades, a post-exilic date for P no longer can be merely assumed. Even if one disagrees with the arguments of Haran, Kaufmann and Milgrom, biblical scholars must consider—at the very least—the possibility of a date for P which is earlier than that proposed by Wellhausen. In the wake of discussions of the term "sons of Aaron" by scholars as Cody, Haran and Cross and the suggestion that Chronicles may preserve some reliable traditions, Wellhausen's view that "sons of Aaron" is an artificial creation also must be questioned.

SIGNIFICANCE FOR THE STUDY OF MALACHI

The scholarly consensus outlined above and the unresolved matter of the date of P are crucial in understanding what the Book of Malachi may indicate about the priesthood at the time of its composition. Based on the assumption of a change in the priesthood and the importance of the Priestly Code in that change, the following questions become central:

- Does Malachi reflect a current notion that all Levites can be priests, or is the smaller priestly group supported by P in control of the priesthood?
- Does the book reflect knowledge of the Priestly Code?
- What is the book's own position? If it reflects P, does it concur with P's program? If it does not appear to reflect P, is the omission due to its ignorance of P *or* to its protest against it?

Scholarly attempts to answer these questions have varied and are described in the next section.

UNDERSTANDINGS OF MALACHI'S VIEW
OF THE PRIESTHOOD

Malachi's lack of explicit references to the sons of Aaron and its mention of a "covenant with Levi" (2:4), a "covenant of Levi" (2:8) and the "sons of Levi" (3:8), along with what many consider to be the Deuteronomic character of the book, raise the questions of whether the author knows the Priestly Code and whether he or she uses the terms "sons of Levi" and "priests" synonymously. Four major positions are taken on these issues.

The large majority of those discussing Malachi contend that in the book the terms are equivalent and, therefore, that Malachi reflects a point in the history of the priesthood prior to the enactment of the reforms of the Priestly Code. Such is the position of Eissfeldt, Chary, M. Smith, and Swetnam.[113] E. Rivkin, a scholar much concerned with P and its "Aaronide revolution," dates P on the basis of Malachi. Pointing to Malachi as the last biblical book which does not reflect P, Rivkin argues that the Priestly Code must have gained prominence after the prophetic book.[114] This majority claim is usually buttressed with the contention that Malachi is a thoroughly Deuteronomic book, employing both the themes and the terminology of Deuteronomy.

Many, however, have suggested that while Malachi relies heavily on Deuteronomy its description of the tithe in chapter 3 resembles more that of the Priestly legislation than that of the Deuteronomic Code. This observation has led some scholars to propose that Malachi reflects the transition from D to P. Wellhausen, J. M. P. Smith, Weaver and Neil explain Malachi in this way.[115] E. Achtemeier, in the same manner, believes that Malachi's characterization of the tithe corresponds to the tithe that was *later* codified by P.[116]

---

[113] Eissfeldt, 442; Théophane Chary, *Aggée, Zacharie, Malachie* (Paris: Gabalda, 1967), 225 (hereafter Chary, *Aggée*); Morton Smith, *Palestinian Parties and Politics that Shaped the Old Testament* (New York: Columbia Univ. Press, 1971), 250, n. 83; James Swetnam, "Malachi 1:11: An Interpretation," *CBQ* 31 (1969): 203, n. 20.

[114] Rivkin, 1-3.

[115] J. Wellhausen, *Die kleinen Propheten übersetzt und erklärt* (Berlin: Walter de Gruyter, 1892/1963), 209-210; J. M. P. Smith, "Malachi," in *A Critical and Exegetical Commentary on Haggai, Zechariah and Malachi*, by Mitchell, Smith and Bewer, International Critical Commentaries (Edinburgh: T & T Clark, 1912), 9, 38; Weaver, 22, 175; W. Neil, "Malachi," in *Interpreter's Dictionary of the Bible*, ed. George Buttrick and others (Nashville: Abingdon, 1962), vol. K-Q, 229.

[116] Elizabeth Achtemeier, *Nahum-Malachi*, Interpretation Series (Atlanta: John Knox Press, 1986), 171-172, 188.

These two viewpoints both maintain that, since in Malachi "priest" and "son of Levi" appear equivalent, the book must predate that final form of P, which recognizes sharp distinctions between Levites and Aaronides. Both imply a late date of P. The second position moreover suggests, as Kaufmann explains, that the prophet rebukes the people for ignoring a regulation that had not yet been officially promulgated.[117]

More importantly, these first two positions concerning Malachi trace a causal relationship between what are in fact two separate issues: the grammatical question of whether the terms "priests" and "sons of Levi" function synonymously and the source–critical question of whether Malachi knows the Priestly Code. Rivkin and others can argue that the grammatical equation of terms implies no knowledge of P only because they assume that the terms could not be treated synonymously from a Priestly viewpoint.

Kaufmann and Glazier-McDonald, taking a different third position, do maintain that Malachi knows P *and* that the terms are equal. Both offer terminological arguments to demonstrate that Malachi does reflect the language of P, and while Glazier-McDonald does not make explicit her dating of P Kaufmann adamantly supports a pre-exilic date for the source. At the same time, both agree that in Malachi priests are called "sons of Levi." According to Kaufmann, Malachi's "...'sons of Levi' are priests, and he assumes that the whole tithe is given over to them."[118] Basing her remarks on the work of Cody and Pedersen, Glazier-McDonald contends that in this period the entire priesthood was subsumed under the genealogy of Levi.[119] In this way, the identity of the terms "priest" and "Levite" rest not on a Deuteronomic notion that all members of the tribe may be priests but rather on the post-exilic notion that the "sons of Aaron" also were "sons of Levi."

A fourth position maintains that in Malachi the terms "priests" and "sons of Levi" are not synonymous but rather in bitter tension; while the book reflects P's distinction between priest and Levite, it does not support P's agenda. Hanson has been the most vocal proponent of this position. According to him, the book contrasts the purity of the "covenant with/of Levi" with the corruption of the priest. The Book of Malachi, for Hanson, portrays the acrid struggle in the early years of the Restoration

---

117 Kaufmann, 446, n. 2.

118 Kaufmann, 436.

119 Beth Glazier-McDonald, "Malachi: The Divine Messenger, A Critical Appraisal" (Ph. D. diss., University of Chicago, 1983), 122-123 (hereafter Glazier-McDonald, "Malachi").

between a Levitical/prophetic group that promoted theocratic rule and the governing Zadokite group that had returned from exile armed with their hierocratic program.[120] Mason has taken a similar position, and Dumbrell adopts Hanson's presentation.[121] Gottwald does not paint so clear a picture. While he recognizes obvious tensions in the book, he is unsure whether the designation "sons of Levi" is intended to directly counter Aaronide claims to the priesthood.[122] Blenkinsopp, though highlighting what he considers to be the pervasive Deuteronomic thought in Malachi, suggests that since the prophet alludes to Aaron's sin at Sinai which was punished by the Levites the book may attack the Aaronide faction.[123]

The matter of whether the terms "priest" and "son of Levi" are synonymous or rather in tension thus remains central to evaluating these various theories and to understanding the priesthood which Malachi addresses. This matter, therefore, properly constitutes the next area of study.

---

[120] Hanson, *People Called*, 253-290.

[121] Rex Mason, *The Books of Haggai, Zechariah, and Malachi*, Cambridge Bible Commentary (New York: Cambridge University Press, 1977), 148; W. J. Dumbrell, "Malachi and the Ezra-Nehemiah Reforms," *Reformed Theological Review* 35 (1976): 43.

[122] Gottwald, 510.

[123] Joseph Blenkinsopp, *A History of Prophecy in Israel* (Philadelphia: Westminster Press, 1983), 242.

CHAPTER II

LĒWÎ AND KŌHĒN: A SYNTACTICAL STUDY

PROBLEM

In five verses of the Book of Malachi, the prophet names persons and/or groups associated with the priesthood. In 1:6 and 2:1, "priests" (hakkōhănîm) are lambasted for failing to honor the deity. A "covenant with Levi" (bĕrît ʾet-lēwî) describes the proper role of the priest in 2:4, as does "the Levitical covenant" (bĕrît-hallēwî) in 2:8. Malachi 3:3 relates that the "sons of Levi" (bĕnê-lēwî), once purified, will present proper offerings to the Lord.

Problematically for understanding the groups that the designations describe, the overall context and connection between these verses are not immediately clear: no distinct markers relate these noncontiguous verses, and the book itself never makes explicit the relationship between the groups. Are, for example, the "sons of Levi" addressed in 3:3 equated or contrasted with those called "priests" in 1:6 and 2:1? Is the "priest" of 2:1 included in or set in contradistinction to the "covenant with/of Levi" in 2:4 and 2:8?

Although the book provides no syntactical clues or lexical indicators for answering these questions, scholars nonetheless have drawn broad conclusions from their understandings of the *implied* relationship between *lēwî* and *kōhēn*—conclusions bearing upon issues ranging from the date of Pentateuchal sources to the nature of post-exilic politics and language. For while only two basic positions on this issue are possible (that is, the terms either are used synonymously or to describe different groups), the range of explanations for either position is not so circumscribed.

While most scholars contend that *lēwî* and *kōhēn* are synonymous in Malachi, they offer different reasons for this synonymity. As outlined more fully in chapter 1, E. Rivkin is followed by many others when he offers this equation of terms as proof that Malachi pre-dates the Priestly Code: recognizing the right of all Levites to serve as priests, Malachi reflects a period in the history of the priesthood prior to the enactment of P's distinction between priest and Levite.[1] While J. M. P. Smith and Wellhausen point to other indications that the book should be considered as transitional in the move from D to P, they yet agree with Rivkin that the reason underlying the synonymity of *lēwî* and *kōhēn* in Malachi is the book's pre-Priestly date.[2]

Kaufmann and Glazier-McDonald likewise contend that Malachi recognizes no difference between priest and Levite, but they explain this usage quite differently. In their view, Malachi is well aware of the Priestly Code and the priestly prerogatives of the sons of Aaron. The book's description of the (Aaronide) priests as sons of Levi, on the contrary, reflects a post-exilic development in which the sons of Aaron are considered sons of Levi, their priestly progenitor.[3]

Just as explanations for the proposed synonymity of *lēwî* and *kōhēn* vary, so too do the explanations for the difference between the terms perceived by other scholars. According to P. Hanson, the "fact" that in Malachi the *kōhănîm* are scathingly rebuked and sharply contrasted with the ideal covenant of the Levites demonstrates the severity of the tension between a dissident priestly group aligned with apocalyptic/theocratic elements and the priestly group wielding power in the Temple.[4] Indeed, judging from the attention that his articles and books devote to these proposed tensions within Malachi, Hanson considers the contrast between *lēwî* and *kōhēn* in the book to be highly significant for tracing the history of Israel's priesthood.[5]

While concurring that the "sons of Levi" and the "priests" are different groups, E. Meyers explains differently the import of this usage. Malachi, instead of describing these groups as existing in tension, rather criticizes both (Aaronide) priests and Levites for corrupting the entire priesthood and, uniquely, occasionally calls the Levite a *kōhēn*. This usage, argues Meyers, reveals no protracted struggle between Levite and priest but rather points to the fusion of the two as a result of which

---

[1] Rivkin, 1-3.

[2] J. M. P. Smith, 8-9; Wellhausen, *Kleinen Propheten*, 209-210.

[3] Kaufmann, 436; Glazier-McDonald, "Malachi," 119.

[4] Paul Hanson, "Biblical Apocalypticism: The Theological Dimension," *Horizons in Biblical Theology* 7:2 (1985): 4.

[5] Ibid., as well as *Dawn, People Called*.

Levites are called priests and priests assume the teaching duties normally associated with the Levites.[6]

As seen from these varying interpretations, the importance of better understanding the relationship between *kōhēn* and *lēwî* in Malachi scarcely can be overstated, since varying assessments of this relationship are used to buttress quite different positions on larger issues of biblical criticism and the history of Yehud in the Persian period. The goal of this chapter, therefore, is to consider how the terms employed by the Book of Malachi to describe priestly groups are used and to evaluate the syntactical/grammatical data upon which these varying scholarly claims are based.

METHODOLOGY

The lack of clear conjunctive or disjunctive indicators to specify whether *lēwî* and *kōhēn* are understood by the author of Malachi as synonymous or different requires the use of a clear methodology by which to assess the *implied* relationship between the terms. None of the studies of Malachi mentioned, however, indicates use of such a methodology. Neither those asserting the synonymity of terms nor those positing tension between them explain the grammatical basis on which their decisions are made. Discussion of the method used in this study, then, is in order.

This approach seeks to consider each of the passages in which priestly groups are named (1:6, 2:1, 2:4, 2:8 and 3:3) and to determine how their contexts may indicate the way in which the author understood these groups. While chapter three will consider the form of the Book of Malachi and attempt to outline the form-critical units of its discourse, the approach taken in this chapter is basicaly contextual, focusing on how the author portrays *lēwî* and *kōhēn*. Are these groups treated similarly or differently? Of what abuses is each group accused? What are considered to be the proper duties and responsibilities of Levites and priests?

The decision to consider the specific canonical context of these occurrences of *lēwî* and *kōhēn* prior to their placement within form-critical units is based upon the recognition that within a given unit the prophet may address or describe more than one group. H. W. Wolff has outlined this problem clearly in his study of Hosea, where he argues that form-critical units do not necessarily coincide with "kerygmatic units"

---

6 Meyers, "Priestly Language," 231.

(defined as that material addressed to or describing a given group).[7] Acknowledging that Malachi may deal with various groups within a canonical unit, then, this method will examine those verses that may be understood to bear directly upon the biblical author's understanding of *lēwî* and *kōhēn*.

Each occurrence first will be treated individually. After its context is defined, the manner in which the priestly group is characterized will be considered. All the occurrences then will be compared in order to determine if the author treats *lēwî* and *kōhēn* synonymously or differently.

OCCURRENCES

1:6

DEFINING THE CONTEXT

In the Book of Malachi, the first identification of a priestly group is that of *hakkōhănîm*, "priests," in 1:6. The context for understanding *hakkōhănîm* is taken to include verses 6-13 for the following reasons.

Verse 6 begins with a proverbial statement that leads to an accusation against the priests, who are addressed in the vocative. No prior verse has mentioned priests; instead, verses 2-5 have focused on the contrasting fortunes of Jacob and Esau.

Once addressed in the vocative, the *kōhănîm* are immediately referred to as "you." The following verses continue to address "you" without indicating any change of referent. This second person address continues through verse 13, with a brief interruption in verse 11. Although 1:14 clearly belongs *thematically* to this section, it does not unequivocally belong to the context for understanding *hakkōhănîm*. In this verse, the earlier second person plural pronouns are replaced with participles, the antecedent of which is indefinite: accusation is made against the *one* who offers inferior animals for sacrifice.[8]

DESCRIPTION OF THE GROUP

The group addressed as *kōhănîm* in 1:6 and as "you" through 1:13 are accused of despising the deity's reputation. More specifically:

1. They are accused of offering defiled food (1:7);
2. They offer improper animals for sacrifice (1:8). These include animals that are blind, lame and sick;

---

7 Hans Walter Wolff, *Hosea*, Hermeneia Series (Philadelphia: Fortress Press, 1974), xxix-xxxiii.

8 According to Glazier-McDonald, verse 14 refers to the laity. "Malachi," 97.

3. The deity wishes that they no longer kindle fire upon the altar vainly (1:10);
4. The deity will not accept *minḥâ* from them (1:10);
5. They profane the altar by thinking that it is despicable (1:12);
6. They disdain the altar (1:13);
7. They bring seized, lame and sick offerings (1:13);
8. They bring *minḥâ* (1:13).

All of these accusations/descriptions attribute to the priests altar functions. Priests are expected to offer proper sacrifices upon the altar and to insure that animals for sacrifice are neither blind, lame, sick or seized (cf. Deut. 15:21). Their kindling of the altar fires and their presentation of *minḥâ* should be done righteously, and the priests are deemed unfit for service when they disregard and scoff at the altar. Due to their failure to honor the deity through proper altar service, the LORD no longer delights in them. He, indeed, yearns for one to close the doors of the Temple.[9]

2:1 and 2:8

DEFINING THE CONTEXT

In 2:1, the *kōhănîm* are again addressed, and as before they are referred to in the second person plural: "this *miṣwâ* is unto you (*ʾălêkem*)." Without any change in referent, this second plural address continues through verse 4, a verse that also includes a third reference to a priestly group—*běrîtî ʾet-lēwî*. Verses 5-7 shift to a third person description of the ideal priest and conclude with the observation that the lips of a *kōhēn* should guard knowledge. In verses 8-9, the prophet resumes his attack on "you." This "you" describes the priests, as is evident from the earlier usage of *ʾattem* and from the sense of these verses.

That the third-person description of the ideal priest in 5-7 must be treated separately from the material that surrounds it (1-4 and 8-9) is mandated not only by the grammatical shift in persons but also by the importance of understanding properly the connection between the "covenant with Levi" in 5-7 and the "priests" who are attacked. The material contained in 2:1-9, indeed, stands as the crux passage for the priest/Levite problem in Malachi. While most commentators suggest that the *kōhēn* is presented as participating in the covenant with Levi,

---

[9] That these doors are those of the Temple is indicated not only by the context of the passage but also by the analogous passage in Nehemiah 6:10 in which closing the doors would prohibit access to the Temple. This term also refers to the Temple doors in 1 Kings 6:34; 2 Kings 18:16; Ezekiel 41:25.

Hanson vigorously argues that *kōhēn* of 2:1-4 and 8-9 is explicitly and sharply contrasted with the Levitical idea described in 2:5-7. According to Hanson, 2:1-4 and 8-9 form a "structural envelope" around 5-7 and place the fallenness of the Zadokite priests in sharpest possible contrast with the Levitical ideal.[10] He further asserts:

> In searching for a model to hold up before a corrupt priesthood, the opposition group coming to expression in the book of Malachi thus goes behind the Zadokite victory to an earlier stage of Israel's history, when the Levites served Yahweh as priests.... In sharp contrast to the division between priests and Levites that had developed under the leadership of the Zadokites, that is reflected in the Priestly Writing and Ezekiel 44, Malachi's "covenant with Levi" recognizes no such distinction. It reflects instead the earlier ideal expressed in Deuteronomy 18:1-8.[11]

Because the relationship between 2:5-7 with its surrounding material is so highly contested and so variously explained, these verses will be treated separately. The characterization of the *kōhēn* in 2:1-4, readdressed as "you" in 2:8-9, will be compared with the description of the *běrît ʾet-lēwî* in 2:5-7.

DESCRIPTION OF THE GROUP

2:1-4

As punishment for failing to honor the reputation of the deity, the *kōhănîm* in 2:1-4 receive the LORD's punishment.[12] This punishment comes as follows:

1. God will curse their blessings. Indeed, He has already done so (2:2);
2. He will rebuke their seed (2:3);
3. He will spread the dung of the festival sacrifices on their faces (2:3).

Determining what information these descriptions give regarding the functions of the priests is rendered difficult by the various translations that are possible for the first two of these punishments. Each, therefore, will be considered in turn.

1. *God will curse their blessings (birkôtêkem).* The precise meaning of *birkôtêkem* in 2:2 is variously assessed. It may refer either to the material blessings that the priests have received from the deity or to the blessings that they pronounce upon others. Glazier-McDonald has offered the

---

10 Hanson, *People Called*, 282.

11 Ibid., 282-283.

12 *wěʿattâ* is often used to draw a conclusion (see BDB, 774) and to introduce punishment (e.g., Hosea 4:16).

former of these interpretations and argues that these blessings are the same material blessings described in 3:10.[13] Michael Fishbane, on the contrary, advocates the second interpretation, viewing Malachi 1:6-2:9 as a post-exilic aggadic exegesis of Numbers 6:23-7 in which the prophet ironically inverts the priests' language, hopes and *actions*. That is, by revoking their prerogative of giving blessings, Malachi condemns the priests with the very language used in Numbers to describe their privilege.[14]

Either of these interpretations of *birkôtēkem* is feasible. Although the noun *bĕrākâ* is never used in the Hebrew Bible to describe the priest's act of blessing, frequent verbal forms attribute to the priest the prerogative of blessing.[15] Determining more precisely the meaning of *birkôtēkem* is not possible through the comparison of other biblical passages and, hence, must be considered in the context of the rest of this description.

2. *He will rebuke their seed (zeraʿ)*. Just as the *birkôtēkem* of 2:1 carries at least two possible meanings, so too does the *zeraʿ* of 2:3. It may indicate that the deity will rebuke either agricultural seed or human progeny. Causing additional translation difficulties, the phrase "I am rebuking the seed on your behalf" is also frequently emended to *hinnĕnî gōdēaʿ lākem ʾet-hazzĕrōaʿ*—"I will cut off your arm"—on the basis of the Septuagint and 1 Sam. 2:31. J. M. P. Smith, as one who reads with the Greek version, argues that the deity's rebuking of agricultural seed would punish farmers rather than priests. He considers the more logical threat to be the cutting of the priest's arm, which continues the previous incapacitation of the priest's act of blessing and more fittingly parallels the "faces" mentioned in 2:3b.[16]

Despite Smith's claims, there is no compelling reason to emend the Masoretic text on the basis of the Septuagint. As seen above, the blessings of the priests in 2:1 are not necessarily actions and, indeed, the rebuking of the priests' seed—however understood—is of no little consequence. The precise meaning of this punishment, however, is debated.[17]

---

13 Glazier-McDonald, "Malachi," 105.

14 Michael Fishbane, *Biblical Interpretation* in *Ancient Israel* (Oxford: Clarendon Press, 1985), 332-334.

15 Deut. 10:8, 21:5, 27:12; 1 Chron. 23:13; 2 Chron. 30:27; Lev. 9:22-23; Num. 6:23; Jos. 8:33.

16 J. M. P. Smith, 36-37. Achtemeier also reads with the LXX (180).

17 A good discussion of this problem is found in Pieter A. Verhoef, *Haggai and Malachi*, New International Commentary (Grand Rapids, MI: Wm. B. Eerdmans, 1987), 240-242.

According to Glazier-McDonald, "seed" is properly translated in its agricultural sense in this passage. As seen in the analogous passage of 3:10ff., Malachi stresses the connection between proper worship and the the material prosperity of the community; as a further parallel, the LORD in 3:11 promises to *rebuke* the devourer who threatens the fruit of the ground. The priests' disrespect for the deity will be punished by the community's lack of food.[18]

Several objections have been raised that contest this agricultural interpretation and suggest that "seed" refers to the offspring of the priests. As noted above, J. M. P. Smith argues that the cutting off of crops would harm the farmer, not the priest; similarly, P. Verhoef asserts that priests did not plant. Verhoef moreover argues that *zeraʿ* is never used to describe fruit or food.[19] Verhoef's statements, though true, prove little. Although priests do not plant, the land may be cursed on their account, and, although no occurrence of *zeraʿ* clearly describes the produce of the land, the restraining of *zeraʿ* would thwart produce.

While Verhoef's arguments are less than compelling, his conclusion that "seed" refers to the priests' offspring is likely correct.[20] *zeraʿ* frequently describes future offspring who will share in the benefits granted to the original recipient: not only do the "seeds" of Ishmael, David, various kings, and the houses of Jacob, Israel, and Ephraim share in what it given to their predecessors, but also the "seed" of Aaron and Phineas are given the responsibilities of priesthood (Exod. 28:43; Num. 17:5, 25:13; Lev. 21:17, 22:4). As a further parallel, in Hosea 4, the LORD threatens to forget the sons of sinful priests.

3. *He will spread the dung (pereš) of their festal sacrifices (ḥaggêkem) on their faces*. The final punishment levelled against the priests in this unit is contained in the second half of 2:3: "I will spread dung on your faces, the dung of your festival sacrifices" (*zērîtî pereš ʿal-pĕnêkem pereš ḥaggêkem*). The term *pereš* occurs elsewhere in the Hebrew Bible only in P texts, where it is used to describe the dung of animal sacrifices, which must be taken outside of the camp and burned (e.g., Exod. 29:14; Lev. 4:11, 8:17, 16:27; Num. 19:5). The use of the term *ḥag* to refer to the animal of the

---

18 Glazier-McDonald, "Malachi," 103-105.

19 Verhoef, 241.

20 This position is supported by James Kodell, *Lamentations, Zechariah, Malachi, Obadiah, Joel, Second Zechariah, Baruch*, The Old Testament Message: A Biblical/Sociological Commentary, 14 (Wilmington, DE.: Michael Glazier, 1983), 100-101.

sacrifice rather than to festivals in general finds its only biblical parallel in Ps. 118:27: "Bind the *ḥag* with cords upon the horns of the altar."

When read in conjunction with one another, these three punishments directed to the priests in 2:1-4 serve to render the priests unfit for their duties. Because of their insubordination, the blessings with which they are charged to bless the people will be—indeed *are*—cursed; the descendants who are to share in their priestly privileges will be cut off; and, the dung—the disposal of which they are responsible—will render them unfit.

2:8-9

Because these verses resume the address of "you" after the intervening passage in verses 5-7, they are understood to address the same group as 2:1-4. In these verses, the priests are lambasted for the following reasons:

1. They have turned from the way (2:8);
2. They have caused others to stumble in/by *tôrâ* (2:8);
3. They have corrupted the Levitical covenant (*běrît hallēwî*) (2:8);
4. They have not guarded "my ways" (2:9);
5. They have not shown favor with *tôrâ* (2:9). As punishment, then,
6. They are therefore made despised and debased (treated as they earlier treated the altar) (2:9).

As seen from even a cursory glance at these verses, the priests are here described much differently than in chapter 1 of the book. The precise nature of these descriptions will be considered in turn.

1. *You have turned from the way (sartem min-hadderek)*. This phrase is frequently used in Deuteronomic and related literature to describe disloyalty. In Exodus 32:8, Judges 2:17 and Deut. 31:29, the people are chastized for "turning quickly from the way" and for corrupting themselves (*šḥt*—a term included in accusation number 3). As M. Weinfeld notes, additional uses of *sûr min-hadderek* to denote rebellion appear in Deuteronomy 9:12, 16 and 11:28.[21]

2. *You have caused many to stumble in tôrâ (hikšaltem rabbîm battôrâ)*. The *hip͑il* of the root *kšl* here is used causatively: by neglecting their duties, the priests have caused others to fall. The *hip͑il* of *kšl* appears elsewhere only in Jeremiah 18:15, where its meaning approximates that of the *qal*. In both the *qal* as well as in the *hip͑il* of Jeremiah 18, *kšl* describes disloyalty. In the Jeremiah passage, the LORD laments that "the people

---

[21] M. Weinfeld, *Deuternomy and the Deuteronomic School* (Oxford: Clarendon Press, 1972), 339 (hereafter, Weinfeld, *Deuteronomy*).

have forgotten me and stumbled in my ways." Similarly, Hosea 4, which bears many affinities with Malachi 2:1-9, accuses the priests of—or perhaps punishes them with—stumbling.[22]

The meaning of *tôrâ* for Malachi is differently evaluated. According to E. Meyers, *tôrâ* in Malachi 2:7-8 (as in Haggai 2:11) refers to a specific priestly ruling on matters of ritual purity.[23] As B. Lindars notes, however, underlying the various nuances of the term *tôrâ* is the base meaning of "instruction":

> [The] three streams of employment of *tôrāh* agree in that there is never any stress laid on the method by which the ruling is obtained, whether it be by priestly regulation, prophetic oracle, or educational instruction. It must be assumed that the method used is that which is appropriate to the person giving *tôrāh*.[24]

Tôrâ in Malachi 2:8 and 9, then, refers to the instructional duties of the priest, be they specific or general. Similarly, in Hosea 4:6 the Lord threatens that since the priests have forgotten *tôrâ*, He will forget their sons.[25]

3. *You have corrupted the covenant of Levi/the Levite (šiḥattem bĕrît hallēwî).* The verb *šḥt* is used both in the *piʿel* and the *hipʿil* and appears both with and without a direct object. When used without an object, it signifies the act of disloyalty (*piʿel*—Hosea 9:9; Gen.6:11; *hipʿil*—Deut. 4:16, 25; Judges 2:19; Ezek. 16:47; 2 Chron. 26:16). Often it is connected with other phrases denoting disloyalty, such as the earlier-mentioned "turning from the way" (Exod. 32:7; Judg. 2:17; Deut. 31:29; compare Ezek. 16:47). The verb's connections with disobedience are further noted by Weinfeld, who explains that *šḥt* is used in the Sefire treaty (I, A:32) in the sense of "devastate, destroy" when referring to the punishment for the breach of treaty.[26]

---

22   For the translation of this passage in Hosea 4, see H. W. Wolff, *Hosea*, 77.

23   E. M. Meyers, "The Use of *Tôrâ* in Haggai 2:11," in *And the Word of the Lord Shall Go Forth: Essays in Honor of David Noel Freedman in Celebration of His Sixtieth Birthday*, ed. Carol L. Meyers and M. O'Connor, ASOR Special Volume Series (Winona Lake, IN: ASOR/Eisenbrauns, 1983), 71. See also E. M. Meyers and C. L. Meyers, *Haggai, Zechariah 1-8*, Anchor Bible Series (Garden City, NY: Doubleday and Co., 1987), 55.

24   Barnabas Lindars, "Torah in Deuteronomy," in *Words and Meanings: Essays Presented to David Winton Thomas*, ed. P. R. Ackroyd and Barnabas Lindars (Cambridge: University Press, 1968), 122.

25   For further discussion of the meaning of *tôrâ* in priestly contexts, see Cody, *History*, 116-119.

26   Weinfeld, *Deuteronomy*, 111.

Šḥt takes a direct object not only here in Malachi 2:8 but also in Hosea 13:9, Isa. 14:20, Jer. 48:18, etc. In these contexts, it signifies total devastation. While various verbs are used in the Hebrew Bible to describe covenant violation,[27] no other passage joins Malachi in describing the breaking of a covenant as *šḥt*.

The proper translation for *běrît hallēwî*, while important in understanding Malachi's priestly agendum, is difficult. The phrase is rendered in two different ways: "covenant of Levi;"[28] and "covenant of the Levites."[29]

Underlying these differing translations is the fact that *lēwî* is used in the Hebrew Bible both as the son of Jacob and Leah (credited as the ancestor of the priesthood) and as the title for members of the priestly tribe. When used in the latter fashion, "Levite" in early texts appears to denote general tribal affiliation but in later literature refers to a specific group of persons with prescribed cultic functions. [30]

No clear criteria exist for distinguishing which of these two meanings of *lēwî* is intended in Malachi 2:8. Although when referring to the priestly tribe the term usually appears in the plural (*hallēwiyyîm*), the singular form (*hallēwî*) may also apply to the group. Examples of this singular usage are found in Exod. 6:19 and Num. 3:20. Num. 26:57, most notably, refers to *pěqûdê hallēwî lěmišpěḥōtām*—in which a plural possessive suffix refers to a grammatically-singular noun.[31]

Raising additional difficulties is the fact that the presence or absence of the article on *lēwî* provides no clue to its meaning. *Lēwî* without the article can describe an individual Levite (Judg. 17:9; 19:1) and, interestingly, *lēwî* with the article often appears to refer to the eponymous ancestor of the tribe even though as a general rule proper names do not take the article. Examples of this unexpected use of the article are found in Neh. 10:40, Deut. 10:8 and Jos. 13:14; and in each case—as in Malachi 2:8—*hallēwî* is attached to a construct noun. Most strikingly in Ps. 135:20 and 1 Chron. 12:27, *hallēwî* stands in parallelism with proper names that bear no article: in Ps. 135:19-20 *bêt hallēwî* parallels *bêt iśrā'ēl* and *bêt ʾahărōn*, and in 1 Chron. 12:27 *běnê hallēwî* parallels *běnê binyāmin* in 12:30 and *běnê ʾeprayîm* in 12:31.

---

27 *ʿbr, hpr, ʿzb, mʾs, nʾr, ḥll, šqr, škḥ.*
28 So RSV; Hanson, *People Called*, 282; Chary, *Aggée*, 252; Verhoef, 243-244 .
29 So JPS; M. Fishbane, 332.
30 Cody, *History*, 33-36.
31 I understand "them" to refer to the Levites.

According to Gesenius, gentilic nouns in which the appellative sense is still evident often take the article.[32] On this basis, then, *bĕrît hallēwî* legitimately may be translated "covenant with Levi." This translation, indeed, is undergirded by Malachi's unambiguous reference to "my covenant with Levi" in 2:4 and by its obvious treatment of Levi as an individual in 2:5-7. While the alternate translation "covenant of the Levites" is equally feasible on grammatical grounds, it does not, however, indicate whether the Levites so mentioned are understood as full priests or as lower-ranking clergy.

4. *Because you are not guarding my ways (kĕpî ᵓăšer ᵓênĕkem šōmĕrîm ᵓet dĕrākay)*. "To keep the way of the Lord" is used in various places throughout the Hebrew Bible to describe loyalty. As M. Weinfeld notes, It "...occurs only once in the Deuteronomic literature (Jud. 2:22) but appears often in the older sources (Gen. 18:19; 2 Sam. 22:22 = Ps. 18:22; Ps. 37:34; Job 23:11)."[33] In these passages, "guarding the way" describes the response expected from the faithful (Gen. 18:19); it is synonymous with cleaving to God (Ps. 37:34) and contrasted with turning from him (Job 23:11) and acting wickedly (2 Sam. 22:22).

5. *Nor are you showing favor with tôrâ (ᵓênĕkem wĕnōśĕᵓîm pānîm battôrâ)*. Scholars disagree regarding the translation and meaning of this accusation. Two issues underlie this disagreement: whether the negative particle *ᵓênĕkem* extends its governance to *nōśĕᵓîm*; and whether *nōśĕᵓîm pānîm* is understood to be a positive or negative act. Asserting that the "lifting of face" here is negative and that *ᵓênĕkem* does not extend to the second clause, Verhoef, Kodell, Hanson, Gruber, Fishbane, J. M. P. Smith and R. Smith translate the phrase as: "but you (rather) are showing partiality in instruction."[34] On the contrary, Chary and Glazier-McDonald understand the negative particle as operative through the end of the verse and *nōśĕᵓîm pānîm* as a positive action, translating: "and neither are you showing favor with *tôrâ*."[35]

Study of the various occurrences of "lift up the face" in Hebrew Scripture underscores its various meanings. It is used positively as "to show favor" in Gen. 32:21, Deut. 28:50, Lam. 4:16, and in Malachi 1:8, 9,

---

32   GKC 125d.

33   Weinfeld, *Deuternomy*, 337.

34   Verhoef, 237; Kodell, 99; Hanson, *People Called*, 282; Mayer Gruber, "The Many Faces of Hebrew *nśᵓ pnym*, <Lift up the Face>," *ZAW* 95 (1983): 258; Fishbane, 332; J. M. P. Smith, 41; Ralph Smith, *Micah-Malachi*, Word Biblical Commentary, no. 32 (Waco, TX: Word Books, 1984), 309 .

35   Chary, *Aggée*, 252; Glazier-McDonald, "Malachi," 69, 112 .

but it bears a negative connotation of "show partiality" in Job 32:21, Deut. 10:17 and Lev. 19:15 [36]

While both positive and negative meanings of "lift up the face" are possible, here the phrase is most likely governed by the negative *'ênĕkem* in accordance with Gesenius' explanation that negatives may extend influence into a second parallel clause. [37] The appearance of both participles in the same masculine plural form supports this interpretation and, indeed, without the continuation of *'ênĕkem* the second participle has no antecedent. The reading of Chary and others is therefore accepted. The import of this accusation, then, is that the priests have failed to benefit others via their instruction.

6. *So I have made you despised and debased before all the people (*'ănî nātatî *'etekem nibzîm ûšĕpālîm lĕkol-hā'ām).* Because of the above accusations, the priests are punished in 2:9a. They will be despised and contemptible—treated just as they treated the altar in 1:6, 7, 12.

As seen from the above analysis, the accusations against the *kōhănîm* in 2:1-4 and 8-9 describe the role of the priest in dual terms. The priest not only oversees and pronounces blessing (2:1-4) but also provides moral leadership and instructs others in *tôrâ* (2:8-9).

2:5

Unlike the surrounding material which levels accusations against the *kōhănîm*, 2:5-7 explains in praiseworthy terms "my covenant with Levi" as first mentioned in 2:4. In these verses, Malachi describes the faithfulness of Levi and the proper conduct of priests.

1. ...that my covenant with Levi might be (2:4);
2. My covenant was with him. Life and peace—I gave them to him (2:5);
3. Fear—he feared me, and bowed before my reputation (2:5);
4. True *tôrâ* was in his mouth and iniquity was not found on his lips (2:6);
5. He walked with me in peace and uprightness (2:6);
6. And he turned many from iniquity (2:6);
7. Because the lips of a *kōhēn* should guard knowledge, and *tôrâ* they will seek from his mouth (2:7);
8. Because he is the messenger of the LORD of Hosts (2:7).

1. *That my covenant with Levi might continue (lihyôt).* The infinitive construct *lihyôt* in this verse has been treated in various ways. Sellin

---

[36] Gruber's just-mentioned article presents further biblical evidence for these contradictory meanings of the same phrase.

[37] GKC 152z.

contends that *lihyôt* is a later modification of an original reading *lḥtt*, "to shatter, destroy."[38] Chary emends the form to *mihyôt* and, reading the prefix *min* partitively, understands this verb to describe the cessation of the covenant.[39] G. R. Driver, while retaining the Masoretic Text, argues that the verb *hāyâ* occasionally means "to fall."[40]

No such emendations or reinterpretations of *hāyâ* however, receive any textual support; they are deemed necessary only when one assumes that the deity is destroying the covenant. As made clear by 3:3, the prophet looks to the purification—and not to the abolition—of Levitical priesthood. The *lamed* prefix likely denotes purpose[41] and, hence, this phrase is best translated as "that my covenant with Levi might be/might continue to be."

2. *My covenant was with him. Life and peace—I gave them to him.* In verses 4-7 Levi is treated as an individual who is referred to with third masculine singular pronouns. The relationship between this individual and the deity is described in terms of a covenant, more particularly in terms of a "grant"-type treaty. The deity grants to Levi life and peace as a reward for Levi's faithfulness and obedience. As outlined by M. Weinfeld, while the grant is basically a promise to the recipient, it nonetheless presupposes the recipient's loyalty.[42] In the case of Malachi, although the parties involved do not share mutual obligations,[43] this grant of priesthood presumes that Levi remain faithful.

As reward for Levi's righteousness, which is detailed in the following verses, God grants to Levi "life and peace." "Life" in wisdom literature as well as in Deuteronomy "...constitutes the framework of reward...'Life' here [Deuteronomy] denotes happiness."[44]

While Malachi clearly treats Levi as an individual figure whose acts of faithfulness were rewarded by God, the book does not offer additional information regarding Levi's identity. According to many, Levi is the corporate "representative of the priestly class"[45] or the "personification

---

38 Ernst Sellin, *Das Zwölfprophetenbuch übersetzt und erklärt*, KAT (Leipzig: A. Deichertsche Verlagsbuchhandlung, 1930), II:599; quoted in Glazier-McDonald, "Malachi," 106.

39 Chary, *Aggée* , 251.

40 G. R. Driver, "Malachi," *JTS* 39 (1938): 399, quoted in R. Smith, 310, n. 4.

41 GKC 114g.

42 Weinfeld, *Deuteronomy*, 74.

43 Contra Glazier-McDonald, "Malachi," 107.

44 Weinfeld, *Deuteronomy*, 307.

45 J. M. P. Smith, 38.

of the early priesthood";[46] according to Kodell, he is the son of Jacob.[47] But while most would agree that Levi represents priesthood, they disagree over whether Levi has been deliberately contrasted with Aaron and Zadok—other preeminent priests. According to Hanson, by identifying proper priesthood with Levi, the Book of Malachi purposefully points to an earlier age when all Levites were priests.[48] Glazier-McDonald, on the other hand, contends that by the post-exilic period all priests (including Aaronides) were understood to share common ancestry from Levi.[49] The identity of Levi, while important, cannot be made on the basis of this passage alone and will receive further attention when the sources underlying Malachi are discussed.

3. *Fear—he feared me (wayyîrā'ēnî) and bowed before my reputation (ûmippĕnê šĕmî niḥat hû').* Levi's acts of reverence are described as *yr'* and *hḥt*—two verbs commonly used to denote fealty. In the diplomatic vocabulary of the ancient Near East, *yr'* signifies the attitude of exclusive allegiance;[50] in Deuteronomy and elsewhere in the Hebrew Bible, the "fear of the Lord" describes covenant loyalty and one's observance of its stipulations.[51]

Yr' and *hḥt* often are used in parallelism to indicate extreme awareness of the power of another. In Deuteronomic military speeches, combatants are encouraged in battle with the admonition, "Do not fear and do not be in dread" (*'al tîrā' wĕ'al-tēḥāt*; Deut. 1:21). Similar phraseology appears in war descriptions within neo-Assyrian royal inscriptions: "fear and dread."[52] While the military connotations of *yr'/hḥt* are not utilized in Malachi 2:5, the intensity of this word pair serves to emphasize Levi's extreme reverence for the deity.

4. *Tôrâ was in his mouth; iniquity was not found in his lips.* As discussed in the treatment of 2:9, *tôrâ* in Malachi 2:1-9 describes instruction; while obviously the instruction here given is priestly, its content is not necessarily limited to rulings or matters of ritual purity. The broader meaning of *tôrâ* in Malachi is underscored by 2:6, where it stands in parallelism to iniquity (*'awlâ*).

---

46 Ralph Smith, 317.
47 Kodell, 101.
48 Hanson, *People Called*, 282-283.
49 Glazier-McDonald, "Malachi," 118-119.
50 Weinfeld, *Deuteronomy*, 83-84.
51 Ibid., 274, 332.
52 Ibid., 50-51.

5. *In peace and uprightness he served (lit: "walked with") me (bĕšālôm ûbĕmîšôr hālak ʾittî).* The description of Levi as "serving in peace and uprightness" parallels closely language used elsewhere in the Hebrew Bible and in the ancient Near East to describe the obedience of a servant to whom, as reward, a grant is bestowed. In the Assyrian grant of Aššurbanipal to his servant Balṭaya, Balṭaya is lauded as one who "stood before me in truthfulness and 'walked' in perfection."[53] Analogous biblical texts describe the faithfulness of the patriarchs as "served me" (*hithallakû lĕpānāyw*; Gen. 24:40; 48:15, etc.) and the loyalty of David as "served you in truth and in righteousness and in uprightness of heart" (1 Kings 3:6).[54] By describing Levi's faithfulness in this way, then, the author both utilizes established terminology and also likens the loyalty of Levi to that of the patriarchs and of David.

6. *And many he turned from iniquity.* As in 2:6, Levi is credited with providing proper religious instruction to others. Not only does he maintain his own integrity but also he fulfills his responsibility of leading others.

7. *For the lips of a kōhēn should guard knowledge (daʿat), and they will seek tôrâ from his mouth.* In verse 7, consideration turns from the figure of Levi to that of the *kōhēn*. Despite this shift in names, however, there appears no shift in description: the priest in 2:7, like Levi in 2:5-6, is responsible for speaking true *tôrâ* and for guarding knowledge. This easy transition between Levi and *kōhēn* indicates that in these verses Levi is understood to be a priest—an ideal priest who fulfills all the duties of priesthood.

As in previously-discussed verses, the priest is here understood as responsible for instruction. The people recognize his didactic authority and seek his guidance; he, in turn, must exercise properly that authority by preserving the knowledge of the LORD. Likewise in Hosea 4:6, the prophet laments that his people lack knowledge of God and accuses the priest of rejecting *daʿat*.

8. *For he is the messenger (malʾāk) of the LORD of hosts.* In no other passage in the Hebrew Bible is the priest called a *malʾāk*. Prophets are so designated numerous times in passages such as Haggai 1:13, Isaiah 44:26 and 2 Chronicles 36:15-16, and prophetic speech patterns have long been associated with ancient Near Eastern messenger speech.[55]

---

53 Ibid., 75.
54 Ibid., 76.
55 E.g., Claus Westermann, *Basic Forms of Prophetic Speech*, tr. H. C. White (Lutterworth, PA: Westminster, 1967).

Malachi's description of the priest rather than the prophet as the LORD's messenger is generally understood as an investiture of the priest with the stature previously enjoyed by the prophet. In the classical statement of this position, J. M. P. Smith maintains that in Malachi 2:7 Yahweh

> who once spoke through angels now has chosen priests for that function. This is a conception of the importance and dignity of the priesthood that is unsurpassed, if it be even equalled, elsewhere in the Old Testament. It renders the work of the prophets superfluous.[56]

Verhoef, perhaps alone, downplays the role here assigned to the priest and denies that Malachi's high estimation of the priest impinges upon the esteem of the prophet. The prophet mediates directly-revealed truths (*dābār*) while the priest mediates that which is handed down to him either in oral or written form (*tôrâ*).[57] Moreover, argues Verhoef, Malachi 2:5-7 describes the early priesthood rather than the book's priestly contemporaries.[58]

Verhoef's remarks, while rightly recognizing the different sources of authority for priest and prophet, nonetheless fail to deal adequately with the fact that the priest is described in terms elsewhere reserved for the prophet. Moreover, while Levi indeed is treated as a past figure, the term *malʾāk* here describes not him but the *kōhēn*, and verses 8-9 make clear that the duties of modern priests are the same as those of Levi.[59]

As *malʾāk*, the priest—like the prophet—is considered as the mediator between the divine and the human.[60] The mediatorial function of the *malʾāk* is made clear both by the prophets who declare the word of the deity in authoritative terms and also by the ancient Near Eastern messengers who functioned as official representative of the Great Kings who sent them.[61]

As seen from the preceding discussion, Malachi 2:5-7 describes the faithfulness of Levi in terms of his personal and relational integrity: he not only leads a virtuous life himself but also properly instructs others in

---

[56] J. M. P. Smith, 40.

[57] Verhoef, 258.

[58] Ibid., 250.

[59] See also the discussion of *malʾāk* in Meyers and Meyers, *Haggai, Zechariah 1-8*, 183. E. Meyers considers the breakdown in traditional barriers between priest and prophet as signalling a new era characteristic of late prophecy.

[60] The implications of this treatment of the priest will be discussed below, 147.

[61] John S. Holladay, "Assyrian Statescraft and the Prophets of Israel," *Harvard Theological Review* 63 (1970): 31.

virtue. Levi, moreover, is understood to be a *kōhēn*; the lips of a *kōhēn* should guard knowledge and Levi fulfills this obligation.

The description of the ideal priesthood of Levi in 2:5-7, then, is sharply contrasted with the "you" of 2:8-9. While Levi walked in peace and uprightness (v. 6), "you" have turned from the way (8). While Levi kept many from iniquity (6), "you" have caused many to stumble in *tôrâ* (8). While God has acted that His covenant with Levi might continue (4), "you" have corrupted the covenant with Levi (8). While others sought *tôrâ* from Levi's mouth (7), "you" will be made despised and debased before everyone (9). While true *tôrâ* was in Levi's mouth (6), "you" have failed to benefit others with *tôra*. This distinction between the covenant with Levi and "you," however, does not neatly coincide with the distinction between *lēwî* and *kōhēn*: while the *kōhănîm* are rebuked, yet Levi is described as *kōhēn*.

3:3

DEFINING THE CONTEXT

The mention of the *bĕnê-lēwî* in 3:3 has little surrounding material by which to understand it. In this verse, the *bĕnê-lēwî* receive neither accusations nor praise but rather the prophet speaks in third-person terms of the day of the purification of the sons of Levi. Although previous verses speak of the circumstances attending this day and although following verses detail its other outcomes, only 3:3 deals specifically with the *bĕnê-lēwî* and their purification.

DESCRIPTION OF THE GROUP

Verse 3:3 relates the following about the *bĕnê-lēwî*:

1. At His coming, the LORD/the messenger will purify the sons of Levi;
2. And refine them like gold and silver;
3. And they will be the LORD's—ones who offer *minḥâ* righteously.

1. *He will purify (ṭihar) the sons of Levi*. The subject of the verb *ṭihar* may be understood in several ways, depending upon the relationship drawn between the three figures mentioned in 3:1: "my messenger (*malʾāk*)," "the Lord (*hāʾādôn*)," and "the messenger of the covenant (*malʾāk habbĕrît*)." Kaufmann treats these titles as describing three separate figures;[62] according to Petersen, the *malʾāk* is equated with *malʾāk*

---

62 Kaufmann, 444-445.

habběrît;[63] Verhoef and Glazier-McDonald maintain that the Lord is linked with the malʾāk habběrît;[64] and, in R. T. France's opinion, all three titles refer to the same messenger.[65] Given this diversity in the relation of these terms, different figures may be understood as purifying the sons of Levi: Petersen identifies the purifier as the messenger/messenger of covenant; Kaufmann gives the role only to the messenger of the covenant; Verhoef and Glazier-McDonald view the LORD himself as cleansing.[66]

This figure, either the LORD and/or the messenger, will cleanse the sons of Levi when he comes. The verb ṭihar here used signifies ritual cleansing and is used elsewhere in the Hebrew Bible for priests, Levites and people. In Lev. 16:30 and 14:11 the LORD cleanses the priests, and in Ezek. 37:23, 36:33 and Jer. 33:8, the LORD cleanses the people. Glazier-McDonald has noted that in Num. 8:6 Moses also cleanses the Levites. She, indeed, draws further conclusions from Num. 8's use of ṭihar for the cleansing of the Levites: according to Glazier-McDonald the similarities between Num. 8 and Mal. 3:3 "are too significant to be ignored."[67]

This close identification, however, of Malachi 3:3 with Num. 8, which sharply contrasts Levites and priests, appears to conflict with Glazier-McDonald's own assessment of the meaning of běnê-lēwî in 3:3. According to her, in Malachi "Levite" signifies not the lower clergy of P but the priestly ideal—while kōhēn refers to the current degenerate priesthood. This passage, then, by signifying "Malachi's announcement of Yahweh's purification of the [altar] priesthood..."[68] denies the bifurcated roles of the clergy as stressed in Numbers. Put more simply, if běnê-lēwî in Malachi 3:3 refers to ideal priests, then it finds an unsteady basis in Num. 8's treatment of Levites as subordinate clergy.

Other scholars join Glazier-McDonald in debating the membership of the group intended by the phrase běnê-lēwî. Most translate the phrase as "Levites" and then debate the stage in the priesthood that it reflects. J. M.

---

[63] David Petersen, "Israelite Prophecy and Prophetic Traditions in the Exilic and Post-Exilic Period" (Ph. D. diss., Yale University, 1972), 152.

[64] Verhoef, 289; Glazier-McDonald, "Malachi," 203.

[65] R. T. France, Jesus and the Old Testament: His Application of Old Testament Passages to Himself and his Mission (reprinted by Grand Rapids, MI: Baker Book House, 1982), 91, n. 31; quoted in Verhoef, 289, n. 12.

[66] See pages cited above. A good discussion of this problem and its various interpretations is found in Bruce Malchow, "The Messenger of the Covenant in Mal. 3:1," JBL 103 (1984): 252-255.

[67] Glazier-McDonald, "Malachi," 232-233.

[68] Ibid., 233-234.

P. Smith understands this group as the Levites who are granted the priesthood in Deuteronomy.[69] Hanson likewise sees these persons as "Levites" but, according to his scheme, they are the second-ranking clergy who though currently excluded from priesthood will again be priests in the future.[70] Like J. M. P. Smith, Glazier-McDonald and Verhoef consider these *běnê-lēwî* as full priests although they consider the priesthood of this group as in no way antithetical to the Priestly Code.[71]

Still another explanation offers that the term *běnê-lēwî* has no necessary connection with an otherwise-known group; it may instead signify the descendants of the enigmatic Levi described in 2:5-7.[72] The determination of exactly whom the author of Malachi intends by the phrase *běnê-lēwî* (as well as by the name Levi) cannot be made on the basis of his language alone and must be considered in connection with Malachi's use of other sources.

2. *And refine (ziqqaq) them like gold and like silver.* Further expanding upon the image of the coming figure as a smelter, this passage indicates that the purification of the *běnê-lēwî* will be like the purification of metal. While further explaining the figure's action, this phrase contributes little to the understanding of the identity of the *běnê-lēwî*.

3. *And they will be to the LORD: those who offer minḥâ in a righteous state (maggîšê minḥâ biṣdāqâ).* The purification of the *běnê-lēwî* will render them fit for the LORD's possession;[73] it moreover will legitimize their offerings. The description of the *běnê-lēwî* as those who will *ngš minḥâ* indicates that their proper function will be to perform altar duties. The language here used parallels that of 1:6-13, in which the priests are accused for offering (*ngš*) improper sacrifices and for vainly offering *minḥâ*.

To summarize the short description of this occurrence, the *běnê-lēwî* are those who need purification and who, once purified, will present proper offerings.

---

69 J. M. P. Smith, 8.
70 Hanson, *People Called*, 283.
71 Glazier-McDonald, "Malachi," 234; Verhoef, 291.
72 For further discussion, see below, 105-106; 145-146.
73 This translation is suggested by the *zāqēp parvum* over *lādōnay*.

COMPARISON OF THE DESCRIPTIONS

As seen in the preceding discussion, Malachi discusses *kōhănîm, lēwî* and *běnê-lēwî* in four separate passages: 1:6-13; 2:1-4 and 8-9; 2:5-7; and 3:3. The description of the group treated in each may be summarized as follows:

1:6-13:   The *kōhănîm* are those responsible for altar duties.
2:1-4 and 8-9: The *kōhănîm*/"you" are those responsible both for priestly functions and for proper instruction.
2:5-7:   *lēwî* is the one who offered proper instruction.
3:3:   The *běnê-lēwî* are those who require purification so that they may in the future perform altar duties righteously.

If this analysis is correct, then Malachi indicates no difference in description between *kōhēn, lēwî* and *běnê-lēwî*. In terms of function, both the *kōhēn* and *lēwî/běnê-lēwî* are responsible for the dual duties of sacrifice and instruction. In terms of context, *lēwî* is effectually called a *kōhēn* in 2:5-7 and in 3:3 the *běnê-lēwî* require purification.

The identity of the functions of the *kōhēn* and *lēwî/běnê-lēwî* as well as the use of both terms in 2:5-7 militate against any theory which depends upon a dogmatic differentiation between them. One such theory is that of Glazier-McDonald, who maintains that the difference between priest and Levite in Malachi is not one of groups but of idea: "Malachi constructed a 'levite/cohen' model in which the term *'cohen'* was used to represent the current degenerate priesthood and 'levite' the priestly ideal."[74]

This theory fails to give weight to the fact that the *kōhēn* is lauded and equated with Levi in 2:7 and that the *běnê-lēwî* in 3:3 are not ideal but in need of purification. Although Glazier-McDonald attempts to counter these objections by maintaining that *kōhēn* in 2:7 is contrasted with actual *kōhănîm* and that in 3:3 the future priests will be Levites, in actuality these two passages demonstrate that Malachi's contrast of the ideal with the actual does not coincide neatly with a contrast between priest and Levite.

While the Book of Malachi equates the functions of *kōhēn* and *lēwî/běnê-lēwî* the book offers no contextual grounds by which to explain this equation. Do, for example, these equal functions indicate that in Malachi's day *běnê-lēwî* actually *were* considered priests or—as Hanson believes—that Malachi championed the rights of the currently-powerless Levites? By treating *lēwî/běnê-lēwî* as full priests, Malachi's language makes clear that it does not deem them to be the lower-ranking Levites

---

74 Glazier-McDonald, "Malachi," 234.

as described by the Priestly Code, and yet its language does not indicate the basis for the difference: that is, whether it precedes, defies or modifies P's ranking of the clergy.

While these descriptions of priestly groups in the Book of Malachi indicate the author of the book treats *kōhănîm* and *lēwî/bĕnê-lēwî* similarly, the uncovering of the ideology underlying these descriptions requires the use of further tools. Chapter 4 considers evidence for the book's use of sources. The next chapter will consider whether an identification of the book's form may inform this problem.

CHAPTER III

THE FORM OF THE BOOK OF MALACHI

As argued in the previous chapter, the author's understanding of the identity of *kōhēn* and *lēwî* in the Book of Malachi cannot be inferred solely from the context of the individual occurrences of these terms. Because *kōhēn* and *lēwî* are attributed with the same functions, the actual sociological groups described by these terms cannot be identified by their unique responsibilities. Other tools, therefore, are needed to discern the groups that the author describes.

The present chapter applies the tool of form criticism to the Book of Malachi in hopes that the book's form may provide some insight into the author's intended message. In so doing, it will consider not only the book's structure (its literary outline) but also its *Gattung* or genre.[1]

The form-critical organization of verses that this chapter considers must be understood separately from the groupings discussed in chapter 2. Chapter 2 sought to identify those verses which form the immediate context for understanding the occurrences of *kōhēn* and *lēwî*; the verses were grouped according to their bearing upon one of these terms and not necessarily according to any literary connection. The task of the present chapter, on the contrary, is to outline the boundaries of passages on the basis of literary considerations.

FORM CRITICISM AND THE PROPHETS

According to its classical presentation by Hermann Gunkel, form criticism has several goals. After outlining the structure of a biblical passage, form criticism then determines its literary type. Such an approach subsequently compares the specific type with analogous literary forms in

---

[1] In keeping with the terminology used in Gene M. Tucker, *Form Criticism of the Old Testament* (Philadelphia: Fortress Press, 1971), 12.

other ancient Near Eastern cultures in order to identify the passage's characteristic patterns and ideas. In the determination of form, Gunkel considered not only literary style and typical introductory phrases but also mood and content. He likewise stressed that each form arose from a particular life setting (*Sitz im Leben*) within Israel's culture:

> Just as among ourselves the 'sermon' belongs to the pulpit, while the 'fairy tale' has its home in the nursery, so in ancient Israel the Song of Victory was sung by maidens to greet the returning war-host.[2]

Biblical form critics since the time of Gunkel have questioned several of his assertions (such as his separation of the divine threat from the prophet's explanation). Muilenberg has challenged the self-sufficiency of the discipline and North has contested attempts to reduce prophecy to a single origin.[3] Despite the constant development of the discipline, however, most scholars continue to recognize the close connection between a prophecy's meaning and its form.

In the course of applying form-critical methodology to the prophetic literature, scholars have produced a long list of discernible literary types as well as quite different vocabularies for describing their constituent parts. W. Eugene March, who has well summarized such debates, describes the major accepted prophetic genres as follows:

1. the prophecy of disaster, comprised of an indication of the situation, a prediction of disaster and a concluding characterization;
2. the prophecy of salvation, comprised of an indication of the situation, a prediction of salvation and a concluding characterization. Related forms include the oracle of salvation (oriented to the present) and the proclamation of salvation (oriented to the future);
3. the woe-oracle, a secondary form;
4. the trial speech, comprised of a summons, a trial and sentencing;
5. the disputation speech, which bears no set pattern but the essence of which consists of answering charges;

---

[2] H. Gunkel, *What Remains of the Old Testament* (New York: Macmillan Co., 1928), 61.

[3] James Muilenberg, "Form Criticism and Beyond," *JBL* 88 (1969): 1-18; Robert North, "Angel-Prophet or Satan Prophet?" *ZAW* 82 (1970): 31-67. A helpful summary of form–critical developments in the study of prophecy is found in W. Eugene March, "Prophecy," in *Old Testament Form Criticism*, ed. John H. Hayes (San Antonio: Trinity University Press, 1977), 141-177.

6. the summons to repentance, comprised of an appeal and a motivation. While not a widely acknowledged genre, this form is discussed by Thomas Raitt.[4]

Various secondary forms, borrowed from diverse spheres of Israelite life, also appear in the prophetic literature. The hymn, the lament and the liturgy, for example, are borrowed from the cult, while the call to battle derives from martial procedures.[5]

Before the Book of Malachi can be analyzed form–critically and compared with these various prophetic genres, attention must turn to the unity of the book. Does the book contain secondary material extraneous to its original form?

THE UNITY & INTEGRITY OF THE BOOK

The passages in Malachi most frequently interpreted as additions to the original composition are the book's superscription (1:1) and its final three verses (3:22-24; Eng. 4:4-6). The authenticity of other verses—such as 1:11, 2:12, 3:1, 3:1b-4, 3:13-15, and 3:16-21—also have been questioned. Each of these passages will be considered in turn.

1:1

The Book of Malachi is commonly treated as an anonymous oracle, the name of which has been borrowed from the reference to "my messenger" in 3:1. Blenkinsopp is representative of many scholars when he suggests that Zech. 9:1-11:17, Zech. 12:1-14:21 and Malachi are three anonymous booklets each introduced by the heading *maśśāʾ*.[6] By granting this final booklet independent status, the editor of the Latter Prophets could boast of "twelve minor prophets and three major ones"—perhaps symbolizing the three patriarchs and the twelve sons of Jacob.[7] Concordant with Blenkinsopp's views, Schneider attributes the addition of Mal. 1:1 to the editor who compiled the Haggai-Zechariah-Malachi corpus.[8]

---

[4] Thomas Raitt, "The Prophetic Summons to Repentance," *ZAW* 83 (1971): 30-49; quoted in March, 168-69.

[5] March, 169.

[6] Blenkinsopp, *History*, 239.

[7] J. Blenkinsopp, *Prophecy and Canon: A Contribution to the Study of Jewish Origins* (Notre Dame, IN: University of Notre Dame Press, 1977), 121.

[8] Dale Schneider, "The Unity of the Book of the Twelve" (Ph. D. diss., Yale University, 1975), 149. While not taking a clear position on the stage at which such a

Undergirding the assessment of 1:1 as an editorial addition is the argument that "Malachi" is not a proper name but rather an appellative borrowed from 3:1. This position is similar to that taken by the Septuagint and Targum, which translate the *maPākî* of 1:1 as "my messenger." Scholars such as Eissfeldt, Sellin/Fohrer and J. M. P. Smith not only point to the similarity between 1:1 and 3:1 as an argument for the secondary quality of 1:1 but also they contend that "Malachi" is not a likely proper name. No parent would name his son "my messenger."[9]

Hence, at least three major reasons for considering 1:1 as secondary have been advanced: the appearance of the heading *maśśāʾ* in Zech 9:1, 12:1 and Malachi 1:1; the unlikelihood that "Malachi" is a proper name; and the presence of the title *maPākî* in Malachi 3:1.

All three of these arguments have been contested, however. As regards the first, Childs has pointed to the differences in the ways in which *maśśāʾ* is used in each of these three passages.[10] Glazier-McDonald also has noted these differences and suggests that Malachi's heading more closely parallels Jer. 50:1 and Hag. 1:1 than Zech 9:1 and 12:1.[11]

Bearing upon the argument regarding the character of the name "Malachi," various scholars have defended the possibility that Malachi may indeed be a proper name. According to Kaufmann, "There is no reason, 'psychological' or other, to deny the possibility of a name such as this, which might be a contraction of 'Malachyahu.'"[12]

Casting doubt upon the third and perhaps most important of these arguments is the observation that the appearance of the term *maPākî* both in 1:1 and 3:1 does not necessarily mandate that either verse be considered secondary. As well argued by Childs, the explanation that 1:1 is based on 3:1 stands in sharp contrast to the fact that 3:1 speaks of a future messenger:

> If an editor believed that the prophet himself had already functioned as the announced eschatological figure in 'preparing the way of Yahweh,' then he

---

corpus was put together, Roland Pierce suggests that Haggai, Zechariah and Malachi form "a useful literary corpus" when read together. "Literary Connnectors and a Haggai/Zechariah/Malachi Corpus," *Journal of the Theological Evangelical Society* 27 (1984): 277-289.

9 J. M. P. Smith, 19. This position is also noted by W. Rudolph, *Haggai—Sacharja 1-8—Sacharja 9-14—Maleachi*, KAT, Bd. 13,4 (Gütersloh: Gütersloher Verlaghaus Mohn, 1976), 247.

10 Brevard Childs, *Introduction to the Old Testament as Scripture* (Philadelphia: Fortress Press, 1979), 491.

11 Glazier-McDonald, "Malachi," 39.

12 Kaufmann, 446, n. 1.

misunderstood the prophetic hope expressed elsewhere with the same formula (cf. Isa. 40:3; 57:14; 62:10).[13]

Such an editorial equation of the prophet with the figure in 3:1, as Childs well argues, renders the text "with a confused and unintelligible meaning"[14]: why will the LORD send a messenger if the messenger has already come? Hence, rather than 1:1 being seen as deriving from 3:1, Childs argues that 3:1 may be seen as a "word-play on the prophet's name in the superscription."[15]

In conclusion, the figure of "Malachi" is indeed anonymous in that we know nothing about such a person, his or her background, family or setting. The title may not be a proper name. Such admissions do not, however, indicate that the title "Malachi" must be understood as secondary to the work itself. It instead—as will be discussed below—may function as a component integral to the message of the book.

3:22-24

Malachi 3:22-24 (English 4:4-6) is most often understood to be composed of two separate appendices to the book. 3:22 (4:4) is seen to be a Deuteronomic appeal to Mosaic authority, while 3:23-24 (4:5-6) is interpreted as an explanatory gloss on the identity of the messenger mentioned in 3:1. A large number of scholars—including Chary, Coggins, R. Smith, Petersen, Childs, Pfeiffer and J. M. P. Smith—point to this twofold character of 3:22-24. Among these scholars, nonetheless, have arisen differing assessments of the origin and intent of these proposed additions.

The first appendix, 3:22, is variously interpreted as either an addition to the book itself or as an appendix to the entire Prophetic collection (perhaps even to the combined Law and the Prophets). Blenkinsopp, Kodell and R. Smith, for example, maintain that the reminder of Mosaic authority serves to unite the Law and the Prophets in purpose and theme.[16]

Other scholars, however, understand this appendix merely as an addition to the book itself. According to J. M. P. Smith, for example, it is "the isolated marginal note of some legalist."[17] Childs has attempted to

---

13 Childs, *Introduction*, 493.
14 Ibid.
15 Ibid., 494.
16 Blenkinsopp, *History*, 240; Kodell, 109; R. Smith, 341. Smith also quotes Childs, "The Canonical Shape of the Prophetic Literature," *Interpretation* 52 (1978): 51-52.
17 J. M. P. Smith, 81.

demonstrate that this addition was likely made to the book to temper its reference to a separation between the righteous and the wicked. Through a reminder that the entire nation of Israel remains under the law of Moses, the editor sought to temper any separatist ideology that might be suggested by the book.[18]

As regards the so-called second appendix (3:23-24), most have suggested that it attempts to define the unnamed messenger of 3:1. Unsatisfied with the anonymity of this figure, an editor connected *malʾakî* with Elijah. Mason explains Elijah's role in turning the hearts of the fathers to the sons and sons to fathers as reflecting the concerns of the Hellenistic age, "...when the younger generation grasped eagerly at Greek customs and thought, to the horror of their more orthodox parents."[19]

Baldwin and Glazier-McDonald belong to a small minority that defends the authenticity of all three final verses of Malachi. Baldwin maintains that the ethical emphasis and style of these verses fit well into the rest of the book and that these features point to Malachi as the likely author.[20]

Glazier-McDonald offers a more extended argument for the authenticity of both proposed additions. Demonstrating that Deuteronomic language permeates the entire book, she suggests that the Deuteronomic character of verse 22 thus is not distinctive or indicative of its secondary nature. Moreover, by reminding that all people remain under the law, verse 22 serves as a proper conclusion to the book as a whole.[21]

Glazier-McDonald also offers arguments defending the authenticity of verses 23-24. First, with regard to the matter of the reconciliation of fathers and sons, she insists that such an exhortation need not refer to the conflicts of the Hellenistic era but instead may reflect the economic conditions of the Persian period.[22] Second and most forcefully, Glazier-McDonald counters the theory that 3:23-24 is an attempt to identify the messenger of 3:1 by suggesting that the two passages refer to the same figure. Demonstrating various common themes found in 3:1 and 3:23-24 (as well as in the entire Book of Malachi and in the Elijah tradition), she

---

18 Childs, *Introduction*, 495.

19 Mason, *Books*, 160-161.

20 Joyce Baldwin, *Haggai, Zechariah, Malachi*, Tyndale Old Testament Commentaries (Downers Grove, IL: Intervarsity Press, 1972), 251.

21 Glazier-McDonald, "Malachi," 390.

22 Ibid., 395.

argues that 3:23-24 should not be considered an interpretative gloss.[23] Interestingly, the very argument advanced by Glazier-McDonald to prove the authenticity of 3:22-24 is the same one employed by Childs to make a quite different point. According to Childs, the identification of the messenger with Elijah represents the intent of the *editor(s)* of the book to provide a larger theological context for understanding Malachi's message:[24]

> This redactional identification went beyond the prophet's original message but did not do injustice to it. Rather, it served to bring together elements from his preaching into a sharper focus, and to set them in a picture, which was enriched by Israel's fuller traditions...the original message of the prophet Malachi was placed within a larger theological context drawn from Israel's tradition which rendered the original prophetic words appropriate as scripture for successive generations of the people of God. The larger context acted both to enrich the prophet's message by the use of typological analogy, as well as to guard against a sectarian misuse of the prophet which would fragment the national solidarity in the name of reform.[25]

As seen from the remarks of Childs, Baldwin and Glazier-McDonald, the final three verses employ themes that comport well with the rest of the book. Whether these verses are to be understood as the author's own conclusion to his or her work or as the effort of an editor (or editors) to expand upon the book's theme cannot be determined solely on the basis of their content. Because the ideas of 3:22-24 do not contradict the earlier portions of the book but rather may expand its ideas, the possibility that they may be original must be considered. A further discussion of the authenticity of these verses must follow a prior consideration of the book's form: only then can one evaluate how these verses fit into the larger form and argument of Malachi.

Internal Additions

While most scholars consider the rest of Malachi to constitute an essential unity,[26] the authenticity of several additional passages within the book also has been questioned:

---

23 Ibid., 399.

24 Childs, *Introduction*, 495.

25 Ibid., 496-497.

26 For example, J. M. P. Smith (3) contends that the essential unity of the book never has been questioned.

1. Blenkinsopp contends that "says the Lord" has been inserted throughout the book in order to bring the work into line with pre-exilic prophecy.[27]

2. 1:11-14 has been described as an "uncharacteristic" assertion of universalism.[28]

3. 2:11-12 is questioned by Mason and Pfeiffer, who explain that this diatribe against mixed marriages was a concern to generations after Malachi.[29]

4. 3:1, according to Malchow, is a post-Daniel addition linked to Qumran ideology.[30] Mason considers 3:1b-4 as an elaboration of the original judgement.[31]

5. 3:13-15 is treated by McKenzie and Wallace as concerning a different audience than that of the previous material: it lacks reference to any historical setting and presumes an inner-Israelite dichotomy.[32]

6. 3:16-21, according to McKenzie and Wallace, is yet another addition, offering a reinterpretation of the first part of Malachi. These two additions—3:13-15 and 3:16-21—have been joined on the basis of the catchwords *zēdîm* and *ʿōśê rišʿâ*.[33] Childs also views 3:16 as a redaction that reports an historical response: "...[The verse] reflects a layer different from the original setting of disputation and provides a new theological perspective."[34]

These positions have not gone unchallenged. Swetnam and others, for example, have considered how 1:11-14 fit into the prophet's message.[35] In addition, 2:11-12 does not necessarily refer to mixed marriages (as will be discussed below). Indeed, the ascription of each of these verses to an editor is based solely upon a given scholar's opinion that its ideas do not comport well with the structure and theme of the work. Attention will therefore turn to the book itself. What is the structure and

---

27 Blenkinsopp, *History*, 240.

28 For example, F. Horst, *Die Zwölf Kleinen Propheten*, Handbuch zum Alten Testament, no. 14 (Tübingen: Mohr/Siebeck, 1938), II: 259-260; quoted in T. Chary, *Les prophètes et le culte à partir de 1'exil*, Bibliothèque deThéologie , series III (Tournai: Desclée and Co., 1955), 184.

29 Mason, *Books*, 150; E. Pfeiffer, "Die Disputationsworte im Buche Maleachi, " *Evangelische Theologie* 19 (1959): 554.

30 Malchow, 252-255.

31 Mason, *Books*, 152.

32 Steven McKenzie and Howard Wallace, "Covenant Themes in Malachi," *CBQ* 45 (1983): 561.

33 McKenzie and Wallace, 562.

34 Childs, *Introduction*, 496.

35 Swetnam, 200-209.

genre of Malachi? Do any portions of the book appear to depart radically from the larger scheme of the book?

SUGGESTIONS OF FORM

Malachi has most often been identified as "disputation speech," a genre in which—according to Gunkel—a prophet quotes his opponents' words and then refutes them. This genre is frequently discerned in Deutero-Isaiah where it has been studied by Begrich, Westermann and others; [36] in Haggai where it has been treated by Long and Whedbee; [37] and in various biblical passages.

While Gunkel points to Malachi as a general example of the form of "statement and counter-statement," E. Pfeiffer has presented the most detailed argument for viewing Malachi as belonging to the genre of disputation speech.[38] According to Pfeiffer, in employing this genre the book follows in the tradition of passages such as Amos 5:18-20 and Isaiah 40:27-31. Malachi is constructed of six prophetic disputations: 1:2-5; 1:6-2: 9;2:10-16; 2:17-3:5; 3:6-12; and 3:13-21 (Pfeiffer treats 2:11-12 and 3:22-24 as secondary).

Each of these disputations is structured in the same manner. Each begins with a statement: (*Behauptung*), is followed by an objection which seeks clarification (*Einrede*), and ends with an explanation that clarifies the issue and leads to a conclusion (*Begründung*). These components vary slightly in the disputations, and a given disputation may contain more than one of each of these elements.

Boecker concurs with Pfeiffer's analysis while yet positing several changes in terminology. Noting that the passages seek more to convince the people of a position rather than to dispute their words, Boecker prefers to designate Malachi as "discussion speech" (*Diskussionsworte*) rather that "disputation speech" (*Disputationsworte*). He also labels the first element of each passage "the opening sentence of the discussion" (*Satz der Gesprächseröffnung*) instead of employing Pfeiffer's term

---

[36] For a summary of these discussions, see A. Graffy, *A Prophet Confronts His People*, Analecta Biblica 104 (Rome: Pontifical Biblical Institute, 1984).

[37] Burke Long, "Two Question and Answer Schemata in the Prophets, " *JBL* 90 (1971): 129-137; J. William Whedbee, "A Question-Answer Schema in Haggai 1: The Form and Function of Haggai 1:9-11," in *Biblical and Near Eastern Studies: Essays in Honor of William Sanford LaSor*, ed. Gary A. Tuttle (Grand Rapids: William B. Eerdmans, 1978), 184-194 .

[38] Pfeiffer, 546-68.

"statement."[39] Wallis' treatment of the book supports both Pfeiffer's analysis of structure and Boecker's adaptation of terminology.[40]

Even those scholars who do not treat Malachi in a careful form-critical manner yet concur with this general perception of Malachi's style as one of disputation. The "question and answer" technique of the book is highlighted by R. Smith and Mason.[41] Fischer deems the book's style "catechetical."[42] Kodell points to the "distinctive dialogue technique" of the book which follows the pattern of affirmation, question or complaint and response.[43] Blenkinsopp suggests that the "quite distinctive category" of the book is "disputation and polemic, featuring question and answer, objection and refutation."[44]

Kaufmann offers his own analysis of Malachi's pattern. He identifies seven prophecies in the book: 1:2-5; 1:6-2:9; 2:10-16; 2:17-3:6; 3:7-12; 3:13-21; and 3:22-24. Kaufmann differs from Pfeiffer not only in treating 3:22-24 as a genuine prophecy but also in his delineation of the fourth and fifth speeches. Each of these seven prophecies, maintains Kaufmann, is composed of a prophetic assertion, a question to the listeners and a response of the prophet.[45]

While Pfeiffer has neatly outlined Malachi's structure and scholars have legitimately perceived the argumentative tone of the book, problems still remain in accurately identifying Malachi's form of prophetic utterance with that of disputation speech. These problems take several avenues.

While agreeing with Pfeiffer's analysis of the structure of the speeches in Malachi, A. Graffy has questioned the description of these oracles as classical disputation speech. Graffy argues that while indeed the *tone* of Malachi is that of disputation, the speeches seek not to reject the people's quoted opinion—as in other examples of the genre—but rather endeavor to convince the listeners of the original stated point.[46] The structure of the speeches, moreover, varies significantly from that of

---

39 Hans Jochen Boecker, "Bermerkungen zur formsgeschichtlichen Terminologie des Buches Malachi," *ZAW* 78 (1966): 78-80; Quoted in Graffy, 16-17.

40 G. Wallis, "Wesen und Struktur der Botschaft Maleachi," *BZAW* 105 (1967): 229-237; quoted in Graffy, 17.

41 R. Smith, 300; Mason, *Books*, 136.

42 James A. Fischer, "Notes on the Literary Form and Message of Malachi," *CBQ* 34 (1972): 315-320.

43 Kodell, 95.

44 Blenkinsopp, *History*, 240.

45 Kaufmann, 437.

46 Graffy, 16.

Isaiah 40:27-31, considered by Pfeiffer to be the classical example of the genre.

In addition, while in disputation speech the quotations of the people are credible and true to life,[47] the same does not hold for Malachi. In the words of Baldwin,

> Such remarks as 'How hast thou loved us?' (1:12), 'How shall we return (to God)?' (3:7), 'It is vain to serve God' (3:14), are rarely heard in public debate...Malachi reads the attitudes of his people and intuitively puts their thoughts into words, and so gains their attention before driving home his word from the Lord.[48]

According to Pfeiffer, the differences between Malachi's employment of this genre and other examples of disputation speech are quantitative rather than qualitative: Malachi presents a late development of the genre and not a new *Gattung*.[49] Graffy, however, has demonstrated quite real differences between Malachi and these other examples. If, indeed, the passage is a "late adaptation" of the genre, then it bears a distinctive character that deserves attention. If the book is disputation speech, how has it attempted to redefine the genre? Why has the form changed? The structure of the book, indeed, is not self-evident, and Baldwin, for example, suggests that Malachi bears no real structure.[50]

More importantly, these treatments of Malachi and other treatments of disputation speech have focused on literary structure and tone but have not addressed the larger issues of form criticism, especially the issue of the genre's *Sitz im Leben*. Graffy suggests that this "disputation" form derives from "real-life disputes," and that the form is assigned to a "specific historical period of approximately a century," during which the people had "reached a peak of skepticism and criticism."[51] The identification of a form's *Sitz im Leben* as "everyday life," however, provides little information for understanding its message. Such an explanation merely describes a passage as a common argument and suggests that other biblical passages also constitute arguments—a conclusion that hardly requires the tools of form criticism.

These scholarly treatments of Malachi, it seems, have drawn little distinction between a book's form (genre) and its style or rhetorical devices. Graffy's quote reveals such a confusion, suggesting that "the dis-

---

47 Ibid., 119.
48 Baldwin, 214.
49 Pfeiffer, 568.
50 Baldwin, 214.
51 Graffy, 119 .

putation speech can be seen as a particular *device* (emphasis mine) designed to confront erring opinions directly and convince the people of the prophet's teaching."[52] Malachi is, quite obviously, constructed as a "rhetorical dialogue."[53] Is "disputation speech, however, the best description of its form?

Perhaps most problematically, treating Malachi as a collection of six disputation speeches fails to account for other significant elements of the book. Not only does such an explanation fail to discern continuity in theme among the oracles but also it ignores Malachi's legal and covenantal characteristics.

Malachi is replete with covenantal terminology and ideology. McKenzie and Wallace perhaps have provided the most thorough treatment of Malachi's covenantal terminology.[54] The following are representative examples:

- the book's use of "love" and "hate" in accordance with ancient Near Eastern treaty language;
- its use of *bāgad* to describe unfaithfulness;
- its employment of the language of curses and blessings;
- its description of the relationship between God and Israel as that between father and son;
- its frequent reference to the deity as a "great king."

McKenzie and Wallace also have studied three covenants mentioned in Malachi: the covenants of Levi (2:8), the fathers (2:10), and marriage (2:14).

While McKenzie and Wallace consider covenant themes and terms in Malachi, others such as Achtemeier have suggested that Malachi's ties to covenant ideology are much stronger. Achtemeier argues that the entire book is "primarily concerned with the fulfillment of the duties of the covenant relationship," and that it has been cast in the form of a court case, "tried before the priest in the temple, with the prophet playing the role of the priest in his imagination."[55] The question and answer style of Malachi noted by Pfeiffer is not, according to Achtemeier, itself the form of the book, but rather reflects the social setting of a court in which question and answer were used. The book, she maintains, employs two genres—the prophetic disputation and the prophetic *tôrâ*—both of which can have a legal setting.

---

52 Ibid., 119.
53 B. 0. Long, 135.
54 McKenzie and Wallace, op cit.
55 Achtemeier, 172.

Achtemeier's remarks are helpful yet overly brief. While she does point to a court setting and the possibility of understanding Malachi in this way, she does not offer a careful analysis of the book's structure or a comparison of Malachi with other examples of this form. The same critique holds true for R. J. Coggins, who suggests that while the structure of the Book of Malachi likely has a legal background and while it shares elements in common with the prophetic *rîb* it yet "would be impossible to reconstruct anything like a complete 'lawsuit' from Malachi."[56]

Verhoef has gone even further than these scholars in considering the pervasive covenant themes and structures within Malachi. He traces the links between Malachi and ancient Near Eastern treaty forms, pointing to the similarities between 1:2-5 and the historical prologue; the tie between the prophet's accusations and covenantal stipulations; Yahweh's self-invocation as a witness; and the book's declaration of blessings and curses.[57] Verhoef traces these major elements of treaty forms, but he concedes that "Malachi's message does not resemble the classical structure of the late second-millenium covenants or even the varying scheme of the covenants from the first millenium."[58]

While offering further analysis of Malachi's full integration of the themes—as well as the very structure—of covenants, Verhoef's presentation yet fails to discern the form of the book. His study focuses on theme and meaning rather than contributing to the questions of structure and genre. Verhoef, moreover, traces the affinities between Malachi and ancient Near Eastern covenant-making instead of the covenant violation for which the prophet accuses the priests and the people.

J. Harvey, on the other hand, has demonstrated that portions of Malachi follow the classical form of the *rîb* or covenant lawsuit. The *rîb*, which finds its parallels in ancient Near Eastern sacral law, takes the following form:

1. Preliminaries;
2. The Interrogation of the judge, in which the judge asks abrupt questions that expect no response;
3. The Indictment, during which in historical terms the accused is charged with disobeying the stipulations of the covenant—especially with following strange gods;

---

[56] R. J. Coggins, *Haggai, Zechariah, Malachi*, Old Testament Guides (Sheffield, England: JSOT Press, 1977), 77.

[57] Verhoef, 180-184.

[58] Ibid., 180.

4. Declaration of guilt (usually in this section, the accused is reminded that ritual acts cannot compensate for guilt);
5. Threats and condemnations, associated with the curses invoked when the covenant was made;
6. A declaration of war *or* an ultimatum threatening punishment if covenant violations are not redressed.[59]

According to Harvey, Malachi 1:6-2:9 employs this *rîb* form:

1. Preliminaries, 1:6a (Sons honor their fathers and servants their masters.)
2. Interrogation, 1:6b (But if am father, where is my honor, and if I am master, where is my fear?)
3. Indictment, 1:7-9 (Priests are charged with their crimes.)
4. Declaration of guilt, 1:10a (God no longer takes pleasure in the priests. Denying the possibility of ritual compensation, God will no longer receive *minḥâ* from them.)
5. Threats, 1:10b (11-14) (Cursed be the one who brings an offering.)
6. Ultimatum, 2:1-9 (If the priests do not honor God's name, He will bring various curses against them; indeed, He has already cursed them.)[60]

Harvey's identification of the *rîb* pattern in 1:6-2:9 offers a valuable contribution to understanding Malachi. His explanation of the passage deals thoughtfully with the issues of genre, and in his discussion of the place of the prophetic lawsuit Harvey wrestles with the matter of the form's *Sitz im Leben*. Harvey's thesis has the additional merit of explaining both the presence of the question/answer scheme (as part of the interrogation) and the presence of covenant terminology and theme. Such a thesis also offers an explanation for the covenantal elements identified by Verhoef: Malachi does not fit classical patterns of covenant making precisely because its form is that of the lawsuit for covenant violation. The reason that it does parallel the elements in treaty-making such as the stipulations, witnesses and curses is that, as Huffmon has demonstrated, the covenant lawsuit is the mirror image of the covenant to which the vassal has assented.[61] The obvious limitation of Harvey's analysis is that

---

[59] J. Harvey, *Le plaidoyer prophétique contre Israël après la rupture de l'alliance*, Scholasticat de l'Immaculée-Conception (Paris: Desclée de Brouwer, 1967), especially chapter 4.

[60] Ibid., 66.

[61] Herbert Huffmon, "The Covenant Lawsuit in the Prophets," *JBL* 78 (1959): 285-295; See also P. A. Rieman, "Covenant, Mosaic," in *Interpreter's Dictionary of the Bible*, Supplementary Volume, ed. Keith Crimm and others (Nashville: Abingdon, 1976), 194-195; and Harvey, 132-133, quoting from F. Sommer, *Die Aḫḫijavā-Urkunden*, Abhandlungen der Bayerischen Academie der Wissenschaften, Philosophisch-historische Abteilung, n. f. 6 (Munich: Verlag der Bayerischen Akademie der

it deals only with one oracle unit in the book. In the course of his discussion of the *rîb*, Harvey mentions elements that may bear upon other portions of Malachi; his demonstration that the terms *tôēbâ* and *şedek* (as well as various idioms) are endemic to the language of the lawsuit may aid in understanding how these terms function in Malachi. As regards structure, however, Harvey's remarks inform only 1:6-2:9. Can this identification of the covenant lawsuit pattern in Malachi be carried further?

THE *RÎB* FORM

The entire Book of Malachi, indeed, employs the form of the covenant lawsuit. The elements that Harvey traces in 1:6-2:9 resound throughout the book, both in the individual units and in the organization of these units into a larger scheme.

Malachi is outlined as follows:

I. Prologue 1:2-5
II. Accusations
    A. First Accusation 1:6-2:9
        1. Preliminaries 1:6a
        2. Interrogation 1:6b
        3. Indictment 1:7-10a
        4. Declaration of guilt 1:10b-14
        5. Ultimatum/Punishment 2:1-9
    B. Second Accusation 2:10-16
        1. Preliminaries 2:10a
        2. Interrogation 2:10b
        3. Indictment 2:11
        4. Declaration of guilt 2:12
        5. Further indictment 2:13-14
        6. Ultimatum/Warning 2:15-16
    C. Third Accusation 2:17-3:5
        1. Indictment 2:17
        2. Ultimatum/Promise 3:1-5
    D. Fourth Accusation 3:6-12
        1. Preliminaries 3:6
        2. Indictment 3:7a
        3. Ultimatum/Promise 3:7b

Wissenschaften, 1932). See also G. E. Wright, "The Lawsuit of God: A Form-Critical Study of Deuteronomy 32," in *Israel's Prophetic Heritage: Essays in Honor of James Muilenberg*, ed. B. W. Anderson and Walter Harrelson (NY: Harper and Brothers, 1962), 26-67.

      4.   Indictment 3:8-9

      5.   Promise.. 3:10-12

   E. Fifth Accusation 3:13-21

      1.   Indictment 3:13-15

      2.   Historical account 3:16-18

      3.   Ultimatum/promise 3:19-21

III. Final Admonition... 3:22

IV. Final Ultimatum 3:23-24

I. PROLOGUE 1:2-5.

These verses serve as a reminder that Israel stands in covenant with Yahweh and affirm the fact that Yahweh has remained faithful to the covenant. Paralleling the historical prologue of a treaty,[62] this section recites the suzerain's beneficent deeds on the vassal's behalf: because Yahweh has been in covenant with Israel ("Jacob I have loved") and not with Edom ("And Esau—I have hated him"),[63] the deity has destroyed Edom and promises to do so again if needed. The fate of Edom is described in language common to ancient Near Eastern treaty curses. Edom has been made a "dwelling place of jackals," and should its inhabitants rebuild their work will be futile.[64] In language also common to treaty terminology, the people themselves will witness this act and will profess the greatness of Yahweh's name.[65]

II. THE ACCUSATIONS.

A. *FIRST ACCUSATION. 1:6-2:9.*

This unit begins the first of several accusations of treaty violation: although Yahweh has been shown to be faithful to the covenant, the priests and the people have not. In this accusation, the deity charges that the priests have violated the stipulations of their agreement. Especially,

---

62 Verhoef, 180-81.

63 William Moran, "The Ancient Near Eastern Background of the Love of God in Deuteronomy," *CBQ* 25 (1963): 77-87; Norbert Lohfink, "Hate and Love in Osee 9,15," *CBQ* 25 (1963): 417.

64 The curse that a site will be made a dwelling place of jackals is invoked by various treaties and various prophets. This curse is discussed by D. Hillers, *Treaty Curses and the Old Testament Prophets*, Biblica et Orientalia, no. 16 (Rome: Pontifical Biblical Institute, 1964), 53. Hillers also considers futility curses such as that in Mal. 1:4 (29).

65 James Muilenberg discusses the importance of self-witnessing in the covenant ("your eyes will see") in "The Form and Structure of the Covenantal Formulations," *VT* 9 (1959): 355. Moshe Weinfeld treats the treaty emphasis on the greatness of the name in "The Covenant of Grant in the Old Testament and in the Ancient Near East," *Journal of the American Oriental Society* 90 (1970): 200

they have profaned the exclusive relationship between parties that the covenant demands.[66]

Preliminaries. 1:6a. A reminder of the intended exclusivity of the relationship serves as the basis for the accusation. Common, proverbial knowledge dictates that inferiors honor superiors (compare Isa. 1:3).

Interrogation. 1:6b. Contrary to proverbial wisdom, the priests have despised the deity's honor. As in classical examples of the *rîb*, the questions asked by the deity do not expect an answer but rather introduce the guilt of the accused.

Indictment. 1:7-10a. The deity's indictment of the priests details the ways in which they have broken covenant. They have improperly maintained the cultus for which they were responsible. Quite sardonic in force is the invitation to "present it to your governor" in 1: 8b: if an offering is unfit for a subordinate official such as a governor, how impudent the priests are in presenting this offering to the Great King!

Declaration of Guilt. 1:10b-14. While Harvey treats 1:10a (*mî...wĕyisgōr*) as part of the interrogation, this phrase is more properly the denial of ritual compensation. It is not interrogative in force but rather expresses the desire that one would shut the Temple doors.[67] The firm declaration of guilt follows in 10b: I have no pleasure in you and will accept no offering from you .

The priests' disregard for the purity of the worship of Yahweh is set in direct contrast with the pure offerings presented by other parties. As used in Psalm 50 and in various ancient Near Eastern documents, the phrase "from the rising of the sun to its setting" stresses the universal power of the sovereign: "It is a comprehensive designation of the whole world—known and unknown."[68] The import of the verse, it seems, is not to stress the purity of gentile offerings[69] but instead to underscore the scope of the deity's influence; although Yahweh is mistreated in Israel, His name is great among the nations.

In contrast to the universal acknowledgement of the deity's greatness, the priests (*wĕʾattem*) have defiled (*ḥll*) the name by violating the stipulations of the covenant. As a conclusion to this indictment, the

---

[66] George Mendenhall, "Covenant," *Interpreter's Dictionary of the Bible*, ed. George Buttrick and others (Nashville: Abingdon, 1962), vol. A-D, 719.

[67] GKC 151a.

[68] Verhoef, 223 .

[69] In *Palestinian Parties and Politics* (93-94), Morton Smith argues that Mal. 1:11 demonstrates that Gentiles worshiped Yahweh.

LORD invokes a curse upon anyone who brings an inferior offering[70]—for, as the people are reminded, Yahweh is a great king and His reputation is acknowledged among the nations.

Ultimatum. 2:1-9. Confronted with these accusations, the priests now receive an ultimatum: "if you do not honor me, I will curse you." This ultimatum is introduced by *wĕʿattâ*, as are accusations in other covenant contexts; in Exodus 19:5 *wĕʿattâ* introduces the conditions of the covenant[71] and frequently in the Deuteronomistic History it introduces the punishment component of the lawsuit (1 Sam. 2:27-36; 2 Sam. 12:7-12, etc.).

The priests, indeed, already are cursed because they fail to honor Yahweh. Their punishment is introduced by *hinĕnî* with a participle, a common formula for introducing the punishment in a covenant lawsuit (see 2 Sam. 12:11; 1 Kgs. 14:10; Jer. 6:19, etc.).

Verses 5-7 serve to describe the proper functioning of the priestly covenant. As discussed in chapter 2, the covenant between the deity and Levi is here described in the terms of an ancient Near Eastern grant. Like a proper subject, Levi feared,[72] walked in peace and uprightness,[73] and respected the deity's name.

In contrast to proper covenant faithfulness, however, "you" (the priests) have failed to show the deity respect. Just as the nations' respect for proper worship in 1:11 was introduced by *kî* and contrasted with the improper worship of "you" (*ʾattem*), so too Levi's faithfulness to the terms of the covenant is introduced by *kî* and contrasted with the unfaithfulness of "you" (*ʾattem*). The priests' breaking of the covenant is described as *šḥt*, a term used in the Phoenician Kilamuwa inscription[74] to describe breaking a treaty or the inscription upon which the treaty is inscribed. As punishment for not obeying the deity, the priests are made despised and debased.

B. SECOND ACCUSATION. 2:10-16.

This unit begins a second accusation of covenant violation.

Preliminaries. 2:10a. Like the previous unit, this passage begins with an almost proverbial reassertion of the exclusive relationship between

---

70 For a similar curse against the one who breaks treaty, see Jeremiah 11:3, as cited in Charles Fensham, "Malediction and Benediction in the Ancient Near Eastern Vassal Treaties and the Old Testament," *ZAW* 74 (1962): 4.

71 Muilenberg, "Form and Structure," 352-353.

72 Weinfeld, *Deuteronomy*, 274, 332.

73 Ibid., 75-76.

74 KAI 24.

Yahweh and Israel. Cast in the style of rhetorical questions, it reminds that all have one father and one God.

Interrogation. 2:10b. Following the preliminaries, the interrogation begins: "Why (if we have one father) are we faithless to one another, so as to profane the covenant of the fathers?" Pfeiffer treats 2:10b as an Objection of the people (*Einrede*) but, on the contrary, it is a question posed by the prophet and not by the people.

The interrogation introduces the accusation that the people have been faithless (*bgd*). The term *bgd* will appear four more times in this unit (verses 11, 14, 15, 16). *Bgd* is used in covenant contexts to describe covenant violation;[75] for example, in Hosea 6:7 *bgd* stands in synonymous parallelism with a phrase signifying the transgression of covenant.

Indictment. 2:11. Various lawsuit-related terms appear in the indictment as well: the deity describes Israel's profanation (*ḥll*) of the sanctuary and its marriage to the daughter of a foreign god (*bat-ēl nēkār*) as treachery (*bgd*) and as an abomination (*tôʿēbâ*). Like *bgd*, which was discussed above, *tôʿēbâ* is also used to describe covenant infidelity. *Tôʿēbâ* describes impurity (usually in the context of idolatry) in Deuteronomy as well as in pre-Deuteronomic and non-Deuteronomic passages (such as Isa. 1:13 and Ezekiel).[76]

Israel is indicted for two offenses that clearly are linked: profaning the sanctuary and marrying the daughter of a foreign god. Most scholars interpret 2:11b as a diatribe against mixed marriages; by marrying foreign women who worship foreign deities, the men of Judah have violated the covenant and profaned exclusive worship of Yahweh. Indeed, so accepted is the notion that Malachi forbids the marriage of non-Jewish women that the book is usually dated in accordance with Ezra's and Nehemiah's abolition of mixed marriages.

Such a widely-held opinion regarding the meaning of this verse is not easily shaken. Several problems with this interpretation, however, must be noted. First, the translation of *bat-ēl nēkār* is not clear. Nowhere else in the Hebrew Bible are foreign women so described and, as Isaakson notes, the phrase "daughter of a god" more logically describes a

---

[75] Arvid S. Kapelrud, "The Prophets and the Covenant," in *In the Shelter of Elyon: Essays on Ancient Palestinian Life and Literature in Honor of G. W. Ahlström*, ed. W. Boyd Barrick and John R. Spencer, JSOTS 31 (Sheffield: JSOT Press 1984), 183.

[76] For discussions of *tôʿēbâ*, see Jean L'Hour, "Les Interdits *Tôʿēbâ* dans le Deutéronome," *Revue biblique* 71 (1964): 481-503; and Weinfeld, *Deuteronomy*, 226, 323.

goddess than a woman.[77] Secondly, the language inveighed against this action is that usually reserved for accusations of idolatry—*tôʾēbâ* and *ḥll*.

In addition, while the interpretation of *bāʿal bat-ēl nēkār* as intermarriage is usually supported by the assertion that 2:13-16 also accuses Judean men of divorcing their Hebrew wives in order to marry more prosperous foreign women, verses 2:13-16 offer their own problems and their interpretation is no less dubious than that of 2:11. The designation of a human marriage as *bĕrît* (2:14b) is unique in the Bible.[78] Also, the translation of *šallaḥ* in 2:16a is unclear: when referring to divorce, *šallaḥ* usually takes an object (Deut. 22:19, 29; 24:1, 3; Jer. 3:1), and if indeed this verse is a blanket condemnation of divorce it stands in direct contrast to Deut. 24:1-4.[79]

For these reasons, a minority of scholars has argued that Malachi 2:11 accuses the people not of intermarriage with foreigners but rather of idolatry. Torrey took such a position late in the last century, maintaining that the "...rebuke is directed against the encroachment of some foreign cult in Israel."[80] Hvidberg likewise maintains:

> The "daughter of a god" is a goddess and the statement that Judah has "married" (bʿl) her is immediately intelligible to the person who e.g. knows the mention by a prophet like Hosea of Yahweh as the husband of Israel.[81]

Isaakson argues that "the interpretation of 2:10-16 as an attack on apostasy to an alien cult is in entire agreement with the rest of the content of the book of Malachi;"[82] according to Matthews "...only by a twist of the imagination can many of the words and phrases be applied to the marriage problem, while they most naturally fit in into the idea of ritual."[83]

These authors also maintain that 2:13-16—the other passage bearing on this issue—likewise concerns idolatry. According to their view, the

---

77　Abel Isaakson, *Marriage and Ministry in the New Temple*, Acta Seminarii Neotestamentici Upsaliensis no. 24 (Lund: Gleerup, 1965), 31. According to Julius Morgenstern, *bat-ēl nēkār* refers to a foreign princess. He maintains that Mal. 2:10-16 records the transactions of a marriage between Menahem ("Judah") and a Tyrian princess. "Jerusalem—485 B.C. (continued)," *HUCA* 28 (1957): 15-47.

78　McKenzie and Wallace, 552-553, n. 14. For another viewpoint, see Paul Kalluveettil, *Declaration and Covenant*, Analecta Biblica, no. 88 (Rome: Pontifical Biblical Institute, 1982), 79-83.

79　Isaakson, 31.

80　C C. Torrey, "The Prophecy of 'Malachi,'" *JBL* 17 (1898): 4.

81　F. F. Hvidberg, *Weeping and Laughter in the Old Testament* (Leiden: E. J. Brill, 1962), 121-122.

82　Isaakson, 32.

83　J. G. Matthews, "Tammuz Worship in the Book of Malachi," *Palestine Oriental Society Journal* 11 (1931): 44.

"wife of your youth" and "your covenanted wife" refer not to an actual human wife but rather, metaphorically, to the covenant religion.[84] According to Isaakson, the wife of the covenant is Yahweh himself. Although the description of Yahweh in feminine terms admittedly is rare in Scripture, Isaakson maintains that such an image is employed to enable the author to extend the image begun in verse 11.[85] Hvidberg carries this description of Malachi's intent much further, suggesting that "covering the altar with tears, weeping and groaning" refers to ritual mourning associated with the Adonis cult: the people have profaned the covenant by marrying the goddess and shedding tears for her lover.[86]

While Hvidberg's position is extreme and his cultic explanation for weeping and laughter reads too much into 2:13, the interpretation of "marriage to the daughter of a foreign god" as idolatry has much to recommend it.[87] Not only does such an interpretation account for why this offense is deemed *tô'ēbâ* and *ḥll*, but also it comports well with the themes of the book: although Israel has one father and God, the people have broken this exclusive relationship by worshipping a female deity.

Declaration of Guilt/Threat. 2:12. Unfortunately, the precise meaning of this curse is unclear. Although most scholars have perceived that *'ēr wě'ōneh* describes two opposing categories the combination of which is intended to include everyone,[88] they disagree concerning the meaning of these two words. Literally, the MT reads "the one who awakes (participle of *'wr*) and "the one who answers (participle of *'nh*). This phrase, however, finds no parallel in the Bible, and ancient translators struggled to interpret the phrase.[89] Several approaches to this problem have been attempted.

One common treatment of the problem is that advocated by Wellhausen, who emends *'ēr* ("one awake") to *'ēd* ("witness") based on

---

84 Torrey, "Prophecy of 'Malachi,'" 5.

85 Isaakson, 33 .

86 Hvidberg, 122 .

87 This position was also taken by David L. Petersen in his paper "Malachi and the Language of Divorce, Mal. 2:10-16," Israelite Prophetic Literature Section, Society of Biblical Literature Annual Meeting, Boston, MA, Dec. 6, 1987. The position is likewise supported by A. S. van der Woude, "Malachi's Struggle for a Pure Community," in *Tradition and Re-Interpretation in Jewish and Early Christian Literature: Essays in Honor of Jürgen C. H. Lebram*, ed. J. W. van Henten and others (Leiden: E. J. Brill, 1986), 65-71.

88 On the contrary, A. van Hoonacker maintains that the two words are synonymous. *Les douze petits propètes* (Paris: Lefebvre, 1906), 724.

89 See G. R. Driver, "Confused Hebrew Roots," in *Occident and Orient: Gaster Anniversary Volume* (London: Taylor 's, 1936), 80.

the reading of the Septuagint. According to Wellhausen, the phrase refers to two legal categories—the "(hostile) witness" and a "(defending) counsel."[90] The curse, then, forbids the accused any legal recourse.

Torrey, Driver, van Hoonacker, J. M. P. Smith and others have criticized Wellhausen's emendation. They argue that ordinary people were little concerned with legal matters and hence scarcely would have been affected by such a threat. Marti adds a further objection, suggesting that if a legal setting were intended, the *ʿēr* and the *ʿōneh* would be cut off from the gates of the city rather than from the tents of Jacob.[91]

Other scholars have attempted to retain the MT while trying to discern other meanings of the phrase. Driver has linked both words with Arabic roots: Hebrew *ʿēr* (from the root *ʿwr*) is related to the Arabic root *ʿyr*, from which the word *ʿyr* ("vagabond") is derived, while *ʿōneh* is linked to the root *ǵny*, on which *mǵʿny* ("stay at home") is based. Based on these parallels, Driver maintains that *ʿēr wěʿōneh* is translated as "gad-about and stay-at-home," and may be an ancient saying originally describing all members of a tent.[92]

Torrey finds a different Arabic parallel in the story of the Ayesha scandal, in which the character laments that in the vacant camp there was neither "one who called and one who answered." The Malachi phrase, according to Torrey, likewise refers to "the one who starts a conversation and one who answers."[93]

Glazier-McDonald remains within Hebrew to suggest that *ʿēr wěʿōneh* bears a sexual connotation. Based on the use of the root *ʿwr* in other passages, she suggests that *ʿēr* refers to "the aroused one." Since the root *ʿnh* (III) in the *piʿel* means "to rape" and since the *piʿel* may refer to "an eager pursuit of an action that may involve causing others to do the same," Glazier-McDonald maintains that the *qal* of *ʿnh* III may express sexual intercourse by mutual consent.[94] Hence, the prophet is threatening those who have joined the fertility rites of their pagan wives.[95]

These suggestions, while dealing admirably with the meaning of the phrase *ʿēr wěʿōneh*, fail to consider other factors involved in the transla-

---

90 Wellhausen, *Kleinen Propheten*, 207. English wording is that of Driver, "Confused Roots," 80.

91 Karl Marti, *Das Dodekapropheten erklärt* (Tübingen: Mohr, 1904); quoted in J. M. P. Smith, 51.

92 Driver, "Confused Roots," 81.

93 C. C. Torrey, "*ʿēr wěʿōneh* in Malachi ii.12," *JBL* 24 (1905): 177.

94 Glazier-McDonald, "Malachi," 148; and "Malachi 2:12: *ʿēr wěʿōneh*—Another Look," *JBL* 105 (1986): 295-298.

95 Glazier-McDonald, "Malachi," 154.

tion of 2:12. Most scholars have interpreted this phrase as further specifying the man (ʾîš) described: may God cut off the man—that is, the waker and the answerer. The grammatical construction of the verse, however, does not permit such an interpretation. The noun ʾîš is introduced by the preposition *lamed*, and, as seen in parallel passages, the *lamed* does not introduce the direct object of "cut off" but rather the person to whose detriment others will be cut off (1 Kgs. 14:10, 21:21; 2 Kgs. 9:8; 1 Sam. 2:33). In addition, while commentators have concentrated heavily on the meaning of *ʿēr wĕʿōneh*, few have considered the relationship between these two participles and the final participle that concludes the verse—*maggîš minḥâ* ("the one who offers *minḥâ*"). Does this final participle serve to qualify the first two (the *ʿēr* and the *ʿōneh*, who *maggîš minḥâ*)? Or does it constitute a separate category (the *ʿēr* , the *ʿōneh*, and the *maggîš minḥâ*)?

As seen in the discussion above, these categories do not further describe the "man," but rather they denote those persons who would be of advantage to the accused. Hence, "the one who offers *minḥâ*" (*maggîš minḥâ*) appears to form a separate category of person; the threat is not against the one who while an *ʿēr wĕʿōneh* yet is an offerer of *minḥâ*, but the man is threatened with the loss of each of these three types of people.

A consideration of the grammatical construction for such a threat/curse offers limited help in determining the meaning of 2:12. It does militate against Glazier-McDonald's view that *ʿēr wĕʿōneh* describes those involved in pagan fertility rites (since these persons would be of little benefit to the man). It also suggests that *maggîš minḥâ* refers to a separate category. Whether the *maggîš minḥâ* refers to any Israelite (as it does in Amos 5:25) or specifically to a priest (as it does in Leviticus 2:8), the man cursed is deprived of ritual compensation for his transgression.

The precise meaning of *ʿēr wĕʿōneh* therefore still remains unclear. Torrey's and Driver's interpretations, both of which treat these words as descriptive of two opposite kinds of persons, are feasible and may suggest that the man is threatened with the abolition of all kin. Wellhausen's view fits nicely into the form of the book by denying to the offender both legal and cultic aid: while Torrey's protest that individuals were not concerned with legal matters may be valid, the form of the covenant lawsuit usually includes the denial of any help for the accused.

The words *ʿēr* and *ʿōneh* may be interpreted as legal terms even without Wellhausen's emendation. *ʿēr* may derived from the Aramaic root *ʿrr*. In Cowley 8:27, *ʿr* means to enter into a lawsuit with someone,[96] and in

---

96 Charles-F. Jean and Jacob Hoftizer, *Dictionnaire des inscriptions sémitiques de l'ouest* (Leiden: E. J. Brill, 1965), 222.

various rabbinic texts, ʿrr refers to protest and objection.[97] In Daniel 4:16, ʿar signifies an adversary. Clearly, the consonantal text would support the derivation of ʿēr from ʿrr although the Masoretic pointing treats the root of ʿēr as ʿwr .[98]

Interpreting ʿēr as deriving from ʿrr is only a suggestion. It, like all other alternatives, finds no parallel in biblical Hebrew. Importantly, however, this verse forms a condemnation against the one who has committed abomination and threatens to cut off any benefit to the accused.

Further Indictment. 2:13-14. These verses form a second indictment within this unit. The meaning of these accusations has been addressed above, although a few additional remarks are in order.

The weeping and groaning described in 2:13 probably do not reflect the ritual mourning described by Hvidberg. These actions appear not to describe offenses but rather the response to God's refusal of their offerings. Although mēʾên may denote that the weeping and groaning either are the cause of God's displeasure or its result,[99] the people in 2:14a inquire of the reasons of His displeasure, a fact suggesting that their transgression has not yet been named.

Noteworthy in 2:14 is that Yahweh stands as a witness against the people's violation of the covenant. Also bearing covenantal connotations is the description of the breach of covenant as bgd.

Ultimatum/warning. 2:15-16. The interpretation of these verses is extremely problematic. Almost every word bears several meanings and several possible subjects. According to one translation of 2:15, the passage indicates that God created but one wife for Adam (or for Abraham)—despite His remaining resources—in order that righteous progeny be produced. According to another translation, the verse affirms that one God created (all of us), that life belongs to Him, and that He seeks righteous seed. Verse 16 also receives various translations: in the view of Hvidberg, "covering the garment" reflects the Adonis rite while according to Glazier-McDonald this phrase describes the ritual of marriage.

These and other translations are often tenuous, usually ignoring Masoretic punctuation and attributing otherwise unknown meanings to

---

97 Marcus Jastrow, *A Dictionary of the Targumim, The Talmud Babli and Yerushalmi, and the Midrashic Literature* (New York: P. Shalom, 1967), II: 1123-24.

98 ʿēr follows the form of the participle of the hollow verb. The participle of ʿrr (stative) would be ʿēr.

99 BDB, 35.

words. Significant, however, is the fact that both 2:15 and 2:16 end with language associated with an ultimatum. In both verses the prophet warns the people to "be on guard for your life" (*nišmartem běrûḥăkem*). This idiom finds a close parallel in Deut. 4:9, 15; Jer. 17:21, and especially in Josh. 23:11, where *nišmartem lěnapšōtêkem* serves as a warning against disobeying the Lord's word.[100] Both 2:15 and 2:16, moreover, caution the people not to be faithless (*bgd*).

C. THIRD ACCUSATION. 2:17-3:5.

Indictment. 2:17. As before, this unit begins with an indictment: the people have wearied God with their doubt. Questioning the Lord's justice, they challenge His goodness.

Punishment/Threat/Ultimatum. 3:1-5. In the most famous passage of the Book of Malachi, the LORD announces that He will send a messenger. The identity and significance of this figure has been much discussed, and the *malʾāk* has been treated as a priestly figure,[101] an eschatological precursor of the Day of the LORD, and as a typification of the prophet as the LORD's messenger. Significant but little discussed, however, is the covenant character of the *malʾāk*.

Noteworthy is the fact that 3:1 begins with *hinněni šōlēaḥ*, a construction commonly used in the lawsuit form to announce punishment (see also 2:3). The messenger functions as agent of God in punishing covenant violators. This assessment is supported by verse 5, in which the LORD reveals that He will be a ready witness in order to bring punishment against adulterers, those who swear falsely, those who mistreat the hireling, widow, orphan and sojourner, and those who do not fear the LORD.

All of these categories describe covenant violation and the prohibitions of all are found in passages that outline covenant obedience. In the Book of the Covenant, which details the conditions of the covenant, the LORD mandates proper treatment of the sojourner, widow and orphan (Exod. 22:21-23) and He describes sorcerers and adulterers as covenant breakers (Exod. 22:18 and 20:14). Leviticus 19, which also lists covenant stipulations, warns against swearing falsely (19:11) and oppressing the hireling (19:13). Proper treatment of the hireling also is mandated by Deut. 24:14-15, a passage likewise outlining covenant obligation. "The one who does not fear the LORD" is a more general description of the person who disregards the covenant.

---

100 Weinfeld, *Deuteronomy*, 357.
101 Malchow, 252-255.

Both in covenant making and covenant lawsuit, the figure of the messenger is central. In each of the accounts of covenant making mentioned above (Exodus 20-23, Deuteronomy and Leviticus), a messenger serves as the mediator. In the *rîb*, the *malʾāk* serves to guard the covenant. The messenger represents the sovereign and guards the covenant made by the sovereign.[102]

Petersen points to a striking parallel between the Malachi passage and Exod. 23:20-22, in which the *malʾāk* is treated as a covenant enforcer: because "the LORD's name is in him," the messenger has the power both to punish those who disobey him and to reward those who listen to his voice.[103] Among ancient Near Eastern examples, the Sefire treaty (III: 8) makes provisions for the sending of a messenger and insists that the messenger be treated with the same respect due the sovereign. In the "Mita of Paḫḫuwa" letter and in various letters, the denial of the messenger is considered a breach of treaty.[104]

As seen in a large number of biblical passages, the messenger announces the punishment ensuing from the *rîb*. In Judges 2:1-5, the *malʾak ʾādônay* pronounces the *rîb* and its punishment, as does the "man of God" (*ʾîš ʾelōhîm*) in 1 Sam. 2:27-36. The same role is assumed by early prophets such as Nathan and Elijah (2 Sam. 12:7-12; 1 Kgs. 21:17-24) and classical prophets such as Jeremiah and Isaiah.

As the agent of the covenant, the *malʾāk* of 3:1 not only will punish covenant violators but also will purify the priests in order to restore Temple worship to its former purity. The image of Yahweh and/or His agent purifying the people as one who purifies metal appears in various biblical passages. In Dan. 11:35, the Lord promises to seduce the ones who violate covenant but to cleanse those who know their God. Zech. 13:9 likewise threatens the two-thirds who have transgressed while promising to refine the remaining third "as one refines silver, and test them as gold is tested." Most strikingly, in Isa. 1, which according to Harvey constitutes a prime example of a *rîb*, the Lord proclaims that He will "turn my hand against you and will smelt away your dross as with lye and remove all your alloy" (1:25).[105] This purification will, as in Malachi, restore the people's former purity: "and I will restore your

---

102 Harvey, 148.

103 Petersen, "Israelite Prophecy," 153.

104 See 0. R., Gurney, "Mita of Paḫḫuwa," *Annals of Archaeology and Anthropology* 28 (1948): 34.

105 Similarly, Isa. 48:10: "Behold, I have refined you, but not like silver; I have tried you in the furnace of affliction" (RSV).

judges as at the first and your counselors as at the beginning. Afterward
you shall be called the City of Righteousness, the faithful city" (Isa. 1:26).

Such an understanding of the role and function of the messenger in
covenant contexts may help explain several problems in 3:1. The fact that
the messenger functions as the "alter-ego" of the sovereign[106] may account for the grammatical fusion of the *mal'āk*, the *'ādôn* and the *mal'ak
habbĕrît*. Also, the statement in 3:1 that the Lord is entering the Temple
may be understood as language appropriate to the covenant lawsuit.
Micah 1, which bears the elements of the *rîb*, declares, "...let the LORD
God be witness against you, the Lord from His holy Temple. For behold,
the LORD is coming forth out of His place, and will come down and
tread upon the high places of the earth" (1:2b-3).

D. FOURTH ACCUSATION. 3:6-12.

Preliminaries. 3:6. Yahweh's assertion that He does not change stands
in direct contrast the faithlessness of Israel described in 3:5. As shown by
N. Waldman, the expression *lō' šānîtî* finds a semantic equivalent in the
Akkadian *enû* which often is used intransitively to mean "going back on
one's word, reneging."[107] Waldman therefore translates Mal. 3:6 as "For
I, the Lord, have not gone back on my word, and you, children of Israel,
have not perished."[108] Within the *rîb*, then, 3:6 serves to remind the people that while they have been faithless, God has kept covenant.

Indictment. 3:7a. The prophet reiterates the fact that Israel's covenant
violation has a long history.

Promise. 3:7b. Despite their persistent faithlessness, the Lord offers
the people the chance to repent.

Indictment/Curse. 3:8-9. Rather than accepting the Lord's offer, the
people immediately question His words. This questioning leads to a
further indictment: they are robbing God. How are they doing so? with
their tithes and offerings. For this reason, they are cursed with a curse.

Promise. 3:10-12. The Lord again makes an offer: "if you will honor
what is due to me, I promise to make you prosper." This promise approximates the language of the covenant blessings. In Deut. 28:11-12,
God promises to bless the faithful by "opening the heavens" (*pth*) and
sending abundant blessings. Here in Malachi, the Lord promises to re-

---

106 Holladay, 31-32.
107 Nahum Waldman, "Some Notes on Malachi 3:6, 3:13 and Psalm 42:11," *JBL* 93
(1974): 543.
108 Ibid., 544.

buke the devourer, and the fruit and the vine will thrive. Moreover, all nations will affirm the blessedness of the land.

E. FIFTH ACCUSATION. 3:13-21.

Indictment. 3:13-15. As do many of the accusations in the Book of Malachi, this accusation begins directly with an indictment. It charges that the people's words have "been harsh" against God (*ḥāzĕqû ʿālay dibrêkem*). Waldman's study helpfully notes Akkadian and Mishnaic parallels to this expression and suggests that the phrase should be translated, "your words have been too much for me."[109]

Following the people's objection, the charge against them is explained further. The people have doubted the importance of serving God, expressing such sentiments as "it is vain to serve God" and "what benefit is there in keeping His charge and walking before him as mourners?" These sentiments underscore that the people have denied the necessity and importance of obeying the covenant. They see no reason to "serve" (*ʿbd*) Him, a term that according to Weinfeld originated in the diplomatic vocabulary of the ancient Near East.[110] The people also consider it "vain" to keep His charge. The phrase *šāmarnu mišmartô* finds a parallel in Gen. 26:4-5, where this same idiom is used to describe the faithfulness of Abraham,[111] and in Akkadian, *naṣāru maṣṣartu* describes faithfulness.[112]

The precise meaning of the final expression "that we walk as mourners" (*qĕdōrannît*) is unclear. While the adverbial form *qĕdōrannît* is a *hapax legomenon* in biblical Hebrew, related forms of *qdr* appear with the verb *hlk* in various laments. In Ps. 38:7, 42:10, 43:2 and in Job 30:28 (less clear), the afflicted supplement the list of their many complaints with the assertion that they "walk about as mourners." Perhaps the intent of this phrase in Mal. 3:14 is to question the efficacy of serving God and in requesting His aid. This indictment ends with the people's further decision to disregard God's standards and to deem "happy" (compare 2:15 with 2:12) the ones who scoff at God.

Historical account. 3:16-18. The nature and integrity of this passage often has been questioned. As noted earlier, Childs considers the passage

---

[109]   Ibid., 546.
[110]   Compare *arādu, ardūtu* in a political context, especially in the Amarna letters. Weinfeld, *Deuteronomy*, 83 and 332.
[111]   Weinfeld, *Deuteronomy*, 75-76.
[112]   Ibid., 335.

to be an editorial insertion. McKenzie and Wallace believe these verses to presuppose a different audience than does the preceding material.[113]

When the covenant character of these verses is considered, however, they are seen to be fully integrated into the book. This passage stands in direct response to the issues raised in 3:13-15, and it uses many of the themes and terms of the earlier passage.

As Waldman notes, the speech of the doubters in 3:14-15 is contrasted directly with the conversation of the righteous in 3:16; and while the words of the wicked are "too much" for the deity, He hears and rewards the words of the righteous.[114] Other ties to 3:14-15 appear as well. While in 3:14 the people deem it vain to serve (ʿbd) God, the LORD in 3:17 promises to reward those who serve (ʿbd) Him. In 3:18 He promises that when He acts all will be able to distinguish between the wicked and the righteous (in contrast to the people's words in 3:15) and between the one who serves and the one who does not serve (in contrast to 3:17).

The language of 3:16-18 is replete with covenant terminology. First, the assurance that God will remember the righteous is described as "a book of remembrance was written before Him." The term *sefer* is often used to describe the text of a treaty in ancient Near Eastern settings[115] as well as in Exod. 24:7 and Deut. 28:58. Second, the LORD will reward the righteous by making them his *sĕgullâ*. *Sĕgullâ*, "treasured possession," is widely used to describe the special status of a favored vassal;[116] by analogy to the sovereign/vassal relationship, it also describes the specialness of Israel to Yahweh (e.g., Exod. 19:5). According to Weinfeld, "it seems that (Ugaritic) *sglt* and (Hebrew) *sĕgullah* belong to the treaty and covenant terminology."[117]

Third, the LORD promises to treat the righteous "as a man pities a son who serves him." Not only is the father/son language of the treaty here reintroduced but also is the reminder that the proper son "serves" his father.

Ultimatum: Promise and Threat. 3:19-21. In this final ultimatum, the LORD reiterates His determination to punish the wicked and reward the righteous. This emphasis on the contrasting fortunes of the wicked and the righteous is not, as many contend, a later introduction of an inner-Israelite dichotomy or an establishment of sectarianism. Rather, this dif-

---

113 For discussion of these positions, see above, 56.
114 Waldman, 546.
115 Hillers, *Treaty Curses*, 45-47.
116 Muilenberg, "Form and Structure," 355.
117 Weinfield, *Deuteronomy*, 226, n. 2.

ferential treatment both serves as a proper conclusion to this unit and utilizes common lawsuit language.

The unit began with the people's denial of the value in serving God. They see no benefit in serving Him and deem the arrogant *(zēdîm)* "happy." In the day of God's action, however, He will make clear the difference between the righteous and the wicked and burn the arrogant *(zēdîm)* as chaff.

The distinction between the righteous and the wicked—far from introducing an alien concept into the book—is an integral part of the *rîb*. As noted by Gemser, "the announcement of different treatment of the obstinate offenders and the repentant" in Isa. 1:24-31 is part of the "protocol of the proceedings of a *rîb*."[118] Similarly, Psalm 50 (also a *rîb*) tells of the contrasting fates of the faithful ones and the wicked.

The punishment against the wicked is, as previously in Malachi, introduced by *hinnĕnî* plus the participle, and the punishment is described in terms strongly tied to covenant curses. The arrogant *(zēdîm)* and the evil-doers will be chaff (compare Obadiah 18) and they will be destroyed "root and branch."

The very imagery of the coming Day of the LORD also may relate to the theme of covenant lawsuit. As George Stuart well argues, "the Day of Yahweh as the prophets describe it may be taken as the military outworking of the covenant sanctions against Israel after Israel is found guilty in the course of the covenant lawsuit proclaimed by the prophets."[119] Fensham also suggests that the Day of the LORD may refer to a day of punishment for covenant violation.[120] Such an interpretation finds strong ancient Near Eastern support in texts such as the letter of the Hittite King Suppiluliuma to Niqmaddu II of Ugarit, in which the king announces the punishment of those "...who let go the covenant and peace agreement with Ḫatti and have become enemies of the great king."[121]

The fate of the righteous, on the other hand, is described in terms associated with blessings. The righteous sun will vindicate them. The righteous will be as well-fed calves, a common symbol of prosperity (see Jer. 46:21, Amos 6:4 and 1 Sam. 28:24), and they will tread down the wicked.

---

[118] B. Gemser, "The *Rîb*—or Controversy—Pattern in Hebrew Mentality," *VTS* 3 (1955): 130.

[119] George Stuart, "The Sovereign's Day of Conquest," *Bulletin of the American Schools of Oriental Research* 221 (1976): 160.

[120] Fensham, "Malediction," 9.

[121] Stuart, 162.

III. FINAL ADMONITION 3:22.

This verse, although usually considered to be a Deuteronomic addition to the Book of Malachi, in fact fits well into the form of the book. The Mosaic covenant, indeed, has formed the basis for the book's accusations: because the people have not kept its stipulations, they are punished. The verse functions as a final admonition and reminds the people to remain faithful to the stipulations transmitted through Moses.

IV. FINAL ULTIMATUM 3:23-24.

These verses may also be seen as a legitimate part of the book rather than a secondary addition. The language in these verses abounds with the themes of the book and the terminology of the lawsuit. After the promise of sending another messenger (once again introduced by *hinnê šōlēaḥ*), the LORD reveals that the goal of Elijah (the messenger *par excellence*) will be to reunite fathers and sons—language familiar to treaties. If this reconciliation is not made, the LORD will smite the land with curse: He will declare complete and total war against the guilty. A similar example in which an ultimatum ends the *rîb* is found in Psalm 50.

MALACHI AS *RÎB*

The above analysis has attempted to demonstrate that Malachi employs much of the terminology, theme and form of the covenant lawsuit. When interpreted within the lawsuit framework, much of the book's language and movement becomes intelligible. Malachi's employment of the *rîb* structure is not wooden nor does every element of the *rîb* appear in every unit, and yet the *rîb* structure and mentality prove integral to Malachi's message. Using this form, the prophet makes clear his conviction that Israel stands under punishment for covenant violation.

Significant, however, are the differences between the classical *rîb* and the form of Malachi. Although the pattern and theme of the covenant lawsuit have remained fairly constant from the time of its origin to its appearance in Malachi—as seen above—the author of Malachi has distinctively shaped this tradition.

As the work of Pfeiffer and others well underscores, the entire tone of the entire book is one of question and skepticism. Every assertion, every indictment that the Lord makes is questioned by the people; they even protest His profession of love. The mighty, all-powerful deity that overwhelmed covenant violators in the classical lawsuit is in Malachi constantly undermined by His subject's doubt. The guilty, previously silent, now are heard to object to every charge. Unlike the classical lawsuit, this form in Malachi invokes no divine witnesses and pays scant attention to the traditional Divine Council setting. It pits accused and accuser in direct debate.[122]

In this author's hand, moreover, the *rîb* becomes no longer the form for a short oracle of prophetic speech but rather the framework for a longer unit of discourse. The form is thoroughly and methodologically employed throughout, with the result that the *mal'āk* as covenant enforcer takes center stage and all of Israel's sins and failures are refracted through the light of the covenant.

Particularly enlightening in this regard are the transgressions against which the *rîb* is invoked. While classical prophets used the lawsuit form to attack economic, social and political injustice, this author employs the *rîb* form to lambast the failure to show the deity the respect of offering proper sacrifice. According to the author of Malachi, true religion is not only defending the fatherless, widow and orphan but also offering the Lord respectful service. The obligations of the covenant combine both "Mosaic" and "priestly" elements, such that the disregard for appropriate sacrifice is as indicative of moral decay as are adultery and sorcery.

THE SIGNIFICANCE OF THIS THESIS

This designation of the book's form as that of the *rîb* integrates rather than replaces the insights that other scholars have provided into the book's structure and message. It accounts for the covenant terminology and themes perceived by McKenzie and Wallace as well as for the courtroom tone noted by Achtemeier. It also explains why Verhoef can discern elements of ancient Near Eastern treaties in Malachi while still admitting that the book fails to follow the standard treaty-making pattern: since the covenant lawsuit mirrors the transacted covenant, the two forms share features such as the historical prologue and stipulations.

Pfeiffer's analysis of Malachi, which long has stood as the standard treatment of the book's form, is also compatible with this approach rather than at variance with it. The scheme of Statement, Objection and Explanation that Pfeiffer discussed is clearly discernible in each of the form-critical units, and Pfeiffer's delineation of the units is generally accepted. This presentation endeavors to demonstrate, however, that the scheme identified by Pfeiffer does not constitute the genre of the book

---

[122] I thank Eric M. Meyers for pointing out the absence of these traditional elements of the *rîb* in Malachi.

but rather functions as a rhetorical or stylistic device employed by the author. Malachi takes the form of the *rîb* but uses the *technique* of question and answer. While the book itself constitutes a *rîb*, the technique in which the people question every statement of God not only serves to elaborate the interrogation segment of the *rîb* but also to underscore through literary means the people's doubt. The people's sin lies not only in their trangressions of covenantal stipulations but also in their refusal to honor the deity and His reputation.

The interpretation of Malachi as utilizing the *rîb* form does not, as it may first appear, constitute a bold anachronism. Admittedly, studies of the *rîb* usually focus on the classical prophets, and since the lawsuit form finds so many parallels with Hittite and Assyrian examples, the time period for the appropriation of these ideas is seen to be that of the classical prophets and—a bit later—Deuteronomy.

While the *rîb* may have originated earlier, it nonetheless persists into the later periods. The lawsuit pattern can be discerned in exilic and post-exilic works such as Ezekiel, the Deuteronomistic History, the Priestly literature, and—as Harvey suggests—2 Chronicles.[123] Likely, it was through such biblical literature that the author of Malachi appropriated the *rîb* form. Although ancient Near Eastern treaty documents were probably unknown to this author, the language and mentality of the prophetic lawsuit were vital parts of Israel's cultural and Scriptural traditions. This author, well-versed in the themes and language of earlier biblical authors, found in the *rîb* form the appropriate vehicle for his message.

IMPLICATIONS FOR THE BOOK'S UNITY

As seen in the course of this analysis, such an understanding of the Book of Malachi as bearing an adapted *rîb* form suggests that many passages usually treated as secondary additions to the book may indeed be integral to it. Those passages already discussed are here summarized:

- Verse 1:11 need not be considered an anomalous universalist standpoint that praises the worship of the Gentiles but rather may underscore the universal reputation and greatness of the sovereign.
- Verse 2:12 utilizes language common to the indictment and may lambast the people for idolatry rather than for mixed marriages.
- Verse 3:22 constitutes a final admonition that comports well with the remainder of the book, and

---

[123] Harvey, 78-79.

- Verses 3:23-24 serve as a final ultimatum. Such a conclusion to a *rîb* finds a parallel in Psalm 50.

Other disputed passages, when seen in light of the lawsuit form, may also be understood as part of the book's original form. Verse 1:1, which introduces the book as a oracle to Israel through the agency of "my messenger," is usually considered as an addition based on 3:1. This identification of the prophet as *malʾāk*, however, properly introduces the agent of covenant prosecution. "My messenger," although not likely a personal name, is nonetheless the personification of the prophet in the central role of the *malʾāk* of the Lord.

Verse 3:1 also focuses centrally on the figure of the *malʾāk* as the agent of covenant prosecution. There is no reason to assume, as Malchow does, that the covenant here mentioned is exclusively the covenant of Levi mentioned in 2:4, that the messenger is a priestly figure and hence that the passage is a post-Daniel addition. Rather, the theme of covenant pervades Malachi and is inseparable from it. The fact that the verse begins with *hinnĕnî* plus the participle (Malachi's common method of introducing punishment) is further reason to understand 3:1 as original to the book.

This treatment of the Book of Malachi as a complete unity is indeed rare. The lawsuit form, however, helps to account for each of the disputed verses and if an editor has added material to the book, he or she has done so with full awareness of the *rîb* form.

THE *SITZ IM LEBEN* OF THE *RÎB*

No real consensus has arisen on the life setting of the *rîb* within Israel, either in the early or the later periods. Harvey argues strongly that in its original form, the covenant lawsuit grew out of international sacral law and found its setting within the justice exercised at the city gate. Other authors such as Huffmon and Wright offer suggestions about the origin of the idea of the lawsuit but never delineate clearly the actual life setting of the *rîb* within Israel.

As K. Nielsen argues, a distinction should be made between a *Gattung's* formal *Sitz im Leben* (that is, the arena in which such language is commonly used) and its actual *Sitz im Leben* (where it actually was employed).[124] While the formal *Sitz im Leben* of the *rîb* is that of treaty

---

[124] Kirsten Nielsen, *Yahweh as Prosecutor and Judge*, JSOTS 9 (Sheffield: Sheffield Academic Press, 1978), 4.

prosecution, the question arises concerning the actual *Sitz im Leben* of the form.

In the case of Malachi, the formal *Sitz im Leben* is that of the lawsuit. The prophet clearly utilizes the imagery as well as the characteristic form of the *rîb* as a literary device in his effort to underscore the people's sins concretely and boldly.

The actual *Sitz im Leben* of the book is less clear. Indeed, such a determination seems impossible. The *rîb* could be employed by a speaker in his oral discourse; it could be a literary device used by an author.[125] While the formal *Sitz im Leben* of Malachi is that of covenant lawsuit, then, the actual *Sitz* is simply that of the prophet's activity—whether that activity be literary or conducted in the streets of Jerusalem.[126]

SIGNIFICANCE OF FORM FOR PRIEST AND LEVITE IN MALACHI

The structure of Malachi suggests several points concerning the relationship between the *kōhēn*, *lēwî* and *bĕnê-lēwî* in the book. According to this analysis 2:1-9, considered as crucial in understanding the relationship between these terms, is not a self-contained unit but rather part of an accusation that extends from 1:6-2:9. In 1:6-14, the prophet outlines the priests' guilt and in 2:1-9 presents to them an ultimatum: it is for the sins of the *kōhănîm* in 1:6-14 that the *kōhănîm* are punished in 2:1-9.

The contrast between 2:5-7 (which describes the covenant faithfulness of Levi) and 2:1-4 and 8-9 (which addresses "you") does not serve to differentiate separate groups but instead contrasts the behavior of the present priests with the stipulations of the covenant. The covenant was granted to Levi for his faithfulness, and only if the priests are included in that covenant can they be held responsible for keeping its stipulations.

Within the lawsuit form, the *bēnê-lēwî* in 3:3 are understood to be a guilty party requiring purification and not a wronged party being vindicated. Similarly, in the *rîb* found in Isaiah 1, the Lord will refine the guilty in order to remove their dross and to restore them to their former purity.

---

[125] Chary suggests that Malachi is primarily a literary creation. *Aggée*, 226.
[126] According to Whybray, modern studies of oral literature suggest that there is no single *Sitz im Leben* for a *Gattung*. *The Making of the Pentateuch: A Methodological Study*, JSOTS 53 (Sheffield: Sheffield Academic Press, 1987), 165.

CONCLUSION

This chapter has attempted to demonstrate that the Book of Malachi employs the language and the structure of the covenant lawsuit. While using the rhetorical device of question and answer, the author draws heavily on the prophetic *rîb*. Such an interpretation of the book, as seen, both suggests that the book may be a unity and also militates against a sociological demarcation between *kōhēn* and *lēwî*.

In employing the lawsuit form, the author of the Book of Malachi demonstrates a thorough knowledge both of the biblical tradition and of covenant mentality. The next chapter, which considers the biblical sources used by the author, will attempt to discern whether this pervasive covenant ideology is due to Deuteronomic influence and whether the author demonstrates awareness of the Priestly Code.

CHAPTER IV

THE SOURCES USED BY THE BOOK OF MALACHI

INTRODUCTION TO THE PROBLEM

As suggested in Chapter 1, two distinct issues emerge in the debate concerning the relationship between the terms priest and Levite that is implied in the Book of Malachi: the contextual question of whether the terms function synonymously in the book, and the source-critical question of whether the book demonstrates knowledge of the Priestly Code. Chapter 2 addressed the first of these issues and suggested that the book itself draws no explicit demarcation between the kōhănîm and the běnê-lēwî. The present chapter considers the second matter, that is, the sources that inform the book.

The most common assessment of the Book of Malachi is that it is thoroughly Deuteronomic, drawing heavily on the language and ideology distinctive to Deuteronomy. Blenkinsopp, Dumbrell and others have forcefully argued such an interpretation, maintaining that Malachi not only draws on general Deuteronomic terms such as "love" and "abomination"[1] but also relies on specific Deuteronomic passages such as Deut. 33:8-11 and Deut. 24:1-4.[2] Many further argue that the book does not demonstrate knowledge of P.[3]

In contrast to such a thesis, other scholars have found evidence of the Priestly Code within the Book of Malachi. Wellhausen and J. M. P. Smith have pointed to minor commonalties between the two works,[4] but Kaufmann and Glazier-McDonald have gone much further to compile

---

[1] Blenkinsopp, *History*, 242.

[2] Dumbrell, 46-7.

[3] W. Stewart McCullough, *The History and Literature of the Palestinian Jews from Cyrus to Herod, 550 B.C. to 4 B.C.* (Buffalo, NY: University of Toronto Press, 1975), 47.

[4] Wellhausen, *Prolegomena*, 389; J. M. P. Smith, 8-9.

substantial lists of terms and practices in Malachi that they believe to indicate the influence of P.[5]

Because the sources with which Malachi is familiar are not immediately evident, the goal of the present chapter is to consider carefully the evidence given for Malachi's use of various sources. It will first consider the claims for Deuteronomic and Priestly influence in the book, questioning whether the book is pervasively Deuteronomic as is often alleged and whether the book demonstrates knowledge of the Priestly Code. After conclusions are drawn concerning the extent of D's and P's influence, attention will turn to other biblical sources reflected in Malachi's language and ideas.

DEUTERONOMY AND THE PRIESTLY CODE

Discussion of the evidence for tracing the influence of Deuteronomy and the Priestly Code within the Book of Malachi may be categorized as follows:

A. General language of the book;
B. Technical cultic language;
C. Description of cultic institutions;
D. Language for describing the priests;
E. Conclusions Regarding D and P.

General Language

DEUTERONOMY

According to most scholars, Malachi is a thoroughly Deuteronomic work, replete with the terms and language distinctive to Deuteronomy. From the work of Blenkinsopp, Dumbrell and others such as Coggins, J. M. P. Smith, Kaufmann, and R. Smith,[6] one can compile a long list of terms used by Malachi that are purported to be Deuteronomic:

1. Love (*ʾāhab*), 1:2;
2. Father/son (*ʾāb/bēn*), 1:6;
3. Fear (*mōrāʾ*),1:6;
4. One God (*ʾēl ʾehād*), 2:10;
5. Abomination (*tôʿēbâ*), 2:11;
6. Special possession (*sĕgullâ*), 2:17;

---

5 Kaufmann, 435; Glazier-McDonald, "Malachi," 113.

6 Blenkinsopp, *History*, 242; Dumbrell, 46; Coggins, 76; J. M. P. Smith, 9; Kaufmann, 435; R. Smith, 300-301.

7. "Sending" (*šallaḥ*) to describe divorce, 2:16;
8. All Israel (*kol-yiśrā'ēl*), 3:22;
9. Law of Moses (*tōrat mōšeh*), 3:22;
10. Horeb (*ḥōrēb*) 3:22.

Attention here turns to a consideration of the nature of these terms. Are these terms, indeed, evidence of Malachi's thorough dependence on the language of Deuteronomy?

While all of the terms are indeed common to the Book of Deuteronomy and often are considered Deuteronomic, careful attention to the biblical contexts in which these terms are used suggests that only a few are exclusively Deuteronomic. This observation holds especially true for the first six items in this list. As demonstrated in the previous chapter, terms such as "love," "father/son," "abomination" and "special possession" belong primarily to the language of covenant-making and accusation for covenant violation. Moreover, "abomination" (*tô'ēbâ*) describes covenant violation in pre-Deuteronomic and non-Deuteronomic contexts,[7] and it also appears in literature ascribed to P (Lev. 20:13; 18:22). The frequent reminder to preserve the reputation of the deity and the insistence upon exclusive worship of Him alone are common to treaty and covenant contexts.[8] The term *šĕgullâ* is integral to the Book of the Covenant (Exod. 19:5).

Each of these first six items do indeed share vocabulary and theme with the Book of Deuteronomy; none of them, however, is exclusively or even primarily Deuteronomic. Rather, these terms belong to the language of covenant—a language which Deuteronomy and Malachi both employ.

An assessment of the seventh item, the use of *šallaḥ*, is less conclusive. The Book of Deuteronomy does describe divorce as *šallaḥ*, in contrast to P which describes a divorced woman as *gĕrûšâ* (for example, Lev. 21:14). If indeed Malachi 2:16 does involve divorce, then the commonality between Malachi and Deuteronomy is supported. As outlined in chapter 3, however, 2:10-16 may not concern divorce but rather may be a polemic against idolatry. A. S. van der Woude supports such an interpretation of Malachi 2:10-16 and contends that

šallaḥ does not mean "send away," "repudiate" or "divorce;" It is much more probable that the verbal form is an abbreviation of the idiomatic ex-

---

7 See above, 67.
8 See above, 65-66.

pression *šallaḥ yad* (the same abbreviation can be found in 2 Sam. 6:6 and Obadiah 13) that designates a morally detestable hostile act.[9]

The final three items, "Horeb, "the law of Moses," and "all Israel," are distinctively Deuteronomic terms. As noted above, Malachi 3:22-23 (in which these words appear) are usually considered to constitute a Deuteronomic editorial addition to the book. Our own discussion in chapter 3 suggested, however, that these verses are integral to the book and indeed may be original. Whatever their origin, these verses do conclude the book with the tone and language of Deuteronomy and suggest that their author intended the Book of Malachi to be viewed as consonant with the Deuteronomic tradition.

THE PRIESTLY CODE

While the large majority of scholars traces the Deuteronomic characteristics of Malachi and maintains that the book demonstrates no affinities with the Priestly Code, a few scholars such as Kaufmann, Wellhausen and Glazier-McDonald suggest that Malachi does utilize some general terms distinctive to P. These terms are as follows:

1. Pleasure (*rāṣôn*) to describe acceptable sacrifice, 2:13;
2. Create (*bārāʾ*), 2:10;
3. Windows of heaven (*ʾărubbôt haššāmayim*), 3:10;
4. Profane the name of God (*ḥll ʾet šēm*), 1:12.

An analysis of these terms immediately indicates that the first and last do not find appropriate parallels in Malachi and the Priestly Code. While Kaufmann suggests that the use of *rāṣôn* is shared by the two, in fact the phrase "to take pleasure"(*laqaḥ rāṣôn*) is unique to Malachi. The Priestly literature, on the contrary, employs the idiom "as a pleasurable thing"(*lĕrāṣôn*). Though common to P, *lĕrāṣôn* appears elsewhere in Isa. 56:7, Jer. 6:20 and Ps. 19:15; the noun occurs alone in various other contexts, including Deuteronomy (33:16, 23), First Isaiah, Jeremiah, Esther and Daniel. The last phrase—"profaning the name of God"(*ḥll ʾet-šēm*)— seen by Glazier-McDonald as a connection between Malachi and P—does not directly appear in Malachi in this form, but is implied in 1:12.

The terms "create"and "windows of heaven"do indeed appear predominately in literature assigned to the Priestly source, but they are not unique to P. Although *bārāʾ* is common to P, it is found also in Second Isaiah (see also Ecc. 12:1). Not only is the phrase "the windows of heaven" used by the P writers in Gen. 7:11 and 8:2 but also is employed

9 van der Woude, 71.

in Isa. 24:18 and 2 Kgs. 7:2 and 19. Such a distribution of the term may suggest that it is late rather than connected exclusively with the Priestly Code.

A quite different discussion of Malachi's knowledge of the Priestly Code proceeds from Michael Fishbane's thesis that Malachi 1:6-2:9 plays upon the key terms of the Priestly Blessing in Numbers 6:23-27. According to Fishbane, Malachi lambasts the unrighteous priesthood of his own day by inverting the originally-positive language of the Priestly Blessing.[10] While in Numbers 6:24-26 the divine countenance serves a favorable function ("may the Lord lift up his face upon you"), in Malachi "lift up the face"is used in the context of condemnation (1:8, 1:9, 2:9). This turning of the Priestly Blessing against the priest is particularly evident in Malachi 2:2, in which God vows to curse the priest's blessings and bless his curses. Fishbane explains that:

> The prophet has taken the contents of the Priestly Blessing—delivered by the priests and with its emphasis on blessing, the sanctity of the divine Name, and such benefactions as protection, favorable countenance, and peace—and *inverted* them. In this way the priests' cultic language is de-sacralized and their actions cursed. By unfolding the negative semantic range of most of the key terms used positively in the Priestly Blessing, the rotten core and consequences of the language and behavior of the priest are echoed throughout the diatribe.[11]

At first glance, such a thorough knowledge of and interaction with the Priestly Blessing would prove unambiguously that Malachi is familiar with the Priestly Code. This inference may, however, be questioned. While incorporated into the Priestly Source, the Priestly Blessing may represent a far more ancient tradition. It is treated as pre-exilic by Sellin-Fohrer,[12] and according to Noth, "It may well belong to the traditions handed down from the earlier period and its simplicity of expression would even argue for great antiquity. It is, of course, impossible even approximately to date its emergence."[13]

Archaeological evidence likewise suggests that the Priestly Blessing may be ancient. Two silver amulets unearthed during excavations at Ketef Hinnom bear texts strikingly similar to the benediction of Num.

---

[10] Michael Fishbane, *Biblical Interpretation in Ancient Israel* (Oxford: Clarendon Press, 1985), 332-334.

[11] Fishbane, 332-334.

[12] Sellin-Fohrer, 181-182.

[13] Martin Noth, *Numbers*, Old Testament Library (Philadelphia: Westminster Press, 1968), 58.

6:24-26. This evidence may suggest "...that a form of the priestly blessing circulated as a popular blessing that possibly influenced the later 'P' strand of Scripture."[14]

Given such information, Fishbane's suggestion that Malachi 1:6-2:9 represents an "aggadic"exegesis of Num. 6 cannot prove conclusively that Malachi was aware of the Priestly source. The author's artful use of this text does however suggest that by the time of the book's composition the blessing had reached an advanced and fixed form.

Technical Cultic Language

One of the major distinguishing factors between Deuteronomy and the Priestly Code is usually perceived to be their differing portrayals of the cult. While attention later will turn to the operation of cultic institutions in Malachi, the technical language describing the cultus will here be considered.

Although the separation of general and technical language is useful in categorization, several problems arise in isolating and in comparing technical terms. Most problematically, words often have both a general and a technical meaning, depending upon their usage. Levine explains this phenomenon as arising from the fact that the cult derives its language from other spheres of life.[15] For this reason, determining whether a word is intended in its general or technical sense is often difficult.

Another problem arises from the fact that the D and P sources are non-analogous corpora. A determination of whether Malachi reflects Deuteronomy's or the Priestly Code's understanding of the cult requires the assumption that both D and P use language precisely and therefore can be contrasted, and yet such may not be the case, since Deuteronomy provides little technical detail regarding the cult. In the words of de Vaux,

> Deuteronomy cannot be used to reconstitute the ritual followed in the Temple during the years after Josiah's reform, because Deuteronomy contains no code of law about sacrifices..... Deuteronomy never mentions offerings, perfumes, incense or the shewbread either, and these things were cer-

---

14 Eric M. Meyers, sidebar for "Gehenna: The Topography of Hell," by Lloyd R. Bailey, *BA* 49 (1986): 190 .

15 Baruch Levine, *In the Presence of the Lord: A Study of Cult and Some Cultic Terms in Ancient Israel*, Studies in Judaism in Late Antiquity, no. 5, ed. Jacob Neusner (Leiden: E. J. Brill, 1974), 17.

tainly used in the pre-exilic liturgy. The picture given in Deuteronomy, therefore, is not complete.[16]

With these considerations in mind, the following discussion will attempt to establish whether cultic language is being used in a precise technical sense or in a more general manner. Where doubt remains, both senses of a given term will be considered as will the implications of each.

COVENANT TRANSGRESSORS

In Mal. 3:5, punishment is invoked against a list of transgressors:

1. Sorcerers (*měkaššěpîm*);
2. Adulterers (*měnāʾăpîm*);
3. Those who swear deceitfully (*nišbāʿîm laššāqer*);
4. Those who oppress the wages of a worker (*ʿōšqê šěkar-śākîr*);
5. Those who oppress the widow and orphan and thrust aside the sojourner (*ʾalmānâ wěyātôm ûmaṭṭê-gēr*).

Such a list implies a prior injunction against these forms of behavior, and the location of such an injunction may indicate the sources upon which Malachi draws. Kaufmann maintains that this list in Mal. 3:5 presupposes the legislation contained in Lev. 19:12-14.[17] Further investigation, however, suggests that in the cataloging of covenant violators the author of the Book of Malachi draws from various sources.

The Priestly Code is indeed represented in this list, although the specific identification of Lev. 19 is of limited applicability. This chapter of Leviticus is generally understood to belong to the Holiness Code, a collection that likely antedates the surrounding P material. Similarities between Malachi and the Priestly Code are nonetheless found in other passages. As in Mal. 3:5, adultery is described as *nʾp* in Lev. 20:10 and "swearing deceitfully" is prohibited in Lev. 5:22 and 24. Lev. 25:50 regulates the payment of wages, although it does not use Malachi's phrase "oppress the wages of a hireling." Similarly, Exod. 7:11 (usually ascribed to P) describes Egyptian "sorcerers" while not expressly addressing sorcery in Israel.

While Malachi's list of covenant transgressors does exhibit similarities with the Holiness Code and with P, it also strongly reflects Deuteronomic guidelines. Indeed, every item in this catalog except "swearing deceitfully" appears in Deuteronomy. Sorcerers are prohibited in Deut. 18:10 and adulterers in Deut. 5:18. In language very close to Mal. 3:5,

---

16 de Vaux, *Ancient Israel*, 425.
17 Kaufmann, 435.

Deut. 24:14 expressly states, "You shall not oppress a hired servant," and the following verses seek to protect the widow, orphan and sojourner (24:17, 19-21). Even closer to Malachi's reference to these three needy classes is Deut. 27:19: "cursed be the one who *thrusts aside* the *sojourner*, the *widow*, and the *orphan*."
Other sources may lie behind this list as well. Both the Covenant Code and the Book of Jeremiah outlaw sorcerers (Exod. 22 :17, Jer. 27: 9) and adulterers (Exod. 20:14; Jer.7:9). Both advocate proper treatment of the widow, orphan and sojourner (Exod. 22:20-21; Jer. 7:6), as do various passages throughout the Hebrew Bible (Isa. 1:17, Zech. 7:10; Ps. 94:6; Job 24:3).
This discussion, which is summarized in table 1, suggests that Malachi's list of covenant violators does not derive from a single source. This passage exhibits close similarities with Lev. 19:12-13, Deut. 24:14 and Deut. 27:19, but it also draws upon various Deuteronomic passages as well as upon language employed in the Book of the Covenant. While Kaufmann properly notes affinities between Mal. 3:5 and Lev. 19, his suggestion that these affinities indicate Malachi's reliance upon P ignores the strong influence of other sources upon this passage.

ANIMALS UNFIT FOR SACRIFICE

A second category of technical cultic terms is the description of the defects that render an animal unfit for sacrifice. In Malachi, such animals are described as

1. Blind (*ʿiwwēr*), 1:8;
2. Lame (*pissēaḥ*), 1:13;
3. Sick (*ḥōleh*), 1:8, 1:13;
4. Seized (*gāzûl*), 1:13;
5. Spoiled (*māšḥāt*), 1:14.

TABLE 1.
TERMS IN MAL. 3:5 COMPARED WITH OTHER SOURCES

	D	P	Bk of Cov	Other
kšp	Deut. 18:10	Exod. 7:11	Exod. 22:17	Jer.27:9
nʾp	Deut. 5:18	Lev. 20:10	Exod. 20:14	Jer. 7:9
nšbʿ		Lev. 5:22, 24		Jer. 5:2, 7:9
lšqr				Lev. 19:12 (H)
ʿšq škr	Deut. 15:18	Lev. 25:50		Exod. 12:45
škyr	24:14			Lev. 19:13 (H)
				22:10 (H)

ʾlmnh,	Deut. 27:19	Exod. 22:20-21	Jer. 7:6
ytwm, gr	24:17,		Zec. 7:10
	24:19-21		Isa. 1:17
			Ps. 94:6
			Job 24:3

While the terms "blind" and "lame" appear in both D and P in the context of sacrifice, these adjectives refer to the sacrificial animal only in Deuteronomy. Deuteronomy 15:21 prohibits the sacrifice of an animal that is *pissēaḥ* or *ʿiwwēr*, but these words in Lev. 21:18 describe human flaws that prevent priests from offering sacrifice. Other passages in P and D more generally warn against the sacrifice of a blemished animal (for example, Num. 6:14, 19:2; Deut. 17:1). Lev. 22:22, for example, specifies that the sacrificial animal may contain no blemish and includes the stipulation that it not be *ʿiwwēr*.

In the Hebrew Bible, only Malachi 1:8 and 1:13 mandate that the sacrificial animal not be *ḥōleh* (sick), although the health of the offering is likely implicitly required by other passages. Similarly, while the use of *gzl* to describe a category of imperfect sacrificial animals is unique to Malachi, a similar idea may underlie Lev. 7:24, 17:15 and 22:18-19.[18] The description of the sacrificial animal as "spoiled" (*māšḥāt*) appears elsewhere only in Lev. 22:25, a passage attributed to the Holiness Code.

In conclusion, the language used by Malachi to describe animals unfit for sacrifice derives primarily from Deuteronomy and from the Holiness Code. The Priestly Code does stand in firm agreement that the sacrificial animal be without defect but it does not use precisely the same vocabulary for these defects as does Malachi. Moreover, the author of Malachi is innovative in introducing a new term to describe impure sacrifice (*ḥōleh*).

OTHER OFFERINGS

The Book of Malachi also uses several other technical terms in describing sacrificial offerings. These include

1. Defiled bread (*leḥem mĕgōʾāl*), 1:7;
2. Table of the Lord (*šulḥan ʾădônay*), 1:7;
3. Dung (*pereš*), 2:3.

Each of these phrases reflects language characteristic of the Priestly Code and of the Book of Ezekiel. The use of *leḥem* to describe offerings is

---

18 Glazier-McDonald, "Malachi," 97.

confined to these two sources (for example, Lev. 3:11, 16; 21:6-22; Ezek. 16:19).[19] The adjective *mg'l* to describe impure sacrifice, however, is limited to Malachi.[20] The description of the altar as the "table of the Lord" appears almost exclusively in P and in Ezekiel (for example, Ezek. 41:22, Lev. 24:6),[21] and the mention of the dung of the animal as unclean occurs elsewhere only in P (for example, Exod. 29:14; Lev. 4:11, 8:17; Num. 19:5).

For the terminology of these other offerings, then, the Book of Malachi utilizes language that is characteristic of P and Ezekiel. The author also utilizes a new term for impure sacrifice (*mg'l*).

PRIESTLY ACTIVITIES

Malachi employs several phrases to describe what may constitute specifically cultic activities:

1. Offer *minḥâ* (*maggîš minḥâ*), 1:11, 2:12, 3:3 (the *hip'il* of *ngš* is used with other nouns in 1:7, 8, 11);
2. Present *minḥâ* (*hābē'tem 'et-hamminḥâ*), 1:13 (the *hip'il* of *bw'* is also used for the bringing of animal sacrifices in 1:13);
3. Keep charge (*šamarnû mišmartô*), 3:14;
4. Purify (*ṭihar*), 3:3;
5. Accept *minḥâ* (*minḥâ lō'-'erṣeh*), 1:10.

Both "offering *minḥâ*" and "presenting *minḥâ*" may have either a general or a technical meaning. In the Priestly Code, the *hip'il* of *ngš* and *bw'* are used in a technical manner. As seen in Lev. chapters 2, 3, and 23, the individual presents the offering (*hip'il* of *bw'*) and the priest offers it (*hip'il* of *ngš*). Other passages in Hebrew Scripture do not use terms so precisely. In Amos 5:25, for example, the people (not the priests) "offer *minḥâ*" (root: *ngš*). Noteworthy is the fact that Malachi does not seem to adhere to P's precise use of the *hip'il* of *ngš* and *bw'* but instead describes the priests' acts with both of these verbs (for example, 3:3 and 1:13). Also, in 1:11 the author lauds the fact that foreign nations "offer *minḥâ*" (*ngš*).

Not only do these verbs for offering *minḥâ* (*ngš* and *bw'*) bear both technical and general meanings, but also the noun *minḥâ* is used throughout the biblical text in various ways. As noted by Levine, *minḥâ* can denote a "gift," a "general offering," or, more specifically, a "grain offering."[22] While the first two of these meanings of *minḥâ* appear in vari-

---

19 Glazier-McDonald, "Malachi," 113.

20 Chary (*Aggée*, 239) notes that *mg'l* appears in other contexts and is almost exclusively post-exilic.

21 BDB, 1020.

22 Levine, 16-17.

ous contexts, *minḥâ* always denotes a grain offering in the Priestly literature.[23] Determining whether *minḥâ* is intended in its technical or general
sense in Malachi is difficult, because the book mentions *minḥâ* along with
other offerings (1:11, 13). *Minḥâ* does appear to be a separate category
from animal sacrifice in 1:13; however, in 1:12, "the one who offers
minḥâ" seems to refer to a general description of a priest, as does the
similar phrase in 3:3.

The term *šamarnû mišmartô*, item 3, also has several different meanings.[24] In the Priestly literature, this term is used technically to describe
the function of the Levites (for example, Num. 1:53), who, unlike the
priests, guard the Temple. Other sources, on the contrary, use this phrase
more generally to describe fidelity (see Lev. 18:30 [H]; Gen. 26:5; 1 Kgs.
2:3; Jos. 22:3).

As noted above, Mal. 3:14 appears to utilize the general meaning of
šamarnû mišmartô.[25] The people find it vain to serve God and keep His
charge. This phrase does not describe the responsibilities of the Levite—
as in Priestly literature—but rather it designates the proper attitude of
the faithful.

In connection with the fourth item, Mal. 3:3 has been purported to
bear connections to the Priestly Code. According to Glazier-McDonald,
"...the parallels between Malachi 3:3-4 and Num. 8:5-22 are too significant to be ignored. In both cases, purification is the means by which the
Levites are separated out and dedicated to the proper performance of
their work."[26]

Linguistically, some connection may link Mal. 3:3 and the Priestly
Code. The *piᶜel* of the verb *ṭhr* is used only in later sources such as
Jeremiah (33:8), Ezekiel (36:33) and especially the Priestly Code. Such a
connection may suggest that Malachi, like P and Ezekiel, employs *ṭhr* in
a technical sense. The specific ideological connections between Mal. 3:3-4
and Num. 8:5-22 that are drawn by Glazier-McDonald, however, are less
instructive. Malachi remarks that once the sons of Levi are purified they
will "offer *minḥâ*" (*ngš*). Such a statement boldly contradicts the position
taken in Numbers and elsewhere in the Priestly Code: in P, the *bĕnê-lēwî*

---

23 BDB, 585.
24 According to Milgrom in *Levitical Terminology*, 12, n. 44, the term developed
semantically over time. While in the early period *šamar mišmeret* referred to physical
guarding or custody (for example, 1 Sam. 22:23, 2 Sam. 20:3), in Deuteronomic and
later literature it signifies duty or service. In the Priestly Code it describes the
function of the Levite (9).
25 See above, 76-77.
26 Glazier-McDonald, "Malachi," 233.

are Temple servants and guardians who are forbidden to *ngš minḥâ* as do the sons of Aaron. If, indeed, Mal. 3:3-4 alludes to Num. 8:5-22, it does so in defiance of the latter's priestly program.

The final item describing cultic activities is found in 1:10, in which Yahweh asserts that He will not accept *minḥâ* from the sinful priests (*minḥâ lōʾ-ʾerṣeh*). This term for not accepting an offering appears to belong to no specific cultic vocabulary. It does not appear in P in reference to the deity's reception of sacrifice but does occur in this context in various biblical passages such as Ps. 51:18, 119:108, Amos 5:22 and Ezek. 20:40.

Regarding its use of terminology to describe cultic activity, then, the Book of Malachi appears to reflect little of P's technical vocabulary. While in P the laity's offering of *minḥâ* is described as "present"(*bwʾ*) and the priests' activity is referred to as "offer"(*ngš*), in Malachi both of these terms appear to apply to priestly activity. In P *šamarnû mišmartô* describes the exclusive function of the Levite, but in Malachi this phrase describes the fidelity of individuals. Malachi does appear to use *ṭhr* in a technical sense as does P and Ezekiel, although Mal. 3:3-4 and Num. 8:5-22 differ ideologically on the proper function of the *bēnê-lēwî*.

Cultic Institutions

The history of Israel's cultic institutions is perhaps the most common battleground of the struggle to prove the sources that were available to the author of Malachi. Indeed, Wellhausen's major contribution to the source-critical enterprise was to undergird earlier suggestions of literary development within the Pentateuch with a parallel scheme of institutional development. While many of the literary bases for isolating sources have been denigrated by biblical scholars in recent years,[27] Wellhausen's analysis of Israel's institutions has remained a sturdy pillar supporting the Documentary Hypothesis.[28]

TITHE

One of the practices through which Wellhausen traced development within Israel's institutions is the giving of the tithe. According to his reconstruction, in Deuteronomy the tithe represents a voluntary offering that was consumed by the family of the individual offerant at a central location. The Priestly Code drastically altered the practice and the ra-

---

[27] E. g., U. Cassuto, *The Documentary Hypothesis*, trans. Israel Abrahams (Jerusalem: Magnes Press, 1983).

[28] Haran, *Temples*, 1.

tionale of tithing, transforming the tithe into compulsory dues given the priests.[29]

Most scholars continue to distinguish between the Deuteronomic and the Priestly tithes.[30] Many argue further that Deuteronomy itself refers to two separate tithes—an annual gift shared by the offerants and a triennial tithe stored locally and designated for the sustenance of the widow, orphan and Levite.[31] Aside from the discussion of dual tithes in Deuteronomy, major agreement prevails that in Deuteronomy the tithes serve to acknowledge God's ownership of the land and are eaten by the offerant or by recipients of charity,[32] while in P the tithes are exclusively designated for the priesthood.[33]

Malachi 3:8-10 briefly concerns the giving of tithes. In response to accusation, the people ask the LORD, "How are we robbing you?" The LORD responds, "In your tithes and offerings....Bring the full tithes into the storehouse that there may be food in my house." Based on this reference, scholars attempting to assess Malachi's knowledge of sources have endeavored to determine whether this portrayal of the tithe more closely reflects the ideology of D or that of P. Blenkinsopp stands virtually alone in maintaining that Malachi's description of the tithe draws upon Deut. 18:1-8;[34] his position is difficult to critique because he offers no explanation for his viewpoint.

J. M. P. Smith is more representative of scholarship in stating that neither Deuteronomy's requirements for the annual tithe eaten by the people nor for those of the triennial tithe eaten by the needy are met by Mal. 3:8-10:

> Neither of these requirements accords fully with the prophet's charge and demand, since the former contemplates no such storage of the tithe as implied in v. 10; and the latter calls for the storage of the tithe in the various

---

29 Wellhausen, *Prolegomena*, 153ff.

30 A minority, however, view these tithes as nearly identical. McConville (*Deuteronomy*, 86) suggests that the D and P tithes are the same, and de Vaux reasons that at least part of the Deuteronomic tithe would have been consumed by the priests (*Ancient Israel*, 381).

31 For example, J. M. P. Smith, 70-71; Kaufmann, 388.

32 E.g., R. S. Sarason, *A History of the Mishnaic Law of Agriculture*, Section Three: *A Study of Tractate Demai*, Studies in Judaism in Late Antiquity, no. 27 (Leiden: E. J. Brill, 1979), 4; H. Jagersma, "The Tithes in the Old Testament," in *Remembering all the Way...*, ed. B. Albrektson and others, Oudtestamentische Studiën, no. 21 (Leiden: E. J. Brill, 1981), 116-128.

33 E.g., H. H. Guthrie, Jr., "Tithe," in *Interpreter's Dictionary of the Bible*, ed. George Buttrick and others (Nashville: Abingdon, 1962), Vol. R-Z, 654-655.

cities, while v. 10 again evidently conceives of it as stored in Jerusalem only.[35]

Hence, contrary to Blenkinsopp's claims, Malachi's tithe does not seem to reflect the tithing legislation of Deuteronomy.

Most scholars maintain that Malachi's reference to the tithe most clearly refers to the Levitical tithe of Lev. 27:30 and Num. 18:21-31. Like the tithe of the Priestly Code, the tithe of Malachi is considered obligatory and is stored for consumption in the Temple—as seen especially in 3:10 where the tithe is deemed the "food"(*ṭerep*) for the house of the Lord. On the basis of the connection between Malachi's understanding of the tithe and the Priestly directives, Weaver, J. M. P. Smith, Wellhausen, Achtemeier and Neil agree that Malachi demonstrates a reliance on the Priestly tithing legislation, although they doubt that Malachi is aware of the entire Priestly Code.[36]

Y. Kaufmann presents a quite different view of Israel's tithing regulations.[37] Tracing a different order of Pentateuchal sources, he maintains that the tithe in the Priestly Code is described much as it is in JE—that is, as a voluntary, free-will offering collected directly by the Levites.[38] With the enactment of the Deuteronomic reforms the tithe became an annual obligation,[39] and—according to Kaufmann—fell into disuse over time. When the generation of Ezra and Zerubbabel returned to the land they knew nothing of the tithe; "...certainly, the Levites (also the singers and the gatekeepers) did not receive a tithe in the early post-exilic period."[40]

Kaufmann identifies the reinstitution of the tithe with the pact enacted by the Great Assembly under Nehemiah (Neh. 12:44; 13:5, 12-13). After a public reading of the Torah (which contained both P and D), the community sought to align its own practices in accordance with biblical law. The resulting guidelines for the tithe arose from a exegetical harmonization of the divergent tithe laws of D and P. As in P, the tithes would be given to the Levites (a class quite different than that intended by P), and, as in D, the tithes would be an annual obligation.[41] The

---

34 Blenkinsopp, *History*, 242.
35 J. M. P. Smith, 71.
36 Weaver, 174-175; J. M. P. Smith, 9; Wellhausen, *Kleinen Propheten*, 209-210; Achtemeier, 138; Neil, 229.
37 A similar view is taken by M. Haran, *Temples*, 109.
38 Kaufmann, 644.
39 Ibid., 388.
40 Ibid., 387.
41 Ibid., 388.

unique stamp given to the tithe by the Great Assembly was the provision that the tithes be stored in the storehouse (Neh. 12:44; 13:5-13).

Based on this reconstruction, Kaufmann argues that the tithe mentioned by Mal. 3:5 represents a post-exilic institution that postdates the reforms of Nehemiah.[42] Contrary to the dictates of the Priestly Code, tithes are stored in the treasury rather than being collected directly by the priests.[43]

As evident from the discussion outlined above, Kaufmann's views on tithing strongly differ from those of other scholars—a difference that largely can be attributed to his quite different understanding of earlier materials and especially of P. Because Kaufmann finds no evidence of centralization of the cult in P, he denies that a Priestly scheme would permit the collection of tithes in a storehouse; because he believes P's tithe to be voluntary and D's to be obligatory, he discerns the influence of Deuteronomic ideology in Malachi's tithe. His analysis of the tithe of Malachi also is based upon his understanding of the actions of the Great Assembly. He does not, however, explain why—if both Nehemiah and Malachi mention the collection of tithes into the storehouse—Malachi must necessarily be later than Nehemiah.

While Kaufmann's portrayal of Israelite history cannot be fully considered here, significant is the fact that Kaufmann stands in basic agreement with other scholars on several key issues involving the tithe:

- With regard to the Pentateuchal sources, all agree that P designates tithes to be given to the Levitical priesthood/Levites.
- With regard to Malachi's tithe, both Kaufmann and others agree that Malachi's tithes are considered obligatory and are designated for the priesthood.
- Importantly, all agree that Malachi's tithe definitely bears the stamp of the tithe of the Priestly Code.

For the purposes of this discussion, this last point is most instructive. Although many (such as Wellhausen, J. M. P. Smith) would deny that Malachi reflects knowledge of the full Priestly document, all but Blenkinsopp concede that in its description of the tithe Malachi presumes the authority of the legislation contained in the Priestly Code.

TĔRÛMÂ

Much like the case of *minḥâ*, the term *tĕrûmâ* bears a wide range of meanings. It may designate general contributions to the sanctuary, dif-

---

42 Ibid., 436.
43 Ibid., 644.

ferent contributions given to the priests and Levites, or the priests' share of the tithe given to the Levites.

Unfortunately for an analysis of cultic institutions, these various meanings of *tĕrûmâ* are scattered throughout the Hebrew Bible, such that no one meaning is limited to a specific source. As Milgrom demonstrates, the Priestly source uses *tĕrûmâ* to describe all gifts to the sanctuary, including first-fruits, the first-born of animals, the tithe of produce and sacred gifts in general.[44] As but one example, in Num. 18:8, 11 and 19, *tĕrûmâ* refers to the priests' portion of the tithe while in Num. 15:19-21 the same word describes general contributions.

In Mal. 3:8 the *tĕrûmâ* and the tithe are mentioned together as gifts to be brought to the sanctuary. Deut. 12:6 and 11 also link these gifts and, according to J. M. P. Smith, this commonality demonstrates that Malachi's description of sanctuary offerings more closely parallels D legislation than P legislation.[45]

While one must acknowledge that Malachi and Deuteronomy share a joint mention of these terms, the fact that P uses *tĕrûmâ* in a variety of ways renders impossible a determination of whether Malachi's reference to *tĕrûmâ* more closely fits one or another source. Since almost all usages of *tĕrûmâ* in the Hebrew Bible refer to some type of sacred offering and since P uses the term in both a general and a more specific manner, Malachi's brief reference to the *tĕrûmâ* as a gift brought to the sanctuary cannot be linked to a specific source.[46]

MALE ANIMAL

The prophetic protest in Mal. 1:14 against one who reneges his vow to sacrifice a male animal has been seen by some as a further indication of the book's connection to a given source. For example, Glazier-McDonald suggests that Malachi follows Priestly stipulations in describing the sacrificial animal as *zākār*—"male."[47] To the contrary, J. M. P. Smith

---

44 Milgrom, *Cultic Theology*, 159.

45 J. M. P. Smith, 9.

46 Milgrom maintains that while in P *tĕrûmâ* includes all sacred gifts, the term in Chronicles and post-exilic literature refers to gifts to the priests from the harvest alone (2 Chron. 31:5, 12; compare 1 Kgs. 3:8; also Neh. 10:38, 40; 13:15) (*Cultic Theology*, 162). Milgrom does not specifically mention Mal. 3:8 and 10 in this regard, but the *tĕrûmâ* of Mal. 3:8 may indeed refer to an agricultural gift--if, like the tithe of 3:10, it is gathered in the storehouse. For the purposes of this discussion, however, Milgrom's schema offers little help: *tĕrûmâ* may refer to agricultural gifts in D and P as well as in the post-exilic era.

47 Glazier-McDonald, "Malachi," 113.

contends that since the Priestly Code permits the sacrifice of both the male and female animal and since Malachi permits only the male, then Malachi may differ from P.[48]

These conjectures fail to discern that the issue involved in Mal. 1:14 is not sacrifice in general but rather sacrifice as payment of a vow. Numerous passages throughout the Hebrew Bible insist that what has been vowed must be done,[49] and the Malachi passage seems more concerned with a broken vow than with the gender of the sacrificial animal. If the gender of the animal is considered, however, Malachi does seem closer to P than to D. Although Glazier-McDonald is incorrect in stating that in P the sacrificial animal is always male (the female is permitted in Lev. 5:6), Lev. 22:18-19 indeed does stipulate that the animal sacrificed as a votive offering must be male. The difference between the Priestly and Deuteronomic regulations on this matter nonetheless is unclear, since Deuteronomy does not outline requirement for votive sacrifices. Malachi does agree with P in referring to a male votive offering, but such a stipulation may be assumed in D as well.

Language for Describing Priests

BĔNÊ-LEWÎ

As generally understood, the various Pentateuchal strata utilize distinctive designations for the priesthood. Deuteronomy and much of the Deuteronomic literature refer to the priests as *hakkōhănîm hallēwiyyîm* ("the Levitical priests") and as *hakkōhănîm bĕnê-lēwî* ("the priests, the sons of Levi"). Although the precise intent of these terms is debated (as will be discussed below), the terms themselves are distinctively Deuteronomic.

Unlike Deuteronomy, the Priestly Code refers to the priests as *bĕnê-ʾahărōn*—"the sons of Aaron"—and clearly mandates that altar clergy must be descendents of Aaron. *Bĕnê-lēwî* in the Priestly Code are unambiguously marked as a different group from the *kōhănîm*. Even though Moses and Aaron are included in the genealogy of Levi in Num. 26:56-59, the Priestly tale of the sons of Korah demonstrates the severity of punishment incurred by Levites who seek priestly privileges. Indeed, so markedly distinct are the priest and the Levite in the Priestly Code that

---

[48] J. M. P. Smith, 8.

[49] For a consideration of the importance and the genre of vow-fulfillment, see the author's article, "Because God Heard My Voice: The Individual Thanksgiving Psalm and Vow-Fulfillment," in *The Listening Heart: Essays in Wisdom and the Psalms in Honor of Roland E. Murphy, O. Carm,* ed. Kenneth G. Hoglund and others, *JSOTS* 58 (Sheffield: JSOT Press, 1987), 289-298.

Milgrom considers the separation of the two to be a major characteristic of P.[50]

Malachi's designations for the priests thus fit the usage of neither the Deuteronomic or Priestly Codes. The book makes no mention of Aaron nor the priestly prerogatives of his descendents, and yet likewise absent from the book are the Deuteronomic titles "Levitical priests"(*hakkōhănîm hallĕwiyyîm*) and "the priests, the sons of Levi"(*hakkōhănîm bĕnê-lēwî*).

While the book does not employ the distinctive language of either source, arguments nonetheless have been advanced identifying specific sources upon which Malachi's terminology for priests is based. By far the most common argument in this regard may be summarized as follows: because Malachi refers to priests as sons of Levi and as participants in a covenant of/with Levi and because it does not mention Aaron, the book therefore must be understood to support the Deuteronomic view of priestly privilege.[51] Since, moreover, Deuteronomy is recognized to allow all Levites to function as priests, then Malachi too must advocate the right of all sons of Levi to serve as priests. [52]

The understanding of Deuteronomy that undergirds this argument (that is, that Deuteronomy recognizes the potential for all Levites to serve as priests) is widely accepted in biblical scholarship but has not gone uncontested. Although Wellhausen and most subsequent scholars have maintained that in Deuteronomy the terms "priests," "Levites," "Levitical priests" and "the priests, the sons of Levi" are equivalent terms, G. E. Wright has questioned this assumption and has argued instead that Deuteronomy's language is more precise. In Deuteronomy, argues Wright, *bĕnê-lēwî* refers to the teaching clergy scattered throughout the country, while "priests" and "Levitical priests" refer specifically to altar clergy.[53] Maintaining that "...the difference between D and P with regard to the Levites has been exaggerated," and that after the Josianic reform the P term "priest" was synonymous with D's term "Levitical priest,"[54] Wright suggests that D—like P—recognizes different ranks within the priesthood.[55]

---

50 Milgrom, *Levitical Terminology*, 10, n. 33.
51 For example, Blenkinsopp, *History*, 242; J. M. P. Smith, 8; Rivkin, 3 .
52 Such also is the assumption of Hanson in his various writings.
53 Wright, "Levites," 328-9.
54 Ibid., 330.
55 This argument recently has been revived by Eric M. Meyers in "Priestly Language," 229.

Wright's position has been directly addressed by J. A. Emerton, who refutes Wright's reading of Deuteronomy and reaffirms the more common view that in D all Levites may be priests.[56] Relying heavily on Deut. 18, Emerton demonstrates that the Deuteronomic writer "...can move easily between one term to the other."[57]

J. G. McConville, in assessing the Wright/Emerton debate, suggests that the comparison between D's and P's descriptions of the Levite "...is not so straightforward as is sometimes thought."[58] McConville concurs with Emerton that Deuteronomy does indeed occasionally refer to priests as "Levites," but he does not accept Emerton's conclusion that such a description indicates that Deuteronomy knows no distinction between the higher and lower clergy.[59] According to McConville, Deuteronomy knows the hierarchy of Levites and priests as enunciated in P and yet uses the term "Levites" to refer to the entire tribe without making distinctions within it. Deuteronomy's usage of terms, he maintains, parallels that of the book of Joshua, in which both precise and more general designations exist in tandem: Joshua demonstrates awareness of the difference between priest and Levite and yet may refer to both as "Levites."[60]

Emerton and McConville convincingly refute Wright's claims that the terminology of D bears the same intent as that of P. As seen clearly in passages such as Deut. 27, Deuteronomy exhibits no compunctions in calling priests "Levites," while on the contrary the P source sharply distinguishes the two.

For this reason, Malachi's apparently synonymous usage of *kōhănîm* and *běnê-lēwî* more closely parallels the usage of Deuteronomy than that of P. Its use of Deuteronomic-sounding terminology, nonetheless, does not necessarily imply that the book advocates the rights of all Levites to serve as priests. McConville legitimately argues that Deuteronomy itself may be aware of the difference between priest and Levite but chooses to soften this distinction for theological reasons. Even if a more traditional view of Deuteronomy's terminology and intent is accepted, however, the fact that Malachi employs Deuteronomy's language does not indicate that it accepts Deuteronomy's ideology.

In conclusion, Malachi's use of *běnê-lēwî* does appear to follow D rather than P, but such a source determination does not undercover

---

56 Emerton, 129-138.
57 Ibid., 133.
58 McConville, 141.
59 Ibid., 138.
60 Ibid., 140.

Malachi's ideological stance. Malachi's language does not necessarily indicate an "every priest a Levite" viewpoint,[61] nor must it be seen to advocate a Deuteronomic-inspired theocratic program in opposition to a hierocratic establishment.[62]

COVENANT WITH/OF LEVI

Source-critical investigation also has focused on a second passage, Malachi 2:4-5, which describes a covenant of/with Levi. Although no other passage in the Hebrew Bible explicitly mentions such a covenant with Levi, various passages have been suggested as the basis for Mal. 2:4-7, including Deuteronomy 33 and Numbers 25.[63]

Blenkinsopp finds Malachi 2:4-7 to be based on the Blessing of Levi in Deuteronomy 33:8-11,[64] and while Verhoef concedes that this Blessing is not explicitly deemed a covenant he likewise sees in Deuteronomy 33 the basis for Malachi 2:4.[65] In Deuteronomy 33, Levi is described both as teacher and priest: he not only teaches "Jacob your ordinances and Israel your law," but also offers incense and burnt offering as well as wielding the Urim and Thummin. This dual function of the priesthood is also highlighted in Malachi 2:5-7, and in both passages Levi is praised as one faithful to the covenant. Contrary to Glazier-McDonald's statement that the "only word in common in these passages is *běrît*,"[66] both mention Levi's role in transmitting *tôrâ* (Deut. 33:10; Mal. 2:7).

But while Malachi does appear to draw upon Deut. 33, the uncertainty in dating Deut. 33:8-11 renders difficult any attempt to trace Malachi's direct dependence upon it. According to Mayes and Cross and Freedman, the Blessing of Levi is a late addition to Deuteronomy.[67] According to Glazier-McDonald, the text of Deut. 33 attempts to give Levi the priesthood and has keen awareness of Levi's enemies, suggesting an historical setting in which Levitical claims to the priesthood were unstable.[68] To the contrary, Weinfeld, Wright and Seeligmann consider the

---

61 Contra Rivkin, 3.

62 Contra Hanson, *People Called*, 277-290.

63 Jeremiah 33 also has been suggested as a possible source. This passage, however, is likely a post-exilic addition, and will be discussed further in chapter 5.

64 Blenkinsopp, *History*, 242.

65 Verhoef, 245.

66 Glazier-McDonald, "Malachi," 120.

67 A. D. H. Mayes, *Deuteronomy*, New Century Bible Commentary (Greenwood, S. C.: Attic Press, 1979), 396; Cross and Freedman, 210.

68 Glazier-McDonald, "Malachi," 120.

passage to be an ancient source,[69] and Cody dates it to no later than the eighth century.[70]

Even if a late date is granted to Deut. 33:8-11, however, most would agree that it pre-dates the post-exilic period. While, therefore, the Blessing of Levi may postdate other portions of Deuteronomy, it likely would have been attached to the Blessing of Moses by the time of Malachi.

More frequently, the covenant of Levi in Mal. 2:4-7 is linked with Num. 25:11-13, in which Phineas the grandson of Aaron is rewarded for his faithfulness with a covenant of perpetual priesthood. E. Meyers points to the connection between these passages,[71] as does Glazier-McDonald, who outlines the vocabulary shared by these texts:

Mal. 2:4-5	Num. 25:12-13
lihyŏt bĕrîtî ʾet-lēwî	*hinnĕnî nōtēn lō ʾet-bĕrîtî*
bĕrîtî hāytâ ʾittô	*wĕhāytâ lō...bĕrît*
(bĕrît) hahayyîm wĕhaššālôm	*bĕrîtî (bĕrît) šālôm*
bĕrît hahayyîm	*bĕrît kehŭnnat ʿôlām* [72]

On the basis of these similarities, Glazier-McDonald contends that Malachi 2:4-5 is based upon Num. 25:12-13.

This shared vocabulary is indeed striking, and an additional example of the possible influence of Num. 25 on Mal. 2 is that both assume that the priestly covenant extends to the "seed" (*zeraʿ*) of the priests (Num. 25:13 and Mal. 2:3). Moreover, Phineas receives this commendation for his action against idolatry and intermarriage—themes often seen as central to Malachi.[73]

Before Mal. 2 can be interpreted as a direct borrowing from Num. 25, however, several issues deserve consideration. First, acknowledgement must be made that the vocabulary highlighted by Glazier-McDonald is not unique to these two passages. Both accounts rely heavily on the language of the grant-type treaty, which surfaces elsewhere in the Hebrew Bible. For example, Gen. 17:19, in recounting the covenant granted to Abraham, also uses much the same language:

Mal. 2:4	Num. 25:12-13	Gen. 17:19

---

[69] Weinfeld, *Deuteronomy*, 153; G. E. Wright, "Lawsuit of God," 26; I. L. Seeligmann, "A Psalm from Pre-Regal Times," *VT* 14 (1964): 75-92.

[70] Cody, *History*, 114.

[71] E. Meyers, "Priestly Language," 232.

[72] Glazier-McDonald, "Malachi," 122.

[73] Ibid., 122.

lihyôt běrîtî ʾet-lēwî   *hinněnî nōtēn lō ʾet-* *wahăqimōtî ʾet-běrîtî*
                              běrîtî
           běrît kehūnnat ʿôlām   *librît ʿôlām*
           lō ûlězarʿô ʾahărāyw   *lězarʿô ʾahărāyw*

Malachi and Numbers are indeed alike in using the language of grant to describe the claims of the priesthood (as does Jer. 33, to be discussed in chapter 5), but the language they use to do so has other biblical parallels.

A second consideration in this discussion is that Malachi differs from Numbers in applying this language to Levi rather than to Phineas or Aaron. Such a change in subjects is significant, especially when seen in light of the fact that the Priestly source traces priesthood through Aaron and not through Levi. Indeed, so to glorify Levi seems quite foreign to the ideology of P.

Third, tracing these similarities between Mal. 2:4-7 and Num. 25 does not account for the elements in Malachi's account that do not derive from Numbers. Especially, it does not explain the strong emphasis on the teaching role of the priest as outlined in 2:5-7. Num. 25:12-13 promises to Phineas a covenant of perpetual priesthood but does not explicate the teaching responsibilities of that office; the teaching and sacerdotal activities of Levi are, however, outlined in the Deuteronomic Blessing of Levi. Rather than drawing upon either Deut. 33 or Num. 25, then, Malachi's description of a "covenant with Levi" appears to integrate these passages into a distinctive portrait of the ideal priest. As in Deut. 33, the eponymous ancestor Levi is lauded for his faithfulness, and the priesthood is described as involving both teaching and sacrifice. As in Num. 25, the faithful priest is the recipient of a covenant of perpetual priesthood—a gift described in the characteristic language of the grant.

Conclusions Regarding D and P

The preceding analysis of the evidence for the influence of D and P upon Malachi suggests that Malachi employs the language and ideas of both sources. As many have noted, the book demonstrates clearly the strong influence of Deuteronomy, and its ending (perhaps original) consciously places Malachi's message within Deuteronomic tradition. The influence of the Priestly Code is likewise evident in the book's vocabulary and ideology.

As also seen in this discussion Malachi rarely uses either source without adaptation. Deuteronomic language is interwoven with language characteristic of other biblical traditions, and while the author obviously knows the Priestly Code he or she feels compelled to replicate neither P's technical terminology nor its language for priests. The author borrows freely from various sources, adapting the language of each for his or her own purposes and thereby creating a new idiom that is deeply rooted in tradition.

OTHER BIBLICAL TRADITIONS

To discern only the influence of D and P within Malachi is to overlook other biblical passages and traditions that undergird the book. Some of these other traditions have already been noted in previous discussion. For example, chapter 3 argued that the book demonstrates a thorough knowledge and mastery of Israel's covenant ideology. Like the writers of the historical and prophetical books, this author artfully wields the language of covenant grant and covenant lawsuit. Passages from other works such as the Holiness Code, the Book of the Covenant, Ezekiel and Jeremiah also were seen as origins of much of Malachi's language, and the description of covenant violators in 3:5 was seen to blend the language of D, P and the Book of the Covenant.[74]

Beyond these previously-noted examples, additional passages in which Malachi employs various biblical traditions may be cited. David Petersen, for example, discerns a "striking" relationship between Malachi 3:1 and Exodus 23:20:[75]

Mal. 3:1:	Behold I send my messenger; he will prepare the way before me.
Exod. 23:20:	Behold I send my messenger[76] before you to guard your way.

Petersen contends that the author of Malachi consciously draws upon and alludes to this passage in Exodus such that "...the passage in Malachi seems to be a reworking of the *maPāk* text in the Book of the Covenant."[77]

The similarities between these passages is evident, but—as in the case of much of Malachi's purported "Deuteronomic" language—the question arises as to whether one work is dependent upon another or whether both may draw upon a common tradition. As noted in chapter 3, *hinnēh/hinnĕnî* plus a participle is a frequent formula for announcement in the Hebrew Bible, especially in the prophetic corpus; in addition,

---

74 Above, 92-93.

75 Petersen, "Israelite Prophecy," 153.

76 Petersen emends the Hebrew text (which does not include the possessive suffix "my") on the basis of other manuscripts and the LXX.

77 Ibid., 153.

šallaḥ is commonly used to describe the commissioning of a prophetic figure (for example, Jer. 7:25; 19:14; 1 Sam 15:1). As Petersen himself well notes, messenger language is used to describe prophetic activity in other prophetic passages (Isa. 42:19, 44:26; Hag. 1:13; and 2 Chron. 36:15-16). The *malʾāk* is also a common figure in the prophetic lawsuit.[78]

Malachi does not, it seems, echo exclusively the language of Exod. 23:20, even though these passages are indeed quite similar. Whether or not Mal. 3:1 borrows directly from Exod. 23, the author's familiarity with the themes and the vocabulary of the prophetic covenant lawsuit is nonetheless evident.

The Book of Malachi also features prominent personalities from Israel's past. The opening oracle of 1:2-5 highlights the fraternity of Jacob and Esau, brothers immortalized in Israelite tradition as well as in the narratives of Genesis. It would be difficult to prove that Malachi's discussion of the contrasting fates of these figures relies directly on the extant literary text of Genesis, and yet this first oracle presumes knowledge of such a tradition.

As has been well noted, the figure of Levi is of central importance in the book. Quite distinctively, the author of Malachi describes Levi with language befitting a patriarch: like Abraham, David and other major figures in Israel's past, Levi receives a grant as reward for his exemplary behavior. The Priestly Code extols Phineas with this language, but Malachi reserves praise for a figure from Israel's more ancient past.

In its closing verses, Malachi recalls two more ancient figures— Moses and Elijah. Israel is admonished to uphold the statutes mediated by Moses and to anticipate the arrival of Elijah, the quintessential prophet.

By pointing to these figures in Israel's memory (Jacob, Esau, Levi, Moses and Elijah), the author of Malachi places the book within the stream of Israel's patriarchal, historical and prophetic traditions. This highlighting of characters does not necessarily indicate that the author borrowed from literary sources, and yet it demonstrates that this author draws—consciously and eclectically—from the wealth of earlier traditions.

---

78 See above, 74.

THE CANON KNOWN TO MALACHI

Malachi's usage of the language, ideas and figures of so many earlier traditions raises the question of the extent of the canon with which its author is familiar. This question is especially significant in light of recent theories regarding the growth of the canon.

For many years, a scholarly consensus has held that the biblical canon developed in three stages: the Torah was compiled under Ezra, the Prophets were completed a few hundred years later and the Writings were finalized ca. 100 C.E.[79] Within such a scheme, Malachi would be familiar with no official canon but rather with various isolated Pentateuchal and prophetic strands. Such indeed, has been the assumption of various commentators on Malachi.

More recently, however, many scholars have attempted to establish earlier dates both for the finalization of the Pentateuch and for the closing of the prophetic corpus. Concerning the Pentateuch, numerous studies have argued that P may not be a late source but may reflect the situation of the exilic or perhaps the pre-exilic era. Israeli scholars have been particularly prolific on this subject,[80] although others have also adopted an early date for P.[81] All the arguments for and against an early date for P cannot be considered here; significant, however, is the fact that these scholars have demonstrated the possibility that P predates the post-exilic era. Accordingly, if P may antedate the return of Ezra and Nehemiah, then the possibility also arises that the Pentateuch may have been completed prior to the Return.

The date of the prophetic collection has also been reevaluated. According to D. N. Freedman, the first component of the canon to be com-

---

[79] E.g., Arthur Jeffrey, "The Canon of the Old Testament," in *Interpreter's Bible*, ed. George Buttrick and others (Nashville: Abingdon, 1952), I: 32-45.

[80] E.g., Avi Hurvitz, "The Language of the Priestly Source and Its Historical Setting--The Case for an Early Date," in *Eighth World Congress of Jewish Studies, Proceedings* (Jerusalem: World Union of Jewish Studies, 1983), 83-93; idem, "The Evidence of Language in Dating the P Code," *Revue biblique* 81(1974): 24-56; M. Haran, "The Character of the Priestly Source: Utopian and Exclusive Features," in *Eighth World Congress of Jewish Studies, Proceedings* (Jerusalem: World Union of Jewish Studies, 1983), 131-138; Ziony Zevit, "Converging Lines of Evidence on the Date of P," *ZAW* 94 (1984): 481-511; M. Weinfeld, "Social and Cultic Institutions in the Priestly Source against Their Ancient Near Eastern Backgrounds," in *Eighth World Congress of Jewish Studies, Proceedings* (Jerusalem: World Union of Jewish Studies, 1983), 95-129; idem, "Bible Criticism," in *Contemporary Jewish Religious Thought*, ed. Arthur Cohen and Paul Mendes-Flohr (New York: Charles Scribner's Sons, 1987), 35-40.

[81] E.g., Milgrom, Hanson, Freedman, Cross.

piled was a Primary History (comprised of the Deuteronomic History and the Tetrateuch). A preliminary edition of the prophetic corpus was then added to this History ca. 550, and by 500 the prophetic collection was completed by the addition of Second Isaiah, Third Isaiah, Jonah, Joel, Haggai, First Zechariah and Malachi.[82] According to this understanding, Malachi's canon would include the Pentateuch, the Deuteronomic History and prophets such as First Isaiah, Jeremiah, Ezekiel, Amos, Hosea, Micah, Nahum, Zephaniah, Habakkuk and Obadiah.[83]

One of the main results of this chapter has been to indicate that Malachi draws upon much of the Pentateuch—including P—and also is fully cognizant of prophetic traditions. It is not possible to ascertain with certainty that the Pentateuch and the Prophets were known to Malachi in their present form, but several clues suggest that the book is indeed aware of such a canon. For example, the book's ability to use "priest" and "Levite" as synonymous while yet demonstrating knowledge of the Priestly Code would be extremely precarious if the book were relying primarily upon an isolated P source. Such a usage would be understandable if, on the other hand, Deuteronomy and P were read as mutually-reinforcing, as in the present canonical arrangement.[84] As a further example, the book's artful use of the literary formulae of the prophetic *rîb* would more likely have developed from a reading of the prophetic corpus rather from a general familiarity with prophetic traditions.

In conclusion, Malachi's usage of various sources demonstrates its author's thorough knowledge of and facility in Israel's Pentateuchal, historical, and prophetic traditions. While this knowledge could have been gleaned from scattered origins, quite possible and reasonable is the suggestion that this author possessed a literary canon including the Pentateuch, Deuteronomic History and a preliminary corpus of the Prophets.

---

82 David Noel Freedman, "Canon of the OT," in *Interpreter's Dictionary of the Bible*, Supplementary Volume, ed. Keith Crimm and others (Nashville: Abingdon, 1976), 132. See also his article "The Earliest Bible," *Michigan Quarterly Review* 22 (1983): 167-175. E. and C. Meyers support Freedman's views on the Primary History and suggest that Haggai and Zechariah were cognizant of such a collection. Meyers and Meyers, *Haggai, Zechariah 1-8*, 16.

83 Freedman, "Canon," 132.

84 Such is the reading of the Pentateuch in traditional scholarship such as that by Curtiss, *The Levitical Priests*.

CONCLUSIONS

The investigation undertaken in this chapter has uncovered numerous examples of Malachi's use of earlier sources. The book exhibits familiarity not only with the Pentateuchal sources of D and P but also with a broad corpus of Israel's historical and prophetic traditions.

Most previous studies of Malachi have overlooked the book's use of these divergent traditions, primarily due to a preoccupation with the problem of tracing Malachi's position within the course of Pentateuchal history. Assuming a late date for the Priestly source and for the compilation of the Pentateuch and prophetic corpora, many scholars have failed to discern other influences within the book. As seen above, for example, much of Malachi's language that has been explained as characteristically Deuteronomic may instead reflect the language of covenant making and covenant violation that is common to Israel's historical and prophetic books.

Focusing narrowly upon identifying Pentateuchal sources within Malachi, scholars have also failed to perceive the ways in which Malachi has adapted the sources from which it borrows. Although several scholars have traced isolated terminological affinities between Malachi and P in order to prove that Malachi is aware of P, few have considered *how* Malachi uses P. This discussion has sought to demonstrate that Malachi interacts with sources and redirects their language to the prophet's own ends.

This recognition of the book's integration of sources also indicates that its use of a given source does not necessarily indicate complicity with that source's ideological goals. As suggested above, Malachi's use of Deuteronomic language does not identify it as pro-Levitical, any more than its use of Priestly language characterizes it as pro-Aaronide. That the Book of Malachi can use the terms "priest" and "Levite" as equivalents while yet knowledgeable of the Priestly Code's distinction between these classes attests to its independence from the politics of the sources from which it borrows.

The conclusions drawn from this and previous chapters suggest that the author of Malachi, fully cognizant of the Pentateuchal, historical and prophetic traditions of Israel, adapted the language of these traditions to describe his or her own understanding and vision of the priesthood. Evoking the memory of the ancient figures of Levi, Moses and Elijah and casting his or her work in the earlier form of the prophetic *rîb*, the author sought to place the contemporary priesthood in the context of Israel's past.

The next chapter turns to a consideration of the possible setting for the composition of the Book of Malachi and to an analysis of other sources that may cast light upon the book's treatment of the priesthood. In doing so, it seeks to determine whether Malachi's usage of terms for the priesthood is anomalous or perhaps reflective of a period in Israel's history. How do sources that are earlier, contemporaneous with and later than Malachi describe the priesthood?

CHAPTER V

MALACHI AND THE PRIESTHOOD
IN CONTEXT

The previous chapters have suggested that in describing the priesthood the author of the Book of Malachi draws substantially from biblical precedent. The author characterizes the priesthood in terms of earlier covenant ideology and recalls such ancient figures as Levi, Moses and Elijah. The book's accusations against the sins of the priests are likewise fashioned according to an ancient model—that of the prophetic lawsuit or *rîb*.

The goal of the present chapter is to consider how Malachi's treatment of the priesthood accords with other literature. In so doing, attention will first turn to a consideration of the date and setting of the book. Subsequently, through a comparison of Malachi with other biblical and extra-biblical literature, effort will be made to determine whether additional literature from this general time frame may be seen to exhibit similar characteristics.

DATE OF THE BOOK

Although the Book of Malachi bears no chronological markers and refers to no concrete dateable event, scholars have reached a surprising unanimity in attributing its composition to the post-exilic period. Perhaps even more surprisingly, most agree on an even narrower time frame for the book. Apart from a few dissenters such as Holtzmann and Spoer,[1] scholars concur in dating Malachi between 520 and 400 B.C.E.

---

[1] O. Holtzmann, "Der Prophet Maleachi und der Ursprung des Pharisaërtums," *Archiv für Religionswissenschaft* 29 (1931): 1-21; Hans H. Spoer, "Some New Considerations Toward the Dating of the Book of Malachi," *JQR* 20 (1908): 167-186. Both Holtzmann and Spoer date Malachi to the Maccabean era.

Scholars point to several factors from which this post-exilic date of the Book of Malachi is inferred:

1. "Historical" references to Edom and to a "governor;"
2. Proposed similarities between the conditions that Malachi describes and those characterized in the Books of Ezra and Nehemiah;
3. Linguistic analysis;
4. Quotes from earlier literature;
5. Style and genre.

In an effort to evaluate the validity of attributing to the book a post-exilic date, each of these factors will be considered in turn.

"Historical" References

EDOM

ln Mal. 1:2-5, the prophet contrasts the fates of Judah and Edom:

> Yet I have loved Jacob, but I have hated Esau. I have laid waste his hill country and left his heritage to jackals of the desert. If Edom says, "We are shattered, but we will rebuild the ruins," the LORD of hosts says, "They may build, but I will tear down, till they are called The Wicked Country, The People with Whom the LORD is Angry Forever."

Through the use of archaeological and comparative literary material, scholars have endeavored to determine to what event and date this destruction of Edom refers. Before these various historical proposals are outlined, however, one must establish that an actual historical event is indeed involved.

According to Peter Ackroyd, no historical context can be determined for Malachi's mention of Edom. In Malachi as in various biblical passages, he maintains, "Edom" does not represent a geographical or political entity but rather signifies a "typical enemy,"[2] the "symbol of a hostile world."[3] Coggins concurs with Ackroyd's assessment, and suggests that, joining Amos, Jeremiah and Obadiah in treating Edom as the typical enemy, " . . . Mal. 1:2-6 may reflect a literary continuum as much as an historical comment."[4]

Often in biblical literature, Edom does indeed symbolically represent Israel's enemies. Such a usage in fact persisted beyond the biblical period, so that both the Jewish and early Christian communities could de-

---

[2] Peter Ackroyd, *Exile and Restoration: A Study of Hebrew Thought of the Sixth Century B. C.*, Old Testament Library (Philadelphia: Westminster Press, 1968), 224.

[3] Ibid., 230-231.

[4] Coggins, 75.

scribe Rome as "Edom." A symbolic interpretation of Malachi's reference to Edom, however, does not accord well with the oracle contained in Malachi 1:2-5. These verses do not voice an eschatological hope that Israel's archenemy will be defeated but rather they refer to a *past* event within the listeners' memory. The success of the argument that the prophet here advances relies on the fact that some event has actually occurred. The deity's concern for Israel *has been* demonstrated in His action, that is, in the destruction of Edom. While various passages in Obadiah, Joel, Ezekiel, Jeremiah, Psalms and Lamentations express the longing that Edom will be punished in the future, Malachi treats Edom as already fallen. Similarly, Isaiah 63:1 considers the destruction of Edom as an event that is both real and reflective of God's faithfulness to Israel.

Having established that Mal. 1:2-5 refers to an actual destruction of Edom, attention now turns to determining the possible date and setting of such an event. Such a determination is rendered difficult by the lack of sufficient information from which to reconstruct the history of Edom. The biblical material provides little evidence; in fact, the Books of Haggai, Zechariah, Ezra and Nehemiah do not even mention Edom. In addition, archaeological study has not resolved some of the major questions regarding Edom's fate. For this reason, Mason considers both the history of Edom and Malachi's reference as insufficient for attempting historical reconstruction.[5]

According to most scholars, Malachi's reference in 1:2-5 refers to the Nabatean invasion of Edom around the beginning of the fifth century B.C.E. This proposal was early advanced by Grätz,[6] and was soon supported by Wellhausen.[7]

In more recent times, this interpretation of Mal. 1:2-5 has been supported by Bright, Winward, Gottwald and R. Smith.[8] Bruce Cresson, in keeping with this understanding, traces similarities between the language of Malachi 1 and what is known of the Nabateans:

> The evidence that the reference of Malachi is to the Nabatean encroachment is found in "I have left his heritage to the jackals of the desert." Seir is usu-

---

5 Mason, *Books*, 138.

6 H. Grätz, "Die Anfänge der Nabatäerherrschaft," *Monatsschrift für Wissenschaft und Geschichte des Judentums* 24 (1875): 60-66.

7 Wellhausen, *Kleinen Propheten*, 214. The positions of Grätz and Wellhausen are noted by T. Cheyne, "Malachi and the Nabateans," *ZAW* 14 (1894): 142.

8 Bright, 377; Stephen Winward, *A Guide to the Prophets* (Atlanta: John Knox Press, 1977), 217; Gottwald, 509; R. Smith, 298.

ally referred to as hill country; the Nabatean invaders would be desert people. [9]

No archaeological evidence has been offered in support of this view. Instead, scholars infer such a scenario from Diodorus' attestation that by the year 312 B. C. E. the Nabateans controlled Petra.[10] As Starcky reasons, since historians possess no record of a Babylonian or Persian campaign in Edom and since the Nabateans controlled Edom by 312, therefore Edom must have fallen to the Nabateans.[11]

Although quite common, this view that Malachi refers to a Nabatean invasion of Edom has various problems. Not only does Cressson's identification of "desert jackals" with the Nabateans attempt to treat historically what is in fact typical language for a treaty curse,[12] but also archaeological investigation fails to support this "Nabatean theory."

The work of Crystal Bennett and J. Bartlett indicates the continuous occupation of sites from Edomite through Nabatean phases.[13] Sites such as Buseirah (biblical Bozrah), Tell el-Kheleifeh and Petra experienced no major upheavals at the hands of the Nabateans .

More significant, however, is evidence demonstrating that the decline of Edom should be placed earlier than the fifth-century date favored by those who see the Nabatean influx as decisive. As noted by J. M. Myers and as the excavations of Bennett show, a large number of sites in Edom were abandoned in the sixth century.[14] While on the basis of his excavations, Nelson Glueck earlier had maintained that Edom experienced a rapid disintegration of power from the eighth century on,

---

9 Bruce Cresson, "The Condemnation of Edom in Post-Exilic Judaism," in *The Use of the Old Testament in the New and Other Essays: Studies in Honor of William Franklin Stinespring*, ed. James Efird (Durham, NC: Duke University Press, 1972), 138.

10 Diodorus Siculus, *Bibliotheca Historica* (Loeb Classical Library, 1954), 19: 94-97; quoted in J. R. Bartlett, "The Rise and Fall of the Kingdom of Edom," *PEQ* 104 (1972): 37 (hereafter, Bartlett, "Rise and Fall").

11 Jean Starcky, "The Nabateans: A Historical Sketch," *BA* 18 (1955): 86.

12 See Hillers, *Treaty Curses*, 53 . Also see above, 64.

13 Crystal Bennett, "Excavations at Buseirah (Biblical Bozrah)," in *Midian, Moab and Edom: The History and Archaeology of the Late Bronze Age and Iron Age Jordan and Northwest Arabia*, ed. John Sawyer and David C. Hines, JSOTS 24 (Sheffield: Sheffield Academic Press, 1983), 9-17: J. R. Bartlett, "From Edomites to Nabateans: A Study in Continuity," *PEQ* 111 (1979): 53-66 (hereafter Bartlett, "Edomites"); Bartlett, "Rise and Fall," 26-37.

14 J. M. Myers, "Edom and Judah in the 6th-5th c. B.C.," in *Near Eastern Studies in Honor of William Foxwell Albright*, ed. Hans Goedicke (Baltimore: Johns Hopkins Press, 1971), 389; Bennett, 17.

Bartlett argues that the seventh century witnessed the height of Edom's prosperity and that decline began in the sixth century.[15]

The reason for this sixth-century decline of Edom is variously assessed. Bennett attributes the decline to destruction by the Babylonian armies, an event also attested by Isa. 63:1, Obadiah 8 and Jeremiah 49:13, 22.[16]

J. Lindsay attempts further precision in dating, and proposes that Edom was destroyed during the campaigns of Nabonidus in 550. Relying exclusively on literary documents such as the biblical text, the Arad ostracon, Josephus and the Nabonidus Chronicle, Lindsay traces evidence for the existence of Edom through 582 and explains that Edom escaped the various campaigns of Nebuchadnezzer. After Nebuchadnezzer's death, however, Edom rebelled and was destroyed by the armies of Nabonidus ca. 550.[17] Lindsay's view is accepted by Bartlett, who argues that since the biblical account blames Edom for helping to destroy Jerusalem, Edom must have escaped the ravages of Nebuchadnezzer's campaigns. Bartlett also argues that Lindsay's reconstruction fits well with biblical and archaeological evidence.[18]

Lindsay's proposal that Edom *must* have fallen to Nabonidus rather than to Nebuchadnezzer is not entirely convincing. For his reconstruction he relies exclusively on literary texts without considering the distinctive aims and concerns of each. Although Bartlett suggests that archaeology may support Lindsay's view, archaeological evidence in fact simply points to a sixth-century date for the fall of Edom—a date which also could include the reign of Nebuchadnezzer.

While the arguments of Lindsay and Bartlett do not clearly demonstrate that Edom fell to Nabonidus, archaeological and literary evidence does suggest that the Babylonian armies destroyed Edom. This evidence therefore links Edom's fall to a date between 605 and 550 rather than to a fifth–century time frame.

Malachi's reference to the destruction of Edom thus also fits into this sixth–century time period. Importantly, Malachi attributes to Edom the hope of rebuilding. According to the discussion outlined above, such a hope would only have remained alive shortly after this 605-550 period. Later in the fifth century, after the Nabateans had effected a gradual and

---

15 Bartlett, "Rise and Fall," 35.
16 Bennett, 17.
17 John Lindsay, "The Babylonian Kings and Edom," *PEQ* 108 (1976): 23-39.
18 Bartlett, "Edomites," 57.

perhaps peaceful takeover of the country, little hope of rebuilding would have survived.

Taking a radically different position, Spoer traces Malachi's reference to Edom to the Maccabean era. He maintains that the destruction of Edom mentioned in Malachi describes Judas' defeat of the Idumeans and that the hope of rebuilding characterizes the years after Judas' death. Spoer's position, however, has little to recommend it. The validity of his proposal relies upon his unproven assertion that Ezekiel's and Jeremiah's prophecies concerning Edom refer to a "different period of history in the life of Judah" than does Malachi.[19] His statement that "Between the denunciations of Ezekiel and those of our prophet there is a long silence in regard to Edom"[20] relies upon his dating of Obadiah, Joel, and Isa. 63. Spoer effectively demonstrates that the oracle of Malachi does not fit with a fourth–century date,[21] but he fails to consider an earlier date.

"GOVERNOR" (*peḥâ*)

A large number of scholars interpret the mention of a "governor" (*peḥâ*) in 1:8 as evidence that Malachi is a document of the Persian period. Such is the position taken by Verhoef, R. Smith, Baldwin and Coggins.[22] Since prior to the exile, Judah was governed by its own kings and since the Persian empire is known to have appointed governors (as in the case of Nehemiah), therefore the presence of a governor is understood to indicate a Persian date.

While indeed local kings ruled Judah prior to the exile and while the Persians did appoint governors over subjugated lands, this exclusive identification of the term *peḥâ* with a Persian date is problematical. Raising initial difficulties is the fact that the term *peḥâ* bears various meanings. As noted by E. Meyers and C. Meyers, *peḥâ* was used by the Persians to describe both a satrap and a provincial governor.[23] Widengren similarly observes that, while Neh. 5:15 implies that various governors ruled the restoration community between the tenures of Zerubbabel and Nehemiah, there exists no information indicating whether these were local or Persian governors.[24] As McEvenue correctly observes, Nehemiah

---

19 Spoer, 183.

20 Ibid., 182.

21 Ibid., 183.

22 Verhoef, 156-157; R. Smith, 298; Baldwin, 213; Coggins, 74.

23 Meyers and Meyers, *Haggai, Zechariah 1-8*, 16.

24 Geo Widengren, "The Persian Period," in *Israelite and Judean History*, ed. John Hayes and J. Maxwell Miller, The Old Testament Library (Philadelphia: Westminster, 1977), 522.

3:7 implies that the restoration community was governed by one *peḥâ* while Nehemiah 2:7-9 suggests that several may have ruled concurrently.[25] The Hebrew Bible does not always clearly define the rank it intends by the term *peḥâ*, and the term is often used flexibly in the biblical text.[26]

Further militating against an easy identification of the term *peḥâ* with Persian administration is the fact that the term *peḥâ* was used by various cultures from the eighth century onwards. The Akkadian equivalent to *peḥâ*—*paḥatu* or *bēl-piḥati*—was used by the Assyrian Empire to describe leaders of provinces. During the reign of Tiglath-Pileser III, the Empire was systematically divided into provinces and over each was placed a *bēl-piḥati*.[27] The Zinjirli Stele attests to this practice. In describing the conquest of Egypt in 671 B.C.E., Esarhaddon boasts:

> The root of Kuš I eradicated from Egypt—leaving not one to do homage (to me). I appointed kings, governors (*bēl-piḥati*), officers, harbor oveseers, commissionaires, and administrative personnel.[28]

Pre-exilic biblical texts such as Isa. 36:9 (= 2 Kings 18:24) employ the term *peḥâ* to describe these Assyrian officials. As McEvenue demonstrates, in pre-exilic biblical usage *peḥâ* appears in military contexts to describe one who marches with the army.[29]

The Babylonian Empire also utilized the term *peḥâ* in describing its officials. Biblical passages such as Jer. 51:57 and likely also Jer. 51:23 refer to Babylonian commanders as *peḥâ*. Extra-biblically, *peḥâ* also appears in the "Adon Letter," a late seventh-century Aramaic document.[30] In this letter, King Adon—whose identity is debated—requests military aid from the Egyptian pharoah. Although the passage in which *peḥâ* appears suffers from lacunae, Adon appears to complain that if the Babylonians

---

[25] Sean E. McEvenue, "The Political Structure in Judah from Cyrus to Nehemiah," *CBQ* 43 (1981): 363.

[26] Hugh Williamson, *Ezra and Nehemiah*, Old Testament Guides (Sheffield: JSOT Press, 1987), 50.

[27] H. W. F. Saggs, "A Lexical Consideration for the Date of Deutero-Isaiah," *JTS* n.s. 10 (1959): 84.

[28] Moshe Elat, "The Political Status of the Kingdom of Judah within the Assyrian Empire in the Seventh Century B.C.E.," in *Investigations at Lachish: The Sanctuary and the Residency* (Lachish V), ed. Yohanan Aharoni (Tel Aviv: Tel Aviv University Institute of Archaeology, 1975), 66.

[29] McEvenue, 362.

[30] Bezalel Porten, "The Identity of King Adon," *BA* 44 (1981): 36-52.

take possession of his territory they will set up a "governor" in the land.[31]

The Persian government appropriated the title *peḥâ* from its predecessors, but—as discussed above—the term in Imperial Aramaic described various offices. From the Persians, the Seleucids adopted the term[32] and, as Spoer outlines, the term is employed in the Mishnah to refer to priests.[33]

One argument for tracing the reference to a governor in Mal. 1:8 to the Persian period is that while the term *peḥâ* was used to describe the governing officials of various empires, Judah was controlled by a *peḥâ* only in the Persian period since prior to the exile independent monarchs ruled. A consideration of Assyrian organizational procedures, however, weakens such an argument. As Moshe Elat effectively argues, when the Assyrians gained control of a region they often placed an Assyrian governor in power alongside the local king. Hence, when Judah came under Assyrian control during the reign of Hezekiah, an Assyrian governor may have been stationed in Lachish to oversee the vassal kingdom.[34] Such an Assyrian governor would have remained in Lachish throughout the Assyrian control of Judah.

Based on the foregoing evidence, the mere appearance of the term *peḥâ* in Mal. 1:8 does not necessarily indicate a date in the Persian period. The term appears in extra-biblical texts from the eighth century onwards, and biblical texts provide pre-exilic examples of the term. Because *peḥâ* was so broadly used and because is was not used uniformly even in the Persian period, it is not possible to determine the historical figure to which *peḥâ* in Mal. 1:8 refers.

Similarities to the Historical Situation of Ezra/Nehemiah

Quite prevalent is the view that the Book of Malachi outlines many of the same problems and issues confronted in the Books of Ezra and Nehemiah. In the words of J. M. P. Smith, "The Book of Malachi fits the situation amid which Nehemiah worked as snugly as a bone fits its socket."[35] Other scholars share this conviction.[36]

---

31 Reading with H. L. Ginsberg, "An Aramaic Contemporary of the Lachish Letters," *BASOR* 111 (1948): 24-27; quoted in Porten, 37.

32 Mason, *Books*, 137.

33 Spoer, 171, citing *Bikkurim*, III, 3.1.

34 Elat, 70.

35 J. M. P. Smith, 7.

36 Baldwin, 213; Winward, 216-217; R. Smith, 298.

Indeed, many scholars are so certain that the Books of Malachi, Ezra and Nehemiah derive from the same period that they attempt to place these books in precise chronological order. Most suggest that the prophet Malachi preceded the return of Ezra and Nehemiah and that his prophecies helped pave the way for reform. J. M. P. Smith, Dumbrell and Chary take this position,[37] and Hanson maintains that the conditions deplored by the prophet Malachi were corrected by Ezra and Nehemiah.[38] Wanke suggests that the prophet Malachi prepared the way for the missions of Ezra, a contemporary.[39] Von Bulmerincq goes further to identify the person of Malachi as an assistant of Ezra.[40]

Verhoef places the work of the prophet Malachi between the two missions of Nehemiah.[41] According to Verhoef, only after Nehemiah's initial work did the community accept the responsibility for the maintainence of the Temple that is assumed in the Book of Malachi.[42] The book, then, lambasts the community for lapsing after initial reform.

This understanding that the prophet Malachi was a contemporary or younger contemporary of Ezra and Nehemiah is based upon the conviction that the books describing the activities of these figures address many of the same issues. These include a concern with:

a. Mixed marriages and divorce;
b. The people's failure to provide tithes and offerings;
c. The corruption of the priests; and
d. A pact known as "a book of remembrance."

Each will be treated in turn.

MIXED MARRIAGES AND DIVORCE

Ezra and Nehemiah's insistence on the dissolution of marriages between members of the restoration community and foreigners is frequently linked to Malachi 2:10-16, which according to most interpreters chastises divorce.[43] According to Glazier-McDonald, the Book of Malachi

---

37 J. M. P. Smith, 8; Dumbrell, 42-52; Chary, *Aggée*, 224.

38 Hanson, *People Called*, 295.

39 Gunther Wanke, "Prophecy and Psalms in the Persian Period," in *The Cambridge History of Judaism*, I: *Introduction; The Persian Period*, ed. Davies and Finkelstein (NY: Cambridge University Press, 1984), 173.

40 A. von Bulmerincq, *Der Prophet Maleachi* (Tartu: J. G. Krüger, 1932), II: 336; quoted in Eissfeldt, 443.

41 Verhoef, 159-160.

42 Ibid., 159.

43 For example, R. Smith, 298 and Verhoef, 159.

must precede the activity of Ezra, since Ezra ended the abuses that Malachi attacks by outlawing further intermarriage.[44] As becomes clear from closer attention, however, the problem confronted by Ezra/ Nehemiah and that addressed by the Book of Malachi are quite different. Mason well observes that Nehemiah does not consider the problem of divorce, but rather encourages Judean men to divorce their foreign wives.[45] In addition, the argument has been made above that the Book of Malachi directs its vehemence not against intermarriage or divorce but rather against idolatry.[46] As shown above, the language of Mal. 2:10-16 is that typically used to combat idolatry: the "daughter of a foreign god" in 2:11 is a goddess rather than a foreign woman, and the deity's attestation that He "hates šallaḥ" may indicate His outrage against treachery rather than His concern with divorce.[47] Even if the Book of Malachi does address the problem of divorce, however, it does not characterize the same situation as found in the Books of Ezra and Nehemiah. As is argued by Kenneth Hoglund in his doctoral dissertation, the restoration community did not stand as a self-governing entity but rather functioned as a dependent population within the Persian Empire.[48] According to Persian imperial policy, "...these dependent populations could continue to enjoy a royal concession to the lands in which they dwelt only if they maintained their ethnic identity separate from the surrounding peoples."[49]

This distinctive social and political situation underlying Ezra-Nehemiah's prohibition of intermarriage does not find parallels in the Book of Malachi. If indeed Malachi addresses intermarriage at all (which it likely does not) it does so in the context of railing against idolatry. While Ezra 10:8 outlines legal recourse against those who refuse to divorce foreign wives (they will forfeit their moveable property),[50] Malachi instead treats divorce as displeasing to the deity and offers no indications that the political standing of the community within the Persian empire is at stake.

---

[44]   Glazier-McDonald, "Malachi," 24.

[45]   Mason, *Books*, 137-138.

[46]   See above, 67-69.

[47]   See above, 89-90.

[48]   Kenneth Hoglund, "Achamenid Imperial Administration in Syria-Palestine and the Missions of Ezra and Nehemiah" (Ph. D. dissertation, Duke University, 1989.)

[49]   Kenneth Hoglund, "We are in Great Distress: Reconstructing the Social Context of Ezra-Nehemiah," Paper presented to the Chronicles, Ezra-Nehemiah Consultat˙ɔn, 1986 AAR/SBL meetings, Atlanta, GA, Nov. 23, 1986, 7.

[50]   Hoglund, "Great Distress," 6.

For the reasons outlined above, the Book of Malachi and those of Ezra-Nehemiah should not be read as mutually corroborating on the issues of intermarriage and divorce. Ezra and Nehemiah addressed a distinctive social situation in which ethnic purity was essential, while Malachi's language addresses the issue of idolatry.

TITHES AND OFFERINGS

The fact that both Malachi 3:6-12 and Nehemiah 13:25-27 accuse the community of failing to provide tithes and offerings is often cited as another indication that these books describe the same historical situation.[51] Verhoef, who dates Malachi's work between the two missions of Nehemiah, maintains that Malachi's appeal to the people to bring the offerings would have gained significance only after the covenant renewal recorded in Nehemiah, in which the people accepted the responsibility of maintaining the Temple. Prior to the arrival of Nehemiah, argues Verhoef, the maintenance of the Temple was sponsored by the Persians.[52]

Kaufmann argues that Malachi 3:6-12, which he describes as entrusting the collection of tithes to the priests, must date to a time after Nehemiah placed the tithes under sacerdotal control. Noting that tithes are not mentioned in Haggai, Zechariah or in Nehemiah prior to the pact made by the community, Kaufmann explains that tithing had fallen into disuse before its reinstatement under Ezra.[53]

Kaufmann finds additional proof that Malachi postdates the pact of the Great Assembly in a dual reference to the tithes being gathered in a "storehouse" (Mal. 3:10; Neh. 10:39). According to his position, this collection of the tithe into a storehouse is an innovation by Nehemiah, since P advocates that tithes be given directly to the Levites.[54]

These similarities between Malachi and Ezra-Nehemiah at first glance are appealing but in part are due to the lack of comparative material. Few biblical passages complain that tithes are not being given, and even fewer prophets lodge such a complaint. Kaufmann's theory regarding the development of the tithe under Nehemiah also suffers from the lack of comparative material. No other biblical work describes the administration of the community and the control of Temple property between the tenures of Haggai-Zechariah and Ezra-Nehemiah. The fact that tithes are not mentioned in Haggai and Zechariah, for example, does not

---

[51] For example, R. Smith, 298.
[52] Verhoef, 159 .
[53] Kaufmann, 436, 446, 387.
[54] Ibid., 644.

necessarily indicate that they were not operative. Moreover, tracing such a clear line of development of the tithe presumes that the Books of Ezra and Nehemiah accurately describe the reforms undertaken by the two.[55]

A comparison of the two passages (Mal. 3:10 and Neh. 10:39) also fails to demonstrate conclusively that they are indeed similar. While Kaufmann assumes the sacerdotal control of the tithe in Malachi, the passage itself does not prove that the priests control the tithe. The prophet, instead, addresses an unclear second person plural audience ("you are robbing me") and calls this same "you" to bring the tithes into the storehouse. Nehemiah 10:39, a bit differently, commands the Levites to bring "the tithe of the tithe" (*not* the tithe itself) to the storehouse.

Kaufmann's argument regarding the collection of the tithe in the storehouse likewise suffers from the lack of sufficient evidence by which to evaluate it. There exists no other literature from this time frame that would indicate whether tithes were gathered in storehouses prior to Nehemiah's reform. There is no reason, for example, that Malachi's reference to storehouse tithes could not precede that of Nehemiah. Joel 1:17 also mentions storehouses, although they are not clearly those of the Temple.

While the Books of Malachi and Ezra-Nehemiah do share a concern with the community's failure to bring tithes, evidence does not permit the direct connection of the books on this basis. The passages in question exhibit some differences, and the lack of other contemporary texts renders tenuous Kaufmann's attempt to trace through the Book of Malachi a clear history of the tithe.

COMPLAINTS AGAINST THE PRIESTS

Verhoef, among others, considers the negligence of priestly functions as a further similarity between the Book of Malachi and those of Ezra and Nehemiah. Malachi's recurrent accusations that the priests fail to offer worthy sacrifices and that they disregard the deity's reputation finds a parallel, he suggests, in Neh. 13:29-30 where Nehemiah laments that various priests have "defiled the priesthood and the covenant of the priesthood and the Levites."[56] Hence, Verhoef maintains, the priestly attitude toward the Temple described in the Book of Malachi is comparable to that found by Nehemiah upon his second visit to Jerusalem.[57]

---

[55] As argued by Coggins (75), one has no means of knowing the nature of the actual work of these figures.

[56] Verhoef, 159.

[57] Ibid.

Such a similarity between books, while perhaps worthy of note, provides little basis on which to relate the books historically. Accusations against corrupt priests constitute a perennial concern of classical prophetic literature.[58] Nehemiah's phrase "the covenant of the priesthood and the Levites" shares some verbal similarity to the "covenant with Levi" in Malachi 2:4, and yet the two "covenants" do not appear to be identical. The precise meaning of the phrase in Nehemiah is not clearly outlined, but it seems to refer to an agreement by the priests to avoid intermarriage. In Malachi the "covenant with Levi" outlines the teaching and sacrificial obligations of the priesthood in ancient and ideal terms, but "the covenant of the priests and Levites" in Nehemiah bears no such connotations. While the reference to a priestly "covenant" is not common in the Hebrew Bible, it does appear in other passages.[59]

"BOOK OF REMEMBRANCE"

The historical account of Mal. 3:16-18, in which the prophet refers to a "book of remembrance" that was written before the LORD has been linked to Neh. 10:1, which refers to a covenant to which the princes, Levites and priests set their seals. Such a linkage, however, has no basis. The two passages do not employ the same phrase, and each describes a different event. In Malachi, the "book of remembrance" refers to God's recognition of the deeds of the faithful; the people do not write the book, but it instead is written before the LORD. In contrast, Neh. 10:1 refers to an agreement made by the community and does not involve the deity's remembrance of the faithful; the action is here taken by the leaders, and not by the LORD.

Although the tracing of connections between Malachi and Ezra-Nehemiah is a commonplace of scholars, the preceding discussion has suggested that little basis in fact exists for making such a connection. The issues of intermarriage and divorce, tithing, accusations against priests and the mention of a "book of remembrance" are not treated equally in these books; often, the accounts describe quite different situations. The books, indeed, bear no necessary connection.

Linguistic Analysis

In addition to historical considerations, attempts also have been made to date Malachi on the basis of its language. While scholars such as Chary and Wellhausen have pointed to isolated words or phrases in the

---

58 Compare Hosea 4:4ff.
59 See Jeremiah 33, discussed below, 135-136.

book that point to a "late" date,[60] a thorough study of the character of the language of the Book of Malachi has been carried out by A. Hill.[61]

Hill's study of the language of Malachi follows the typological method developed by Robert Polzin, which as Hill describes it:

> involves systematic application of nineteen grammatical and syntactical categories developed by Polzin for the express purpose of distinguishing the relative chronological relation of Early and Late Biblical prose.[62]

Hill has adopted and refined Polzin's approach in order to utilize it in analyzing Malachi. According to him, the typological approach has advantages over other research because it seeks to relate Malachi to other literature rather than to specific historical events that bear absolute dates.[63]

From his application of Polzin's methodology to the Book of Malachi and from his comparison of these results with those obtained from analyzing other biblical literature, Hill concludes that Malachi broadly should be dated between 520 (the tenures of Haggai and Zechariah) and 458-445 (to which he dates Ezra-Nehemiah and the P[S] corpus).[64] More narrowly, he considers Malachi most likely to have been written between 500 and 475. Since Hill maintains that Malachi's language is similar to that of the exilic writers, he suggests that the Book was written by a first-generation returnee.[65]

Hill's study produces a date amenable to the results produced by other endeavors. Practically all scholars agree in placing the book within Hill's broad time range of 520-445. The narrower time frame of 500-475, which Hill prefers, does not radically challenge many theories of the date of Malachi.

---

[60] Chary considers *mgʾl* late term; Wellhausen argues that *brʾ* is late and related to the Priestly Code. See above, 88-89, 94.

[61] Andrew E. Hill, "The Book of Malachi: Its Place in Post-Exilic Chronology Linguistically Considered" (Ph. D. diss., University of Michigan, 1981) (hereafter Hill, "Book of Malachi"); Also, "Dating the Book of Malachi: A Linguistic Reexamination," in *And the Word of the Lord Shall Go Forth: Essays in Honor of David Noel Freedman in Celebration of his Sixtieth Birthday*, ed. Carol L. Meyers and M. O'Connor, ASOR Special Volume Series (Winona Lake: Eisenbrauns and ASOR, 1983): 77-89 (hereafter Hill, "Dating").

[62] Hill, "Dating," 77.

[63] Ibid.

[64] Hill accepts Polzin's isolation of four strata in the Priestly Code. The two treated here are P[g] (the base text of P) and P[S] (supplements to P).

[65] Hill, "Book of Malachi," 135.

An analysis of Hill's study, however, reveals that his work does not offer independent verification of these commonly-accepted dates. Rather, he draws conclusions that accord with those of other scholars simply because he shares many of the common assumptions regarding the Book of Malachi and its setting. Rather than deriving his dates from a purely typological scheme, Hill bases many of his dates on historical assumptions. In addition, Hill's data often fail to support the conclusions that he draws.

Although Hill claims to employ a primarily typological approach—comparing the Book of Malachi to other literature rather than to dateable historical events—he in fact often determines the chronology of pieces of literature on the basis of such historical events. For example, Hill maintains that although the Books of Haggai and Zechariah are *not* similar typologically they nonetheless must be dated to the same year on the basis of their date formulae.[66] Confronted with two books dated to the same year that do not produce similar ratios when Polzin's criteria are applied, Hill is forced to attribute these differences to "style" or to "alternative language development."[67] In much the same way, Hill relates his typological analysis to specific dates in a manner that is often quite subjective. He conjectures that "the official demise of the period of classical BH [Biblical Hebrew] *no doubt* came with the fall of the Judean monarchy in 586 B.C.,"[68] and he "*prefers*" to date the Ps corpus to Ezra-Nehemiah[69] (emphasis mine). Quite interesting is his statement that, "It is *likely* that the Pg corpus, to which the *post-exilic* prophets are typologically similar, dates to the Exile"[70] (emphasis mine). Hill gives no explanation or legitimation for these dates, although his chronological ordering of biblical materials is dependent upon them. Despite his claims to the contrary, Hill's analysis relies heavily on the relation of literature to events rather than only to other literature.

---

66 Hill, "Dating," 84.
67 Ibid., 84.
68 Ibid., 83.
69 Hill, "Book of Malachi," 78.
70 Ibid., 79.

TABLE 2.
CHRONOLOGICAL ORDER OF WORKS AS CONSTRUCTED
BY HILL

	LBH features	BH features
JE		12
CH		12
Dtr		12
Pg	4	7
Haggai	5	8
Zech 1-8	3	10
Malachi	3	9
Zech 9-14	4	8
Ps	8	2
Est	6	6
N¹	8	5
Ezra	10	0
N²	10	0
Chr	13	0

NOTE: For each work, Hill identifies Late Biblical Hebrew (LBH) and Biblical Hebrew (BH) features. LBH features include nineteen characteristics such as the reduced use of ʾet before a noun in the nominative case and expression of possession by prospective pronominal suffix with a following noun, or lĕ plus noun, or šel plus noun. The absence of these characteristics constitutes a BH feature.

NOTE: JE = Yahwist and Elohist traditions; CH = Court History (2 Sam 13-1 Kings l); Dtr = Deuteronomy and parts of Deuteronomic History; Est = Esther; N¹ = memoir portions of Nehemiah; N² = non-memoir portions of Nehemiah; Chr = Chronicles ("Dating," 79). Chart found in "Dating," 85.

TABLE 3.
CHRONOLOGICAL ORDER OF WORKS BASED ON
HILL'S STATISTICS

	LBH features	BH features
JE		12
CH		12
Dtr		12
Zech 1-8	3	10
Malachi	3	9
Zech 9-14	4	8
Pg	4	7
Haggai	5	8
Est	6	6
N1	8	5
Ps	8	2
Ezr	10	0
N2	10	0
Chr	13	0

Although Hill concludes from his study that Malachi likely dates between 500 and 475, his own data in fact suggest an earlier date for the book. In various statements, Hill acknowledges that Malachi's language bears affinities with pre-500 literature. He notes that, "Typologically, nothing precludes one from dating Malachi to the same general time frame [as Haggai and Zechariah 1-8]."[71] He observes that Malachi's language is closest to that of the exilic writers,[72] and his findings indicate

---

71 Hill, "Dating," 84.
72 Hill, "Book of Malachi," 132.

that while Malachi bears a low density of Late Biblical Hebrew (LBH) features, it exhibits a high density of classical Biblical Hebrew (BH) characteristics.[73] Despite this evidence, however, Hill persists in assigning to Malachi a traditional date between Haggai-Zechariah and Ezra-Nehemiah.

Hill's failure to rely solely on his data is also evident in the typological continuum of BH that he constructs. Hill places biblical literature in the chronological order outlined in table 2, supposedly on the basis of typological analysis.

A consideration of the numbers of LBH and BH features given for each piece of literature, however, indicates that Hill has not relied solely on his typological data. Indeed, when his own calculations are placed in numerical order, they produce a different order of biblical works, as seen in table 3.

As seen in table 3, Pg (which Hill dates on other grounds to the Exile) in fact bears close affinities with Zech 9-14; in addition, Malachi is typologically more akin to Zech. 1-8 than Zech. 1-8 is to Haggai—although both of the latter date to the same year. Significantly, Hill gives no data for exilic and immediate pre-exilic literature such as Ezekiel and Jeremiah.

In the second part of his dissertation, Hill supplements his typological study with lexical analysis, and, as before, his results suggest that the language of Malachi is most similar to literature that dates prior to 520. He finds no presence of any of the features considered by Polzin to be distinctive to LBH,[74] and he gives numerous examples in which the book follows the pre-exilic usage of a term. Examples include the terms *bḥn*, *bky*, and *npḥ* , which as he notes are common to Jeremiah and Ezekiel; *ḥlm* and *piʿ ôm*, which is common to Jeremiah; *ʾayyēh*, the usage of which fits pre-exilic patterns; and *segullâ*, which fits earlier rather than later usage. From his lexical study, Hill concludes that

- 37 items in Malachi are found in no other post-exilic prophet, while 36 items are concurrent with pre-exilic and exilic BH;[75]
- Malachi's vocabulary is closest to that of Jeremiah and Ezekiel;[76]
- Malachi's language is more akin to exilic and poetic literature than to LBH.[77]

---

73 Ibid., 79.
74 Hill, "Book of Malachi," 103.
75 Ibid., 129.
76 Ibid., 130.
77 Ibid., 132.

As may be seen in the above analysis, Hill's study of the language of Malachi does not offer solid grounds for dating the book to 500-475. Methodologically, his analysis is not strictly typological but rather relies heavily on his dating of individual biblical works—dating that is usually "preferred" rather than rigorously defended. Often, Hill's assumptions concerning the date of a particular work or the proper order of biblical books overrides his own data. While he himself acknowledges Malachi's strong linguistic ties to pre-exilic and exilic literature, he ignores this data when placing the book within the continuum of BH. If Hill's typological method bears any validity, his findings suggest that the language of the Book of Malachi accords best with exilic and immediate post-exilic usage. The book demonstrates few LBH features, and lexical analysis indicates its many affinities with the Books of Jeremiah and Ezekiel. On the basis of these findings, the composition of the book likely should be placed between the advent of LBH and the composition of Chronicles, which is replete with LBH features.

Quotes From Other Literature

Another argument for dating the Book of Malachi is that since the book quotes from other literature it therefore must be dated subsequent to that literature. While the evidence for the book's use of sources was treated in chapter 5, consideration here turns to the implications of such source usage in establishing the book's date.

As suggested in chapter 4, Malachi draws upon much of the Pentateuch—including P—and is fully cognizant of prophetic traditions.[78] Although it is not possible to determine whether the author had access to a completed Pentateuch, his use of the terms "priest" and "Levite" as synonyms would be most understandable if Deuteronomy and the Priestly literature were read in the present canonical arrangement.[79]

Although recognizing the book's employment of a large portion of the Pentateuch is important, it contributes little to establishing a precise date for the book. Malachi's knowledge of JE, the Book of the Covenant, the Holiness Code and Deuteronomy merely confirm the almost universal opinion that Malachi postdates Deuteronomy. The book's probable knowledge of the Priestly Code would be a much more significant clue to dating if a standard date for P were accepted. As noted above, scholars are sharply divided on the date of P—some dating it to the pre-exilic pe-

---

[78] See above, 111-112, for conclusions.
[79] See above, 111.

riod and others maintaining its post-exilic date.[80] To suggest here a possible date for Malachi on the basis of its knowledge of P would constitute a circular argument, since, indeed, one of the goals of this study is to evaluate the assertion of Rivkin and others that P can be dated on the basis of Malachi.

Similar difficulty arises in attempts to date Malachi on the basis of proposed references to other prophetic literature. Although Spoer points to isolated words that are shared by Malachi and Deutero- and Trito-Isaiah,[81] tracing commonalties between two corpora on the basis of a single shared usage (such as the *hip‛il* of *yg‛*) is quite tenuous. Chapter 4 does suggest that Malachi reflects the work of various prophetic writers, but it is not possible to establish the precise canon known to the author of the book or to know the date of that canon.

In sum, although this study does indicate that the author of Malachi reflects knowledge of various Pentateuchal, historical and prophetic works, the inability to determine the shape of the canon known to the author of the Book of Malachi and the inability to date corpora such as the P code preclude any determination of Malachi's date from its use of other literature.

Genre and Style

As demonstrated in chapter 3, Malachi's form represents an adaptation and not a duplication of the earlier prophetic *rîb*. In earlier literature the *rîb* form characterized short oracles, but in Malachi it becomes the pattern for the entire book. In earlier lawsuits, the *rîb* delivered accusations of a political and ethical nature, but in Malachi the accusations of the *rîb* are directed against improper sacrifice and worship.

These differences between the *rîb* contained in the Book of Malachi and those found in earlier prophetic literature, while significant for understanding the style and intention of the book, do not contribute significantly to dating Malachi. These differences cannot be linked to any concrete historical period. Although it is perhaps possible to argue from these findings that Malachi reflects a later period than First Isaiah, Amos and Hosea, further inferences regarding date cannot be substantiated from the genre of the book.

---

[80] See above, 19-21 and 109. Compare, for example, the positions of Kaufmann and Vink.

[81] Spoer, 172.

Conclusions Regarding Date

The foregoing analysis has demonstrated the weaknesses of many arguments that have been advanced concerning the date of the Book of Malachi. The book's references to Edom and to a governor fit a broad range of dates, and, despite claims to the contrary, Malachi bears no necessary connection to the Books of Ezra and Nehemiah. Hill's typological and lexical studies stress the book's commonalties with exilic works rather than conclusively indicating a post-exilic date.

In highlighting the problems inherent in many of these scholarly theories, this analysis also has shown that many elements of the Book of Malachi are consonant with an earlier date than is generally assumed. The book's historical referents, its linguistic characteristics, its usage of other literature, its genre and its reference to a Temple—as well as its diatribes against idolatry and insincere worship—are as consonant with the years immediately preceding the Exile as they are with the Persian period.

The presence of these elements does not, however, permit a precise dating of the Book of Malachi, for while many of the elements find parallels in exilic literature they appear in post-exilic literature as well. The reference to a governor fits any period from the Assyrian to the Hellenistic. If Edom was destroyed ca. 605-550, as argued above, then a reference to its destruction and hopes of rebuilding could reflect any time from 605 through the late sixth century. Typological and lexical studies not only underscore the continuity between Malachi and the Books of Jeremiah and Ezekiel but also point to commonalties between the language of the Book of Malachi and that of First and Second Zechariah.

MALACHI'S DESCRIPTION OF THE PRIESTHOOD COMPARED WITH OTHER LITERATURE

Previous discussion has argued that in describing the priesthood, the Book of Malachi remains independent of the ideology of the sources upon which it draws. For example, although the book demonstrates knowledge of P, it does not emulate P's precision with technical terminology or P's clear demarcation between priest and Levite.

Having considered various arguments for the date of the book and having suggested a broad range of dates for its composition, attention now turns to a comparison of Malachi's treatment of the priesthood with biblical and extra-biblical literature. While this analysis cannot treat adequately the problems raised in each work, it does endeavor to deal with such question as: in each work, what is the role of the priest understood to be? How does the work treat the terms "priest" and "son of Levi"? Does the text follow the technical cultic language of P? Does the work demonstrate a concern with earlier forms, traditions and biblical precedents? While this discussion does not seek to place books or ideas in a precise historical sequence, works will be considered in the chronological order in which they are commonly placed.

Deuteronomistic History (DH)

Although the Deuteronomistic History bears various references to Levites, its lack of precise language precludes a ready judgement of whether "Levites" (*hallĕwiyyîm*) are understood to be synonymous with or distinct from "priests" (*hakkōhănîm*). This problem is easily noted in DH's description of who carries (*nś᾿*) the ark. In 2 Sam. 15:24-29, the Levites (*hallĕwiyyîm*) carry the ark, but in 1 Kgs. 2:26 Abiathar, a priest, exercises this function. Particularly frustrating are two continuous verses in 1 Kings. In 8:3, the *kōhănîm* are reported as bearing the ark, but in 8:4 the priests *and* the Levites carry the ark and the holy vessels. Joshua 3:3 grants the same function to the Levitical priests (*hakkōhănîm hallĕwiyyîm*).

These references indicate the lack of precision with which the terms "priest" and "Levite" are used in DH. While some passages employ the common Deuteronomic phrase "Levitical priests" (e.g., Jos. 3:3)—implied to be identical with the "priests" (cf. Jos. 3:6)—other verses indicate a separation between priestly classes (1 Kgs. 8:4). Noteworthy in this regard is Jos. 18:7, in which Levites are described as having the priesthood (*khnt*) as their portion. Clearly, while DH may occasionally recognize the difference between priest and Levite, it does not recoil from describing a Levite as part of the priesthood.

Perhaps even more significant is that even in passages that recognize distinctions within the priesthood, DH stresses that priests must be from the "sons of Levi." Joshua 21:4, which clearly distinguishes the prerogatives of the sons of Aaron, yet describes them as "the sons of Aaron the priest, from (among) the Levites" (*libnê ᾿ahărōn hakkōhēn min-hallĕwiyyîm*). Joshua 21:10 also stresses the descent of the sons of Aaron from Levi: *libnê ᾿ahărōn mimmišpĕḥôt haqqĕhātî mibbĕnê lēwî*. Similarly, 1 Kgs. 12:31 criticizes Jeroboam for choosing priests who were not from the sons of Levi (*mibbĕnê lēwî*).

Unlike Malachi, DH does not stress the sacrificial role of the priest. The priest (and the Levite?) primarily carries the ark; others may sacrifice

(1 Sam. 6:15). DH does not use cultic terms technically as does P. For example, *minḥâ* in I Sam. 2:17 refers to general offerings rather than to a cereal offering.

In sum, DH devotes none of the same concern with priesthood that is expressed by the author of Malachi. DH neither treats Levi as a personal figure nor discusses the sacrificial duties of the priesthood. Like Malachi, however, DH demonstrates a looseness in its description of priests and Levites, and it does not make explicit its understanding of the relationship between the two.

Jeremiah and Ezekiel

Since Hill's lexical study suggested that Malachi's language is similar to that of Jeremiah and Ezekiel, a comparison of the way in which all treat the priesthood should prove instructive. The Book of Jeremiah, however, provides little information regarding the priesthood. Exclusive of chapter 33, which is treated below,[82] the Book of Jeremiah does not mention the terms "Levi" or "Levite," although it refers to "priests" (*kōhănîm*) and to various rankings within the priesthood (*ziqnê hakkōhănîm*—19:1; *pāqîd nāgîd bĕbêt ᵓădônay*—20:1; *kōhēn hārōᵓš*—52:24).

Ezekiel 40-48, on the other hand, devotes much attention to priestly matters. These chapters generally use cultic terms technically (e.g., 42:13, where *minḥâ* is a distinct category from *ḥattāᵓt* and *ᵓăšām*)—although Ezekiel does use some terms differently from P. These chapters do not treat Levi as a figure, but they do maintain that priests are descendents of Levi. Hence, while these chapters rail against "the Levites who went far from me," they nonetheless describe the proper Zadokite priests as sons of Levi: *hakkōhănîm hallĕwiyyîm bĕnê ṣādôk* (44:13; cf. also 43:19).

Miscellaneous Prophetic Writings

Jeremiah 33, Third Isaiah and Joel bear numerous affinities with the Book of Malachi. These works are here treated as "miscellaneous" because they are not easily dated.

JEREMIAH 33

Jeremiah 33 is considered separately from the rest of the Book of Jeremiah because many scholars date it later than the rest of the book. Glazier-McDonald notes that the passage is missing in Greek and sug-

---

82 See below, 135-136.

gests that it likely is contemporary with the Book of Malachi.[83] Bright shares this assessment.[84] Couturier argues for the lateness of the passage on the basis of its ideology. He maintains that the prominence of the Levitical priests and of David does not fit the age of Jeremiah but rather combats the same pessimism confronted by the post-exilic community.[85] The late date assigned to Jeremiah 33 is not without detractors, however. J. A. Thompson supports the authenticity of the passage, since its ideas fit Jeremiah's own thought.[86] Indeed, Couturier's statement that such of view of the priesthood fits only the post-exilic era rests solely on his opinion of what ideas were "appropriate" to the Jeremianic age and of the ethos of the restoration community.

Jeremiah 33:17-22 describes the priesthood in language similar to that found in Malachi, although Jeremiah uses the term *hallĕwiyyîm* while Malachi uses "sons of Levi" (*bĕnê-lēwî*). Levites are apparently considered as priests, since those called *hakkōhănîm hallĕwiyyîm* in 33:18 and 21 are called *hallĕwiyyîm* in 33:22. As in Malachi, Jer. 33:20-22 describes the deity's promise of a perpetual priesthood as a covenant (*bĕrît*).

Most striking, however, is the similarity between Malachi 2:12 and Jeremiah 33:18. The curse formula of Mal. 2:12 parallels closely the deity's promise in Jer. 33:18 to withhold the curse from the Levitical priests:

Mal. 2:12	Jer. 33:18
yakrêt ʾădōnay lāʾîš	*wĕlākkōhănîm hallĕwiyyîm lōʾ yikkārēt ʾîš*
mĕʾăhălê yaʿăqōb	*millĕpānāy*
ûmaggîš minḥâ	*ûmaqṭîr minḥâ*

In both passages, the priest is responsible for sacrifices, and the Levites are considered full priests.

THIRD ISAIAH

Arguments for the date of Isaiah 56-66 will not be considered here. Sufficient for our purposes is the recognition that these chapters exhibit a different character from the preceding portions of the Book of Isaiah.

---

[83] Glazier-McDonald, "Malachi," 121.

[84] John Bright, *Jeremiah*, Anchor Bible (Garden City, NY: Doubleday and Co, 1965), 298.

[85] Guy P. Couturier, "Jeremiah," in *Jerome Biblical Commentary*, ed. Raymond Brown and others (Englewood Cliffs, NJ: Prentice-Hall, Inc., 1968), 328.

[86] J. A. Thompson, *Jeremiah*, New International Commentary on the Old Testament (Grand Rapids: Wm. B. Eerdmanns, 1986), 598.

Third Isaiah describes Levites in much the same way as does Deuteronomy. Isa. 66:21 looks to a time when the LORD will take foreigners for "Levitical priests."[87] Isa. 56:6 may be a word play on the term "Lewi," for in it the deity promises to accept foreigners who "join themselves to the LORD" (*běnê hannēkār hannilwîm ʿal-ʾādônay*).

Although these chapters are similar to Deuteronomy in using the term "Levitical priests," they sometimes use cultic terms technically as does P. In 57:6, 66:3 and 66:20, *minḥâ* seems to be intended technically and is contrasted with other types of offerings.

Like Malachi, Third Isaiah marks a return to earlier traditions. Especially noteworthy is the figure of Moses in 63:11. As in Mal. 3, Moses is called the LORD's "servant," and the prophet reminds his listeners of the Mosaic age. Third Isaiah also recalls such figures as Abraham (63:16) and Jacob (58:14) and repeats the sinfulness of the fathers (Isa. 63:10; compare Mal. 3:7). These chapters, like Malachi, also hark back to earlier prophetic traditions. They twice repeat the opening of Isa. 40: "prepare ye the way" (57:14; 62:10).[88]

JOEL

The Book of Joel does not treat the priesthood in any extensive way as does the Book of Malachi. It makes no mention of "Levi" or "Levites." It does, however, mention "priests" (*hakkōhănîm*) and three times places *kōhănîm* in parallelism with "ministers" (*měšortê ʾādônay*, 1:9; *měšortê mizbēaḥ*, 1:13; and *měšortê ʾělōhāy*, 1:13). The book does use some of P's technical cultic terminology, distinguishing *minḥâ* from *nesek* in 1:9 and 1:13. Hence, while Joel does share other similarities with Malachi,[89] its description of the priesthood is little like that of Malachi.

Haggai and Zechariah 1-8; Zechariah 9-14

Although, like Joel, Haggai and First Zechariah make no mention of "Levi" or "Levites," these works do provide some indications of how their authors understood the priesthood. Both books refer to ranks within the priesthood, identifying Joshua as *hakkōhēn haggādōl* (Hag. 1:1;

---

87 RSV reads, with several manuscripts, "for priests *and* for Levites."

88 Hanson accounts for these similarities between Malachi and Third Isaiah by positing that the two corpora were written by social groups with common political and religious goals. Hanson's thesis regarding these and other books will be considered in the conclusion to this chapter.

89 For example, the use of the term "storehouses" (*ʾōṣārôt*) in 1:17 and the historical account in 2:18-19, comparable to the account in Mal. 3:16-18.

Zech. 3:1). Both also attribute to the priest the role of making rulings or discerning *tôrâ*. In Hag. 2:11ff., the priests answer a question regarding impurity and in Zech. 7:1ff. the people of Bethel inquire of the priests regarding festal observances.[90] Neither book employs technical cultic terminology.

Second Zechariah does refer to "Levi." In 12:12-13, the LORD speaks of a time when the land will mourn. This mourning shall be carried out by families: the family of the house of David, the family of the house of Nathan, the family of the house of Levi, and the family of Shimeites. While the passage provides no explanation for these groupings, it appears obvious that "the house of Levi" serves as a broad designation for all of the priesthood (and not just the lower clergy).

Ezra and Nehemiah

Unlike Malachi, the Books of Ezra and Nehemiah clearly distinguish between priests and Levites. Priests are traced through a different genealogy than are Levites, and the two are assigned different functions. The genealogy of the priests is traced to Aaron (Ezra 7:2-4, Neh. 10:39), and the priests are often called "sons of Aaron" (Neh. 12:47). Other ranks within the priesthood are recognized as well: *hakkōhēn hārō'š* (Ezra 7:5); *śārê hakkōhănîm* (Ezra 10:5); and *hakkōhēn haggādōl* (Neh. 3:1).

The Books of Ezra and Nehemiah do not attempt to describe their own situations in terms of earlier forms and types. They do, however, recognize the authority of earlier traditions, and Ezra 6:18 records that the priests and the Levites are assigned their respective duties according to what is written in the Book of Moses.

Chronicles

The work of Sara Japhet and others has provided various arguments for considering Chronicles as a separate work from Ezra and Nehemiah.[91] The manner in which these two corpora treat the priesthood also suggests that they are discrete works.

Although Chronicles clearly distinguishes between priests and Levites, granting them different genealogies and functions, its language is often imprecise, much like that of Deuteronomy. For example, in 2

---

90 For a consideration of this function of the priest in the context of Hag. 2:11ff. see E. M. Meyers, "The Use of *tôrâ*," 69-76; for Zech. 7:3, see Meyers and Meyers, *Haggai, Zechariah 1-8*, 384-387.

91 Sara Japhet, "The Supposed Common Authorship of Ezra-Nehemiah Investigated Anew," *VT* 18 (1968): 330-371.

Chron. 29:4 Hezekiah gathers both the priests and the Levites but then addresses them as "Levites" (*hallĕwiyyîm*, 29:15). Following this address, not only do the Levites act (29:12) but so too do the priests (29:16). Similarly, in 1 Chr. 15:14, both priests and Levites sanctify themselves to bring up the ark, but the Levites alone carry it (15:15).

In describing the Levites, the Chronicler uses several different terms. Levites are designated not only as *hallĕwiyyîm* (as they are most frequently called elsewhere) but also as *bĕnê-lēwî*. This reference to the Levites as *bĕnê-lēwî* is significant, because the Chronicler apparently also describes the priests as "the sons of Levi." Such a usage is implied in 1 Chron. 24:20, where, after the priests are listed, the *"rest* of the Levites" (*bĕnê-lēwî*) are recorded. This treatment of the priest as a "son of Levi" in a corpus in which priest and Levite are separated is striking, even when Chronicles' partiality toward the Levites is taken into consideration.

Old Testament Pseudepigrapha

No attempt is made here to treat the Pseudepigrapha comprehensively. Rather, a few significant texts will be considered: the Testament of the Twelve Patriarchs, Jubilees, and Third Enoch (the Hebrew Apocalypse of Enoch).[92]

In keeping with the character of the genre of "testament," Levi is treated as a distinct figure throughout the Testament of the Twelve Patriarchs. This corpus, usually dated to the second century B.C.E., treats Levi not only the ancestor of the priesthood but also as its epitome. The Testaments of Simeon, Judah and Issachar frequently remind their readers that while the kingship belongs to Judah, Levi retains the priesthood.

The Testament of Reuben describes the duty of Levi: he knows *tôrâ* and he blesses Israel. The Testament of Levi, in which this figure is central, also indicates that Levi has been granted the blessing of the priesthood (5:2).[93]

The Book of Jubilees, also usually dated ca. the second century B.C.E., likewise makes of Levi a personal character. As in the Testaments of the Twelve Patriarchs, this Levi is endowed with the priesthood, and the right of the priesthood is given to his sons after him (ch. 32).

---

[92] Unless otherwise noted, texts are read from *The Old Testament Pseudepigrapha*, ed. James H. Charlesworth, 2 vols. (Garden City, NY: Doubleday & Co., Inc., 1983).

[93] Interestingly, however, Levi's posterity is divided into three branches: while the first will be great and the second priestly, the new priesthood will arise from Judah (8:1lf.).

Although the Hebrew Apocalypse of Enoch (Third Enoch) is dated by P. Alexander to the fifth to sixth centuries C.E., Alexander recognizes that the book "...contains some very old traditions and stands in direct line with developments that had already begun in the Maccabean era ...."[94] In this work, priesthood is associated not with Levi but with Aaron (1:3). Metatron, however, legitimizes R. Ishmael by explaining that Ishmael is:

> of the tribe of Levi, which presents the offering to his name. He is of the family of Aaron, whom the Holy One blessed be he, chose to minister in his presence and on whose head he himself placed the priestly crown on Sinai (2:3).

Noteworthy is the fact that, although priesthood is connected with Aaron, descent through Levi is highlighted.

Qumran

As seen in various documents, the Qumran community distinguished between priests and Levites. Although, as Vermes notes, the duties of these groups are not specifically outlined,[95] numerous passages indicate that the two were separate. For example, the Community Rule records that in the covenant ceremony, "the priests shall enter first . . .; then the Levites; and thirdly, all the people one after another."[96] In the ceremony, priests pronounce blessings on the congregation, and the Levites invoke curses against evil ones.[97] Both, however, join in pronouncing the final curses.[98]

Throughout documents associated with Qumran, priests are usually designated as "sons of Zadok." In the Damascus Rule III-IV, the title is explained as deriving from Ezekiel's description; later, reference is made to Zadok himself (V). Occasional references are also made to the "sons of Aaron." While no text clearly outlines the membership of these groups,

---

94 P. Alexander, "3 (Hebrew Apocalypse of) Enoch," in *Old Testament Pseudedigrapha*, ed. James Charlesworth (Garden City, NY: Doubleday and Co., 1983), I: 229.

95 Geza Vermes, *The Dead Sea Scrolls in English*, 2d ed. (NY, NY: Penguin Books, 1975), 24.

96 Column 5. As found in Vermes, 74. Unless otherwise noted, translations are from Vermes.

97 Vermes, 73.

98 Ibid., 73-74.

the terms "sons of Zadok" and "sons of Aaron" appear to be used interchangeably.[99]

Conclusions Regarding Context

The foregoing overview, however cursory, has outlined some similarities between the Book of Malachi and other biblical and extra-biblical texts. Although Malachi exhibits some unique features, the manner in which it characterizes the priesthood is not anomalous.

While the developmental scheme of the priesthood proposed by the Documentary Hypothesis posits extreme tension between priestly groups in the exilic and post-exilic periods, such tension is not always evident in biblical literature. On the contrary, terms for priestly groups often are used loosely, with the result that the terms "priest" and "Levite" often overlap or blur. This lack of clarity in describing priestly groups characterizes not only such works as the Deuteronomistic History, which may endeavor to establish the equality of these groups, but also such works as Chronicles in which the groups are clearly distinguished.

In the various corpora of literature the priesthood is associated with Levi. Although some works may use other designations for the priests such as "sons of Aaron," Levi retains his connection with the priesthood. The prominence of Levi is attested by Ezekiel's phrase "the Levitical priests, the sons of Zadok," by Second Zechariah's treatment of the "house of Levi," and by Third Enoch's mention of Aaron's descent from Levi. Malachi's description of the priests as "sons of Levi," then, accords well with exilic and post-exilic understandings of priestly genealogy even if other designations (such as "sons of Aaron") were more commonly used.

In dealing with the priests as "sons of Levi," Malachi personifies Levi as an ideal priest. This treatment of Levi as a personal figure finds its only real parallel in the Pseudepigraphical literature. In the Testaments of the Twelve Patriarchs and in Jubilees, Levi likewise is characterized as an individual with whom the priesthood began. The Pseudepigraphical

---

[99] Such is the position of Michael A. Knibb, *The Qumran Community* (Cambridge: Cambridge University Press, 1987), 105. A similar view is taken in Emil Schürer, *The History of the Jewish People in the Age of Jesus Christ* (175 B. C.—A.D. 135), rev. and ed. Geza Vermes, Fergus Millar, Matthew Black (Edinburgh: T & T Clark, 1979), II: 253. A different position is taken by J. Liver, "'The Sons of Zadok the Priests' in the Dead Sea Sect," *Revue de Qumran* 6 (1967/68): 14-15. Liver maintains that the "sons of Zadok" are the high priestly family, while the "sons of Aaron" are other priests.

literature, however, places greater emphasis on the eschatological roles of Levi and his partner Judah,[100] and attributes even greater honor to Levi than does the Book of Malachi. Hence, while the Book of Malachi is unique among prophetic and biblical literature in treating Levi as an individual and in using the distinctive language of the grant-type treaty in describing this ideal priest, the characterization of Levi in later literature may be seen as a further development of this type of description.

In conclusion, the Book of Malachi stands broadly within the stream of exilic and post-exilic biblical literature in its description of the priesthood. Its characterization of the priests as the "sons of Levi" accords with the genealogy of the priesthood presented by other literature and need not be construed as specifically Deuteronomic or as deliberately contrasted with the present ruling priesthood. The return to earlier traditions and forms exhibited by the Book of Malachi finds parallels in Second Zechariah, Third Isaiah and other literature.[101] The Book of Malachi, however, provides its own unique description of the priesthood, and its personification of Levi in chapter 2 stands alone in the biblical literature.

---

100 H. C. Kee, "The Testaments of the Twelve Patriarchs," in *Old Testament Pseudepigrapha*, ed. Charlesworth, I: 779.

101 Hanson's thesis that the similarities between Malachi, Third Isaiah and Second Zechariah are due to the common political and religious goals of the communities that produced this literature fails to account for the fact that other literature shares many of these characteristics.

CHAPTER VI

CONCLUSIONS AND IMPLICATIONS

In their attempts to correlate the Book of Malachi's description of the priesthood with the developmental scheme of priesthood advanced by the Documentary Hypothesis, scholars have produced several different theories. Most argue that by calling priests "sons of Levi" and by drawing heavily on Deuteronomic language, the Book of Malachi demonstrates its dependence on Deuteronomy and its ignorance of the Priestly Code. Other theories have portrayed the book as revealing the transition between D and P; as displaying hostility between rival claimants to the priesthood; and as utilizing language distinctive to the post-exilic period.

The goal of this dissertation has been to evaluate these diverse claims and theories concerning the priesthood as described in the Book of Malachi. In so doing, it has reached numerous conclusions regarding the book's language and genre, the sources it may be seen to utilize and the relationship between its characterization of the priesthood and the descriptions found in other literature. The most important of these conclusions will be summarized here, and some implications of these findings will be considered.

CONCLUSIONS

In evaluating the many scholarly theories regarding the view of the priesthood presented by the Book of Malachi, this study has argued that two issues, usually joined together, must in fact be treated separately: the contextual relationship between the terms "priest," "Levi," and "sons of Levi" as inferred from the book; and the evidence for the book's use of sources. For example, while Rivkin has maintained that since the book equates "priests" and "sons of Levi" its author therefore cannot have known the Priestly Code, one cannot in fact assume *a priori* a causal link between these two issues. This study, indeed, has concluded that the

Book of Malachi simultaneously treats the terms "priests" and "sons of Levi" synonymously and demonstrates a familiarity with the Priestly Code.

A study of the book's description of *kōhēn*, *lēwî* and *běnê-lēwî* has revealed that the terms are treated as equivalent in the book. Contrary to the position of Hanson, the book demonstrates no evidence of acrimony between the groups described by these terms. All of these groups are described as exercising the same functions, those of sacrifice and of teaching. The canonical context of these terms cannot prove that these groups actually were identical in the author's own historical setting, and yet the author's treatment of *kōhēn*, *lēwî* and *běnê-lēwî* does cast doubt on any theory that posits bitter tension between them.

An analysis of Malachi's dependency or familiarity with other biblical texts has revealed the broad range of sources with which its author is familiar. Among Pentateuchal sources, the book demonstrates knowledge not only of Deuteronomy but also of the Priestly Code. While it does not follow P's use of "sons of Aaron," the book reflects much of the language and ideology of P. The author draws freely from P and yet remains independent of its politics.

Source analysis also has indicated that although Malachi clearly borrows from Deuteronomy—as most scholars recognize—the book's "Deuteronomic"character has often been exaggerated. Much of the language usually deemed "Deuteronomic" in Malachi is in fact characteristic of the covenant language used throughout biblical and extra–biblical literature. Covenant language is especially prominent in Malachi because, as argued above, the book takes the form of an adapted covenant lawsuit or *rîb*. Employing common prophetic accusations against covenant violation and patterning the book after the structure of the *rîb*, the author describes the contemporary failings of the priests in terms of an ancient prophetic model.

The recognition that the Book of Malachi takes the form of an adapted *rîb* is significant for understanding the book as a whole. Such a recognition, on the one hand, facilitates the interpretation of various passages. For example, while Mal. 2:10-16 is usually explained as a denunciation of divorce, it in fact draws from the classical prophetic repertoire of language for combatting idolatry. As argued above, this oracle unit accuses the people of worshipping other deities; it does not concern intermarriage.

The recognition of the *rîb* form in the Book of Malachi has the additional merit of underscoring the author's thorough familiarity with a broad range of Israel's historical and prophetic traditions. In modifying the lawsuit genre to characterize contemporary problems, the author not only reveals a knowledge of the type of lawsuits found in the Deuteronomistic History and in the prophetic works of Isaiah and Jeremiah, but also a desire to place this message within the the the stream of prophetic tradition.

The book also bears other indications that its author sought to establish biblical precedent for his or her message. The promise to send Elijah (3:23) and the reminder of the "law of Moses my servant"(3:22) fit with this tendency. Although these latter passages are often treated as secondary additions to the book, they in fact are consonant with the book's attention to earlier figures.

The description of Levi in 2:4-7 is a prime example of the author's return to earlier figures. The exalted language with which Levi is described parallels closely the language used to describe the recipient of a grant-type treaty—language elsewhere in the Hebrew Bible reserved for such great figures as Abraham and David. Although Levi is also treated as a personal figure in Deut. 33, nowhere else in Scripture is he treated with such honor as in Mal. 2. This attention to ancient figures and the personification of Levi persist beyond Malachi into the pseudepigraphical literature.

IMPLICATIONS

The conclusions highlighted above, as well as the study from which they are derived, indicate that the description of the priesthood presented in the Book of Malachi cannot be readily placed within a developmental scheme of the priesthood. The book does not exhibit a simple Deuteronomic (and hence pre-Priestly) understanding, as Rivkin maintains, or even a viewpoint that can be identified as midway between D and P, as Wellhausen suggests. Neither does the book reveal the sociopolitical struggle between priest and Levite perceived by Hanson.

The Book of Malachi instead characterizes the priesthood according to its own agenda and in its own terms. In an effort to place this message within the biblical tradition, the author describes the priests as descendents of the ancient and exalted figure Levi. Hence, while Hanson's position is based on the assumption that the term "sons of Levi" refers to a distinct social group, the identity of which remained essentially the same over a period of centuries, the author in fact uses "sons of Levi" to characterize the current priesthood in the terms of an earlier period.

Many of the theories regarding the Book of Malachi have assumed that all biblical works employ terms precisely and uniformly; for example, if the author of a prophetic book knew the Priestly Code, he or she then would call priests "sons of Aaron." The results of this study have challenged such an assumption and have suggested that a work such as Malachi can both borrow from P and use language for priests that differs from that of P. Later works may borrow from sources without following those sources in all details. Each work addresses its own concerns and utilizes its sources according to its own needs.

Malachi's representation of priests as "sons of Levi" reflects a different socio-political situation than do the sources from which it draws. While Deuteronomy takes great effort to establish that all "sons of Levi" may serve as priests if they come to the central sanctuary, Malachi readily assumes that "sons of Levi" may serve as priests. While the Priestly Code devotes much energy to distinguishing between the "sons of Aaron" and the Levites, Malachi exhibits no reluctance to call priests "sons of Levi." The book, quite clearly, endeavors not to differentiate ranks within the clergy but to highlight the corruption of the priests and the people.

The fact that biblical works utilize language according to their specific goals underscores the difficulty in uncritically tracing a development of the priesthood through the entire Hebrew Bible. Pentateuchal sources may indeed be separated on the basis of their designations for the priesthood, but such a criterion cannot be directly applied to other literature. Hence, while D's reference to priests as "sons of Levi" may indicate a certain stage in Pentateuchal and priestly development, Malachi's reference to priests as "sons of Levi" may not reflect the same situation as Deuteronomy. As indicated in a consideration of Malachi and of other biblical and extra-biblical texts, many non-Pentateuchal works use terms for the priesthood less precisely than do Pentateuchal sources.

Not only do the conclusions of this study bear implications for interpreting the relationship between "priests" and "sons of Levi," but also they offer some suggestions regarding the status of the biblical canon at the time of the composition of the Book of Malachi. As argued above, the book demonstrates a broad knowledge of Israel's Pentateuchal, historical and prophetic traditions. The author not only appears familiar with D and P but also seems to have access to these sources in some type of integrated form. The author's adaptation and modification of these sources further indicates that he or she likely lived some time after the completion of these works.

The book offers no means by which to discern the precise shape of the canon known to its author. This study, however, has suggested that the book may be dated any time between 605 and 500 B.C.E. and hence the possibility arises that much of the canon was taking near-final shape during this period. By the time of Malachi's composition, the Pentateuch may have been complete and many of the historical and prophetic writings may have been accessible.[1] The author's use of the literary style of the *rîb* may further indicate that he or she used these historical and prophetic writings in written form.

Finally, this study also bears upon the understanding of the status of the priesthood in the period ca. 600-500. The attention that the Book of Malachi devotes to the priesthood stands without precedent in biblical literature. Nowhere else does the priesthood receive such extended or scathing beratings: the priests will, indeed, have dung spread upon their faces. Conversely, nowhere else is such exalted language used for the priest. Levi, the priests' ancestor, is characterized as an exemplary servant, and the lips of the priest are said to guard knowledge. In 2:7, the priest is described as the *malʾāk* of the LORD of hosts—a term usually applied to the prophet. The author here grants to the priest an exalted classical role, and the priest assumes the role of the prophet in communicating the divine will.[2]

In its description of the priesthood, the Book of Malachi frequently refers to the dual role of the priest: the priest is responsible not only for proper sacrifice but also for proper teaching. Most scholars have maintained that while priests in Israel's early history were primarily responsible for consulting oracles and giving rulings, over time priests became increasingly responsible for sacrifice.[3] Although Malachi devotes most of its accusations against the priests to lambasting their inappropriate sacrifices, the book clearly stresses the priest's teaching responsibilities.

Although the Book of Malachi cannot be effectively utilized in evaluating the developmental scheme of priesthood outlined by the Documentary Hypothesis, it does demonstrate inordinate concern with

---

[1] David Noel Freedman contends that during the Exile (ca. 550) Jehozadak put together a collection of the Pentateuch and Former Prophets ("Canon," 132). Meyers and Meyers concur with this assessment (*Haggai, Zechariah 1-8*, 16).

[2] E. Meyers considers the increasing prominence of the priesthood as a hallmark of late prophecy and of the post-exilic period ("The Use of *tôra*").

[3] This position is, for example, taken by Weaver (66).

the priesthood, its failings and its ideal. Despite its stern accusations against sinful priests, Malachi urges the purification and not the abolition of the priesthood. The priests are corrupt and must be radically purged, but the priesthood remains an ordained channel for the deity's communication with His people.

WORKS CITED

Abba, R. "Priests and Levites." In *Interpreter's Dictionary of the Bible*, ed. George Buttrick, 876-889. Nashville: Abingdon, 1962.

Aberbach, Moses and Leivy Smolar. "Aaron, Jeroboam, and the Golden Calves," *Journal of Biblical Literature* 86 (1967): 129-140.

Achtemeier, Elizabeth. *Nahum-Malachi*. Interpretation Series. Atlanta: John Knox Press, 1986.

Ackroyd, Peter. *Exile and Restoration: A Study of Hebrew Thought of the Sixth Century B.C.* Old Testament Library. Philadelphia: Westminster, 1975.

Alexander, P. "3 (Hebrew Apocalypse of) Enoch." In *The Old Testament Pseudepigrapha*, ed. James Charlesworth, I: 223-254. Garden City, NY: Doubleday and Co., 1983.

Baldwin, Joyce. *Haggai, Zechariah, Malachi*. Tyndale Old Testament Commentaries. Downers Grove, IL: Intervarsity Press, 1972.

Bartlett, J. R. "From Edomites to Nabateans: A Study in Continuity," *Palestine Exploration Quarterly* 111 (1979): 53-66.

_____. "The Rise and Fall of the Kingdom of Edom," *Palestine Exploration Quarterly* 104 (1972): 26-37.

_____. "Zadok and His Successors at Jerusalem," *Journal of Theological Studies* n. s. 19 (1968): 1-18.

Baudissin, Wolf. "Priests and Levites." In *Hasting's Dictionary of the Bible*, ed. James Hastings, vol. IV, 67-97. New York: Charles Scribners' Sons, 1902.

Bennett, Crystal. "Excavations at Buseirah (Biblical Bozrah)." In *Midian, Moab and Edom: The History and Archaeology of the Late Bronze Age and Iron Age Jordan and Northwest Arabia*, ed. John Sawyer and David Clines. Journal for the Study of the Old Testament, Supplement Series 24, 9-17. Sheffield: Sheffield Academic Press, 1983.

Blenkinsopp, Joseph. *A History of Prophecy in Israel.* Philadelphia: Westminster, 1983.

_____. *Prophecy and Canon: A Contribution to the Study of Jewish Origins.* Notre Dame, Ind.: University of Notre Dame Press, 1977.

Boecker, Hans Jochen. "Bermerkungen zur formsgeschichtlichen Terminologie des Buches Malachi," *Zeitschrift für die alttestamentliche Wissenschaft* 78 (1966): 78-80.

Bright, John. *A History of Israel,* 3rd ed. Philadelphia: Westminster Press, 1981.

_____. *Jeremiah.* Anchor Bible Series. Garden City, New York: Doubleday and Co., 1965.

Brown, Francis, S. R. Driver and Charles Briggs. *A Hebrew and English Lexicon of the Old Testament.* Oxford: Clarendon Press, 1979.

Buber, Martin. "Priest." In *The Jewish Encylopedia,* ed. Isidore Singer and others, vol. 10, 192-197. New York: Funk and Wagnalls, 1905.

Bulmerincq, A. von. *Der Prophet Maleachi.* Vol. II. Tartu: J. G. Krüger, 1932.

Buss, Martin. "The Study of Forms." In *Old Testament Form Criticism,* ed. John H. Hayes, 1-56. San Antonio: Trinity University Press, 1977.

Cassuto, Umberto. *The Documentary Hypothesis.* Translated by Israel Abrahams. Jerusalem: Magnes Press, 1983.

Charlesworth, James, ed. *The Old Testament Pseudepigrapha.* 2 vols. Garden City, New York: Doubleday and Co., 1983.

Chary, Théophane. *Aggée, Zacharie, Malachie.* Paris: Gabalda, 1967.

_____. *Les prophètes et le culte à partir de l'exil.* Tournai: Desclée and Co., 1955.

Cheyne, T. "Malachi and the Nabateans," *Zeitschrift für die alttestamentliche Wissenschaft* 14 (1894): 142.

Childs, Brevard. "The Canonical Shape of the Prophetic Literature," *Interpretation* 32 (1978): 51-52.

_____. *Introduction to the Old Testament as Scripture.* Philadelphia: Fortress Press, 1979.

Cody, Aelred. *A History of the Old Testament Priesthood*. Rome: Pontifical Biblical Institute, 1969.

_____. "An Excursus on the Priesthood in Israel." In *Ezekiel*. The Old Testament Message: A Biblical-Theological Commentary, 256-263. Wilmington, Del: Michael Glazier, Inc., 1984.

Coggins, R. J. *Haggai, Zechariah, Malachi*. Old Testament Guides. Sheffield, England: Journal for the Study of the Old Testament Press, 1977.

Couturier, Guy P. "Jeremiah." In *Jerome Biblical Commentary*, ed. Raymond Brown and others, 301-336. Englewood Cliffs, NJ: Prentice-Hall, Inc., 1968.

Cresson, Bruce. "The Condemnation of Edom in Post-Exilic Judaism." In *The Use of the Old Testament in the New and Other Essays. Studies in Honor of William Franklin Stinespring*, ed. James Efird, 125-148. Durham, NC: Duke University Press, 1972.

Cross, Frank Moore. *Canaanite Myth and Hebrew Epic*. Cambridge: Harvard University Press, 1973.

Cross, Frank M. and D. N. Freedman. "The Blessing of Moses," *Journal of Biblical Literature* 67 (1948): 191-210.

Curtiss, Samuel Ives. *The Levitical Priests: A Contribution to the Criticism of the Pentateuch*. Preface by F. Delitzsch. Edinburgh: T & T Clark, 1877.

Day, John. "Pre-Deuteronomic Allusions to the Covenant in Hosea and Psalm LXXVIII," *Vetus Testamentum* 36 (1986): 1-12.

Donner, H. and W. Röllig. *Kanaanäische und aramäische Inschriften*. 3 vols. Weisbaden: Otto Harrassowitz, 1966-1969.

Driver, G. R. "Confused Hebrew Roots." In *Occident and Orient: Gaster Anniversary Volume*, ed. Bruno Schindler, 73-83. London: Taylor's, 1936.

_____. "Malachi," *Journal of Theological Studies* 39 (1938): 399. Quoted in Ralph Smith, *Micah-Malachi*. Word Biblical Commentary. Waco, TX; Word Books, 1982.

Dumbrell, W. J. "Malachi and the Ezra-Nehemiah Reforms," *Reformed Theological Review* 35 (1976): 42-52.

Eissfeldt, Otto. *The Old Testament: An Introduction*. Translated by Peter R. Ackroyd. New York: Harper and Row, 1965.

Elat, Moshe. "The Political Status of the Kingdom of Judah within the Assyrian Empire in the Seventh Century B.C.E." In *Investigations at Lachish: The Sanctuary and the Residency*, ed. Yohanan Aharoni, 61-70. Tel Aviv: Tel Aviv Institute of Archaeology, 1975.

Emerton, J. A. "Priests and Levites in Deuteronomy," *Vetus Testamentum* 12 (1962): 129-138.

Fensham, F. Charles. "Father and Son as Terminology for Treaty and Covenant." In *Near Eastern Studies in Honor of W. F. Albright*, ed. Hans Goedicke, 121-25. Baltimore: Johns Hopkins Press, 1971.

_____. "Malediction and Benediction in Ancient Near Eastern Vassal–Treaties and the Old Testament," *Zeitschrift für die alttestamentliche Wissenschaft* 74 (1962): 1-9.

Fischer, James A. "Notes on the Literary Form and Message of Malachi," *Catholic Biblical Quarterly* 34 (1972): 315-320.

Fishbane, Michael. *Biblical Interpretation in Ancient Israel*. Oxford: Clarendon Press, 1985.

France, R. T. *Jesus and the Old Testament: His Application of Old Testament Passages to Himself and His Mission*, reprint edition. Grand Rapids, MI: Baker Book House, 1982. Quoted in Pieter Verhoef, *Haggai and Malachi*. New International Commentary on the Old Testament, 289, n. 12. Grand Rapids, Mich.: Wm. B. Eerdmanns, 1987.

Freedman, D. N. "Canon of the OT." In *Interpreter's Dictionary of the Bible*, Supplementary Volume, ed. Keith Crimm and others, 130-136. Nashville: Abingdon, 1976.

_____. "The Earliest Bible," *Michigan Quarterly Review* 22 (1983): 167-175.

Gemser, B. "The *Rîb*—or Controversy—Pattern in Hebrew Mentality," *Vetus Testamentum, Supplements* 3 (1955): 120-137.

Gesenius, William, E. Kautzsch and A. E. Cowley. *Gesenius' Hebrew Grammar*, ed. and enlarged by E. Kautzsch. 2d English ed. by A. E. Cowley. Oxford: Clarendon Press, 1910.

Ginsberg, H. L. "An Aramaic Contemporary of the Lachish Letters," *Bulletin of the American Schools of Oriental Research* 111 (1948): 24-27.

Glazier-McDonald, Beth. "Malachi 2:12: ʿēr wěʿōneh—Another Look," *Journal of Biblical Literature* 105 (1986): 295-298.

_____. "Malachi: The Divine Messenger, A Critical Appraisal." Ph. D. diss., University of Chicago, 1983.

Gottwald, Norman K. *The Hebrew Bible: A Socio-Literary Introduction.* Philadelphia: Fortress Press, 1985.

Graffy, Adrian. *The Prophet Confronts His People.* Analecta Biblica, 104. Rome: Pontifical Biblical Institute, 1984.

Grätz, H. "Die Anfänge der Nabataërherrschaft," *Monatsschrift für Wissenschaft und Geschichte des Judentums* 24 (1875): 49-67.

Gray, George B. *Sacrifice in the Old Testament: Its Theory and Practice.* Oxford: The Clarendon Press, 1925.

Greenberg, Moshe. "A New Approach to the History of the Israelite Priesthood," *Journal of the American Oriental Society* 70 (1950): 41-47.

Gruber, Mayer. "The Many Faces of Hebrew nśʾ pnym 'lift up the face,'" *Zeitschrift für die alttestamentliche Wissenschaft* 95 (1983): 252-260.

Gunkel, Hermann. *What Remains of the Old Testament.* New York: Macmillan Co., 1928.

Gunneweg, A. H. J. *Leviten und Priester.* Göttingen: Vandenhoeck and Ruprecht, 1965.

Gurney, O. R. "Mita of Paḫḫuwa," *Annals of Archaeology and Anthropology* 28 (1948): 32-47.

Guthrie, H. H., Jr. "Tithe." In *Interpreter's Dictionary of the Bible,* ed. George Buttrick and others. Vol. R-Z, 654-655. Nashville: Abingdon, 1962.

Hanson, Paul. "Biblical Apocalypticism: The Theological Dimension," *Horizons in Biblical Theology* 7:2 (1985): 1-20.

_____. *The Dawn of Apocalyptic: The Historical and Sociological Roots of Jewish Apocalyptic Eschatology.* Revised Edition. Philadelphia: Fortress Press, 1979.

_____. *The People Called: The Growth of Community in the Bible.* San Francisco: Harper & Row Publishers, 1986.

Haran, Menahem. "Behind the Scenes of History: Determining the Date of the Priestly Source," *Journal of Biblical Literature* 11/3 (1981): 321-333.

_____. "The Character of the Priestly Source--Utopian and Exclusive Features." In *Eighth World Congress of Jewish Studies, Proceedings*, 131-138. Jerusalem: World Union of Jewish Studies, 1983.

_____. "Priests and Priesthood." In *Encyclopaedia Judaica*, vol. 13, 1069-1086. Jerusalem: Keter Publishing House, 1971.

_____. "Shiloh and Jerusalem: The Origin of the Priestly Tradition in the Pentateuch," *Journal of Biblical Literature* 81 (1962): 14-24.

_____. *Temples and Temple Service in Ancient Israel: An Inquiry into the Character of Cult Phenomena and the Historical Setting of the Priestly School*. Oxford: Clarendon Press, 1978.

Harvey, Julien. *Le plaidoyer prophétique contre Israël après la rupture de l'alliance. Etude d'une formule littéraire de l'Ancien Testament*. Scholasticat de l'Immaculée Conception. Paris: Desclée de Brouwer, 1967.

Hauer, Christian E., Jr. "Who was Zadok?" *Journal of Biblical Literature* 82 (1963): 89-94.

Hayes, John H. and J. Maxwell Miller, eds. *Israelite and Judaean History*. Old Testament Library. Philadelphia: Westminster Press, 1977.

Hill, Andrew Elmer. "The Book of Malachi: Its Place in Post-Exilic Chronology Linguistically Considered." Ph. D. diss., University of Michigan, 1981.

_____. "Dating the Book of Malachi: A Linguistic Reexamination." In *And the Word of the Lord Shall Go Forth: Essays in Honor of David Noel Freedman in Celebration of His Sixtieth Birthday*, ed. Carol L. Meyers and M. O'Connor. American Schools of Oriental Research Special Volume Series, 77-89. Winona Lake: Eisenbrauns and ASOR, 1983.

Hillers, D. R. *Treaty Curses and the Old Testament Prophets*. Biblica et Orientalia, no. 16. Rome: Pontificial Biblical Institute, 1964.

Hoglund, Kenneth. "Achamenid Imperial Administration in Syria-Palestine and the Missions of Ezra and Nehemiah." Ph. D. diss., Duke University, 1989.

_____. "We are in Great Distress: Reconstructing the Social Context of Ezra-Nehemiah." Paper presented to Chronicles, Ezra-Nehemiah Consultation, Society of Biblical Literature Annual Meeting, Atlanta, GA, November 23, 1986.

Holladay, John S. "Assyrian Statescraft and the Prophets of Israel," *Harvard Theological Review* 63 (1970): 29-51.

Holtzmann, O. "Der Prophet Maleachi und der Ursprung des Pharisaërtums," *Archiv für Religionswissenschaft* 29 (1931): 1-21.

Hoonacker, Albin van. *Les douze petits prophètes.* Paris: Lefebvre, 1906.

Hoppe, Leslie J. "The Origins of Deuteronomy." Ph. D. diss., Northwestern University, 1978.

Horst, F. *Die zwölf Kleinen Propheten.* Handbuch zum Alten Testament, 14, 2. Tübingen: Mohr/Siebeck, 1938. Quoted in T. Chary, *Les prophètes et le culte à partir de l'exil* Bibliothtèque de Théologie, Series III, 259-260. Tournai: Desclée and Co., 1955.

Huffmon, Herbert. "The Covenant Lawsuit in the Prophets," *Journal of Biblical Literature* 78 (1959): 285-295.

Hurvitz, Avi. "The Evidence of Language in Dating the P Code," *Revue biblique* 81 (1974): 24-56.

_____. "The Language of the Priestly Code and its Historical Setting—The Case for An Early Date." In *Eighth World Congress of Jewish Studies, Proceedings,* 83-93. Jerusalem: World Union of Jewish Studies, 1983.

Hvidberg, F. F. *Weeping and Laughter in the Old Testament.* Leiden: E. J. Brill, 1962.

Isaakson, A. *Marriage and Ministry in the New Temple.* Acta Seminarii Neotestamentici Upsaliensis, 24. Lund: Gleerup, 1965.

Jagersma, H. "The Tithes in the Old Testament." In *Remembering all the Way....* Oudtestamentische Studiën, no. 21, ed. B. Albrektson and others, 116-128. Leiden: E. J. Brill, 1981.

Japhet, Sara. "The Supposed Common Authorship of Chronicles and Ezra-Nehemiah Investigated Anew," *Vetus Testamentum* 18 (1968): 330-371.

Jastrow, Marcus. *A Dictionary of the Targumim, the Talmud Babli and Yerushalmi, and the Midrashic Literature.* New York: P. Shalom, 1967.

Jaubert, A. *La notion de l'alliance dans le Judaïsme aux abords de l'ère chrétienne* Patristica sorbonensia, 6. Paris: Seuil, 1963.

Jean, Charles-F. and Jacob Hoftizer. *Dictionnaire des inscriptions sémitiques de l'ouest.* Leiden: E. J. Brill, 1965.

Jeffrey, Arthur. "The Canon of the Old Testament." In *Interpreter's Bible,* ed. George Buttrick and others, I, 32-45. Nashville: Abingdon, 1952.

Judge, H. G. "Aaron, Zadok, and Abiathar," *Journal of Theological Studies,* n.s. 7 (1956): 70-74.

Kalluveettil, Paul. *Declaration and Covenant.* Analecta Biblica, 88. Rome: Pontifical Biblical Institute, 1982.

Kapelrud, Arvid S. "The Prophets and the Covenant." In *In the Shelter of Elyon: Essays on Ancient Palestinian Life and Literature in Honor of G. W. Ahlström,* ed. W. Boyd Barrick and John R. Spencer. Journal for the Study of the Old Testament, Supplement Series, 31, 175-183. Sheffield: Sheffield Academic Press, University of Sheffield, 1984.

Kaufmann, Ezekiel. *A History of the Israelite Religion: From Antiquity to the End of the Second Temple.* Tel Aviv: Dvir, 1937-1948. Quoted in Moshe Greenberg, "A New Approach to the History of the Israelite Priesthood," JAOS 70 (1950): 41-47.

_____. *The History of the Religion of Israel.* Vol. IV: *From the Babylonian Captivity to the End of Prophecy.* New York: KTAV, 1977.

Kee, H. C. "The Testaments of the Twelve Patriarchs." In *The Old Testament Pseudepigrapha,* ed. James Charlesworth, I: 775-828. Garden City, NY: Doubleday and Co., 1983.

Kelly, James C. *The Function of the Priest in the Old Testament.* Rome: Pontificum Athenaeum Antonianum. Sectio Biblica Hierosolymitana, 1973.

Kennett, R. H. "The Origin of the Aaronite Priesthood," *Journal of Theological Studies* 6 (1905): 161-86.

Knibb, Michael A. *The Qumran Community.* Cambridge: Cambridge University Press, 1987.

Kodell, James. *Lamentations, Zechariah, Malachi, Obadiah, Joel, Second Zechariah, Baruch.* The Old Testament Message: A

Biblical/Sociological Commentary, 14. Wilmington, Del: Michael Glazier, 1983.

Lattey, Cuthbert. "The Tribe of Levi," *Catholic Biblical Quarterly* 12 (1950): 277-291.

Levine, Baruch A. *In the Presence of the Lord: A Study of Cult and Some Cultic Terms in Ancient Israel.* Leiden: E. J. Brill, 1974.

L'Hour, Jean. "Les Interdits *Tô‛ēbâ* dans le Deutéronome," *Revue Biblique* 71 (1964): 481-503.

Lindars, Barnabas. "Torah in Deuteronomy." In *Words and Meanings, Essays Presented to David Winton Thomas,* ed. Peter Ackroyd and Barnabas Lindars, 117-136. Cambridge: Cambridge University Press, 1968.

Lindsay, John. "The Babylonian Kings and Edom," *Palestine Exploration Quarterly* 108 (1976): 23-39.

Liver, J. "'The Sons of Zadok the Priests' in the Dead Sea Sect," *Revue de Qumran* 6 (1967/68): 3-30.

Lohfink, Norbert, "Hate and Love in Osee 9,15," *Catholic Biblical Quarterly* 25 (1963): 417.

Long, Burke O. "Two Question and Answer Schemata in the Prophets," *Journal of Biblical Literature* 90 (1971): 129-137.

Malchow, Bruce. "The Messenger of the Covenant in Malachi 3:1," *Journal of Biblical Literature* 103 (1984): 252-255.

March, Eugene. "Prophecy." In *Old Testament Form Criticism,* ed. John H. Hayes, 141-177. San Antonio: Trinity University Press, 1977.

Marti, Karl. *Das Dodekapropheten erklärt.* Tübingen: Möhr, 1904. Quoted in J. M. P. Smith, "Malachi." In *A Critical and Exegetical Commentary on Haggai, Zechariah, Malachi, Jonah,* by Mitchell, Smith and Bewer. International Critical Commentaries, 51. Edinburgh: T & T Clark, 1912.

Mason, Rex. *The Books of Haggai, Zechariah, and Malachi.* Cambridge Bible Commentary. New York: Cambridge University Press, 1977.

Matthews, J. G. "Tammuz Worship in the Book of Malachi," *Palestine Oriental Society Journal* 11 (1931): 42-50.

Mayes, A. D. H. *Deuteronomy.* New Century Bible Commentary. Greenwood, SC: Attic Press, 1979.

Mazar, Benjamin. "The Cities of the Priests and Levites," *Vetus Testamentum, Supplements,* 7. 1959 Congress Volume, 193-205. Leiden: E. J. Brill, 1960.

McCarthy, Dennis. "Notes on the Love of God in Deuteronomy and the Father-Son Relationship between Yahweh and Israel," *Catholic Biblical Quarterly* 27 (1965): 144-47.

_____. *Treaty and Covenant: A Study in Form in the Ancient Oriental Documents and in the Old Testament.* Analecta Biblica. Rome: Pontifical Biblical Institute, 1963.

McConville, J. G. *Law and Theology in Deuteronomy.* Journal for the Study of the Old Testament, Supplement Series, 33. Sheffield, England: Department of Biblical Studies, The University of Sheffield, 1984.

McCullough, W. Stewart. *The History and Literature of the Palestinian Jews from Cyrus to Herod, 550 B.C. to 4 B.C.* Buffalo, New York: University of Toronto Press, 1975.

McEvenue, Sean E. "The Political Structure in Judah from Cyrus to Nehemiah," *Catholic Biblical Quarterly* 43 (1981): 353-364.

McKenzie, Steven and Howard Wallace. "Covenant Themes in Malachi," *Catholic Biblical Quarterly* 45 (1983): 549-63.

Mendenhall, George. "Covenant." In *Interpreter's Dictionary of the Bible,* ed. George Buttrick and others, vol. A-D, 714-723. Nashville: Abingdon, 1962.

Meyers, Eric M. Sidebar for "Gehenna: The Topography of Hell," by Lloyd R. Bailey, *Biblical Archaeologist* 49 (1986): 190.

_____. "Priestly Language in the Book of Malachi," *Hebrew Annual Review* 10 (1987): 225-237.

_____. "The Use of *tôrâ* in Haggai 2:11 and the Role of the Prophet in the Restoration Community." In *And the Word of the Lord Shall Go Forth: Essays In Honor of David Noel Freedman in Celebration of His Sixtieth Birthday,* ed. Carol L. Meyers and M. O'Connor, 69-76. American Schools of Oriental Research Special Volume Series. Winona Lake: Eisenbrauns and ASOR, 1983.

Meyers, Eric M. and Carol L. Meyers. *Haggai, Zechariah 1- 8,* Anchor Bible Series. Garden City, NY: Doubleday and Co., 1987.

Milgrom, Jacob. "Profane Slaughter and a Formulaic Key to the Composition of Deuteronomy," *Hebrew Union College Annual* 47 (1976): 1-17.

_____. *Studies in Cultic Theology and Terminology.* Studies in Judaism in Late Antiquity, ed. Jacob Neusner, 36. Leiden: E. J. Brill, 1983.

_____. *Studies in Levitical Terminology. I: The Encroacher and the Levite. The Term ʿAbodah.* London: University of California Press, 1970.

Moran, William. "The Ancient Near Eastern Background of the Love of God in Deuteronomy," *Catholic Biblical Quarterly* 25 (1963): 77-87.

Morgenstern, Julius. "Jerusalem—485 B.C. (continued)," *Hebrew Union College Annual* 28 (1957): 15-47.

Mowinckel, Sigmund. *The Two Sources of the Predeuteronomic Primeval History (JE) in Gen 1-11.* Oslo: J. Dybwad, 1937. Quoted in Ernst Sellin and Georg Fohrer. *Introduction to the Old Testament.* Translated by David E. Green, 146, 154. Nashville: Abingdon, 1965.

Muilenberg, James. "Form Criticism and Beyond," *Journal of Biblical Literature* 88 (1969): 1-18.

_____. "The Form and Structure of Covenantal Formulations," *Vetus Testamentum* 9 (1959): 347-365.

Myers, J. M. "Edom and Judah in the Sixth-Fifth Centuries B.C." In *Near Eastern Studies in Honor of William Foxwell Albright,* ed. Hans Goedicke, 377-392. Baltimore: The John Hopkins Press, 1971.

Neil, W. "Malachi ." In *Interpreter's Dictionary of the Bible,* ed. George Buttrick and others, vol. K-Q, 228-232. Nashville: Abingdon, 1962.

Nielsen, K. *Yahweh as Prosecutor and Judge.* Journal for the Study of the Old Testament, Supplement Series, 9. Sheffield: Department of Biblical Studies, University of Sheffield, 1978.

North, Francis Sparling. "Aaron's Rise in Prestige," *Zeitschrift für die alttestamentliche Wissenschaft* 66 (1954): 191-199.

North, Robert. "Angel-Prophet or Satan-Prophet?" *Zeitschrift für die alttestamentliche Wissenschaft* 82 (1970): 31-67.

Noth, Martin. *A History of Pentateuchal Traditions*. Translated by Bernhard W. Anderson. Englewood Cliffs, NJ: Prentice-Hall, Inc., 1972.

_____. *Numbers. A Commentary*. Old Testament Library. Philadelphia: Westminster Press, 1968.

O'Brien, Julia M. "Because God Heard My Voice: The Individual Thanksgiving Psalm and Vow-fulfillment." In *The Listening Heart: Essays in Wisdom and the Psalms in Honor of Roland E. Murphy, O. Carm.*, ed. Kenneth Hoglund and others, 289-298. Journal for the Study of the Old Testament, Supplement Series, 58. Sheffield, England: Journal for the Study of the Old Testament Press, 1987.

Olmstead, A. T. *History of the Persian Empire*. Chicago: University of Chicago Press, 1948.

Petersen, David Lee. "Israelite Prophecy and Prophetic Traditions in the Exilic and Post-Exilic Periods." Ph. D. diss., Yale University, 1972.

_____. "Malachi and the Language of Divorce: Mal. 2:10-16." Paper presented at the Society of Biblical Literature Annual Meeting, Israelite Prophetic Literature Section. Boston, MA, Dec. 6, 1987.

Pierce, Roland. "Literary Connectors and a Haggai/Zechariah/Malachi Corpus," *Journal of the Evangelical Theological Society* 27 (1984): 277-289.

Pfeiffer, E. "Die Disputationsworte im Buche Maleachi," *Evangelische Theologie* 19 (1959): 546-568.

Polk, Timothy. "The Levites in the Davidic-Solomonic Empire," *Studia Biblica et Theologica* 9 (April 1979): 3-22.

Polzin, Robert. *Late Biblical Hebrew: Towards a Typology of Late Biblical Hebrew Prose*. Harvard Semitic Monographs, 13. Missoula, Montana: Scholars Press, 1976.

Porten, Bezalel. "The Identity of King Adon," *Biblical Archaeologist* 44 (1981): 36-52.

von Rad, Gerhard. *Old Testament Theology*. 2 vols. Hagerstown: Harper and Row, 1965.

Radday, Yehuda, et al. "Genesis, Wellhausen and the Computer," *Zeitschrift für die alttestamentliche Wissenschaft* 94 (1982): 467-481.

Raitt, Thomas. "The Prophetic Summons to Repentence," *Zeitschrift für die alttestamentliche Wissenschaft* 83 (1971): 30-49.

Rieman, P. A. "Covenant, Mosaic." In *Interpreter's Dictionary of the Bible*, Supplementary Volume, ed. Keith Crimm and others, 192-197. Nashville: Abingdon, 1976.

Rivkin, Ellis. "Aaron, Aaronides." In *Interpreter's Dictionary of the Bible*, Supplementary Volume, ed. Keith Crimm and others, 1-3. Nashville: Abingdon, 1976.

Rowley, H. H. *Worship in Ancient Israel: Its Forms and Meanings*. London: SPCK, 1967.

Rudolph, W. *Haggai—Sacharja 1-8—Sacharja 9-14—Maleachi*. Kommentar zum Alten Testament, 13,4. Gütersloh: Gütersloher Verlaghaus Mohn, 1976.

Saggs, H. W. F. "A Lexical Consideration for the Date of Deutero-Isaiah," *Journal of Theological Studies* n.s. 10 (1959): 84-87.

Sarason, Richard S. *A History of the Mishnaic Law of Agriculture*. Section III: *A Study of the Tractate Demai*. Studies in Judaism in Late Antiquity. Leiden: E. J. Brill, 1979.

Schneider, Dale Allan. "The Unity of the Book of the Twelve." Ph. D. diss., Yale University, 1979.

Schürer, Emil. *The History of the Jewish People in the Age of Jesus Christ (175 B.C.—A.D. 135)*. Rev. and ed. Geza Vermes, Fergus Millar, Matthew Black, II. Edinburgh: T & T Clark, 1979.

Seeligmann, A. "A Psalm from Pre-Regal Times," *Vetus Testamentum* 14 (1964): 75-92.

Sellin, Ernst. *Das Zwölfprophetenbuch übersetzt und erklärt*. Kommentar zum Alten Testament, 12. Leipzig: A. Dieichertsche Verlagsbuchhandlung, 1930. Quoted in Beth Glazier-McDonald, "Malachi." Ph. D. diss., University of Chicago, 1985.

Sellin, Ernst, and Georg Fohrer. *Introduction to the Old Testament*. Translated by David E. Green. Nashville: Abingdon, 1978.

Seters, John van. *Abraham in History and Tradition*. New Haven: Yale University Press, 1975.

Sklba, Richard. "The Teaching Function of the Pre-Exilic Israelite Priesthood." Ph. D. diss., Pontifica Universitas A. S. Thomas Aq. in Urbe (Rome), 1965.

Smith, J. M. P. "Malachi." In *A Critical and Exegetical Commentary on Haggai, Zechariah, Malachi*, by Mitchell, Smith and Bewer. International Critical Commentaries. Edinburgh: T & T Clark, 1912.

Smith, Morton. *Palestinian Parties and Politics that Shaped the Old Testament*. New York: Columbia Univ. Press, 1971.

Smith, Ralph. *Micah-Malachi*, Word Biblical Commentary. Waco, Texas: Word Books, 1984.

Smith, W. R. "The Deuteronomic Code and the Levitical Law." Chap. in *The Old Testament in the Jewish Church*. New York: D. Appleton and Company, 1881.

Smith, W. R. and A. Bertholet. "Levites." In *Encyclopaedia Biblica*, ed. T. K. Cheyne and J. S. Black, vol. III, 2770-2776. New York: MacMillan and Co., 1902.

_____. "Priest." In *Encyclopaedia Biblica*, ed. T. K. Cheyne and J. S. Black, vol. III, 3837-3847. New York: MacMillan and Co., 1902.

Sommer, F. *Die Aḫḫijavā-Urkunden*. Abhandlungen der Bayerischen Akademie die Wissenschaften, Philosophisch-historische Abteilung, n.f., 6. Munich: Bayerischen Akademie die Wissenschaften, 1932.

Spoer, Hans H. "Some New Considerations Toward Dating the Book of Malachi," *Jewish Quarterly Review* 20 (1908): 167-186.

Starcky, Jean. "The Nabateans: A Historical Sketch," *Biblical Archaeologist* 18 (1955): 84-106.

Stuart, George. "The Sovereign's Day of Conquest," *Bulletin of the American Schools of Oriental Research* 221 (1976): 159-164.

Swetnam, James. "Malachi 1:11: An Interpretation," *Catholic Biblical Quarterly* 31 (1969): 220-209.

Thompson, J. A. *Jeremiah*. New International Commentary on the Old Testament. Grand Rapids: Wm. B. Eerdmanns, 1986.

Torrey, C. C. "*ᶜēr wĕᶜōneh* in Malachi ii.12," *Journal of Biblical Literature* 24 (1905): 1-15.

_____. "The Prophecy of 'Malachi,'" *Journal of Biblical Literature* 17 (1898): 1-15.

Tucker, Gene. *Form Criticism of the Old Testament*. Guides to Biblical Scholarship, Old Testament Series. Philadelphia: Fortress, 1971.

Vaux, Roland de. *Ancient Israel: Its Life and Institutions.* New York: McGraw-Hill Book Co., Inc., 1961.

Verhoef, Pieter A. *Haggai and Malachi.* New International Critical Commentary. Grand Rapids, Mich.: Wm. B. Eerdmans, 1987.

Vermes, Geza. *The Dead Sea Scrolls in English,* 2d ed. New York, New York: Penguin Books, 1975.

Vink, J. S. "The Date and Origin of the Priestly Code in the Old Testament." In *The Priestly Code and Seven Other Studies.* Oudtestamentische Studiën, 15, 1-144. Leiden: E. J. Brill, 1969.

Waldman, Nahum. "Some Notes on Malachi 3:6, 3:13 and Psalm 42:11," *Journal of Biblical Literature* 93 (1974): 543-549.

Wallis, G. "Wesen und Struktur der Botschaft Maleachi," *Beihefte zur Zeitschrift für die alttestamentliche Wissenschaft* 105 (1967): 229-237.

Wanke, Gunther. "Prophecy and Psalms in the Persian Period." In *Cambridge History of Judaism.* Vol. I: *Introduction; Persian Period,* ed. Davies and Finkelstein, 162-188. Cambridge: Cambridge University Press, 1984.

Waterman, Leroy. "Moses, the Pseudo Levite," *Journal of Biblical Literature* 59 (1940): 397-404.

Weaver, Horace Robert. "The Priesthood of Judaism in the Persian Period." Ph. D. diss., Boston University Graduate School, 1949.

Weinfeld, Moshe. "Bible Criticism." In *Contemporary Jewish Thought,* ed. Arthur Cohen and Paul Mendes-Flohr, 35-40. New York, NY: Charles Scribner's Sons, 1987.

_____. "The Covenant of Grant in the Old Testament and the Ancient Near East," *Journal of the American Oriental Society* 90.2 (1970): 184-203.

_____. *Deuteronomy and the Deuteronomic School.* Oxford: Clarendon Press, 1972.

_____. "Social and Cultic Institutions in the Priestly Source Against their Ancient Near Eastern Backgrounds." In *Eighth World Congress of Jewish Studies, Proceedings,* 95-129. Jerusalem: World Union of Jewish Studies, 1983.

Welch, Adam. *Post-Exilic Judaism.* Edinburgh and London: Wm. Blackwood and Sons, Ltd., 1935.

Wellhausen, Julius. *Die kleinen Propheten übersetzt und erklärt*. Berlin: Walter de Gruyter and Co., 1892/1963.

_____. *Prolegomena to the History of Ancient Israel*. Preface by W. Robertson Smith. Reprint edition. Gloucester, Mass.: Peter Smith, 1973.

Westermann, Claus. *Basic Forms of Prophetic Speech*. Translated by C. White. Philadelphia: Westminster, 1967.

Whedbee, J. William. "A Question-Answer Schema in Haggai 1: The Form and Function of Haggai 1:9-11." In *Biblical and Near Eastern Studies: Essays in Honor of William Sanford LaSor*, ed. Gary A. Tuttle. Grand Rapids: William B. Eerdmans Publishing Co., 1978.

Whybray, R. N. *The Making of the Pentateuch: A Methodological Study*. Journal for the Study of the Old Testament, Supplement Series, 53. Sheffield, England: Sheffield Academic Press, 1987.

Widengren, Geo. "The Persian Period." In *Israelite and Judean History*, ed. John H. Hayes and J. Maxwell Miller. Old Testament Library, 489-538. Philadelphia: Westminster Press, 1977.

Williamson, Hugh. *Ezra and Nehemiah*. Old Testament Guides. Sheffield: Journal for the Study of the Old Testament Press, 1987.

Winward, Stephen. *A Guide to the Prophets*. Atlanta: John Knox Press, 1977.

Wolff, Hans Walter. *Hosea*. Hermeneia Series. Philadelphia: Fortress Press, 1974.

Woude, A. S. van der. "Malachi's Struggle for a Pure Community." In *Tradition and Re-interpretation in Jewish and Early Christian Literature: Essays in Honor of Jürgen C. H. Lebram*, ed. J. W. van Henten, and others, 65-71. Leiden: E. J. Brill, 1986.

Wright, G. Ernest. "The Lawsuit of God: A Form-Critical Study of Deuteronomy 32." In *Israel's Prophetic Heritage: Essays in Honor of James Muilenburg*, ed. B. Anderson and W. Harrelson, 26-67. New York: Harper and Brothers, 1962.

_____. "The Levites in Deuteronomy," *Vetus Testamentum* 4 (1954): 325-330.

Zevit, Ziony. "Converging Lines of Evidence Bearing on the Date of P," *Zeitschrift für die alttestamentliche Wissenschaft* 94 (1982): 481-511.